Tailwinds

Past

Florence

DOUG WALSH

ALSO BY DOUG WALSH
One Lousy Pirate

ISBN: 978-1-7327467-0-1

Library of Congress Control Number: 2018911848

The characters and events portrayed in this book, other than those clearly in the public domain, are either products of the author's imagination or are used fictitiously. Any resemblance to actual persons, living or dead, is purely coincidental.

Cover and book design by Scarlett Rugers of TheBookDesignHouse.com

Printed and bound in the United States of America

Published by Snoke Valley Books

P.O. Box 564

Snoqualmie, WA, USA 98065

Visit www.dougwalsh.com

For Kristin, my world

Natalie,
Thank you for the terrific, insightful feedback... and the laughs. Best wishes!
Doug Wolf

PART ONE

Chapter 1

WEDNESDAY, FEBRUARY 11 — SEATTLE,
WASHINGTON, USA

Edward Vaughan cursed the midday stillness as his wedding band tapped a jittery S.O.S. against the granite countertop.

He stood in the same spot every morning at five, mug in hand, scanning his news feed, checking the pre-market indicators. Even at that early hour, the apartment would buzz with Kara's presence. He'd kiss her forehead goodbye as she slept, anticipating another on her lips fifteen hours later to bookend his workday. She'd be in sweats and a tee, a cold, food-streaked plate beside her on the couch, wine glass within reach. His dinner would be waiting on the stove, the television chugging through a YouTube playlist on mute, a book unfurled on her lap.

That was their routine.

He'd never forget overhearing Kara on the phone, raving to a friend back east about the Space Needle views and luxury finishes when they moved in. Her excitement fueled him for months, but his tank needed a refill. Edward had hoped to surprise her tonight with a move to the junior penthouse. Now they couldn't even afford what they had.

Good thing the lease is up next month.

He adjusted his suit cuff and checked the time. She'd be home soon. He needed an explanation.

The words would come. Eventually. But he had to get moving. Fortune never favored anyone who stood around, going cross-eyed in an unlit kitchen.

Edward knocked the counter twice, gaveling himself into action.

He tugged the half-Windsor loose and undid the top button on his shirt. Custom or not, the damn collar had been strangling him since the drive home. He pulled off the jacket and kicked his shoes ahead down the hall. One took a bad bounce, scuffing the wall, ricocheting into Kara's studio.

The door was typically closed.

With no kids on the horizon or in-laws willing to travel *all that way*, the second bedroom had become a land of forgotten hobbies. Dust-covered mountain bikes leaned where a dresser may have stood, a paint-splattered drop cloth took the place of a guest bed, an empty easel in lieu of a mirror.

As he rose from picking up the shoe, an unexpected absence caught his eye. The map was gone. For months it had hung opposite the door, above a bookcase lined with old college texts and a copious collection of brushes and paint tubes. Now, in its stead, only thumbtack holes in the same not-quite-white (Kara called it *Saffron Lace*) that covered every wall in their Seattle apartment.

She brought the map home last fall, a laminated Rand-McNally depicting every country on earth in shaded relief. Accompanying it was a proposal to bicycle around the world. She wanted him to take a sabbatical—a laughable notion in the world of venture capital—and spend a year or three traveling.

Issues of *Adventure Cyclist* appeared in the bathroom soon after, borrowed travel guides rotated across her nightstand, and seemingly every conversation held an air of wanderlust, with Kara pining for small towns and country roads, campfire beers at sunset. *Just the two of us,* she'd say in a coquettish whisper. *While we're still young.* Edward could only guess what spurred her restlessness and expected it to vanish as abruptly as it emerged.

The map hadn't gone far. A quick search found it crunched into a football of discarded fantasy, punted behind a pile of bags and boxes. By the looks of things, she'd cleaned out the closet.

He unfurled the map, exposing a runaway squiggle of black ink. His eyes locked on the map's northwest corner, where a star marked the departure point. Home. From there, the line dipped and danced across the northern United States and Canada before dashing south from London to Spain. Onward it went, around the Mediterranean to Greece, Turkey, and beyond. Edward followed the trail, past a who's who of countries he knew nothing about, to China and Vietnam and a hand-drawn smiley face clear on the other edge of the poster, in Bali.

She'd given up on it. No. *She gave up on me.*

A car alarm echoed between the high-rises, drawing his attention. He carried the map to the living room window, trying to recall the last time she'd mentioned the trip. Several weeks, at least. Probably not since New Year's.

In no mood to deal with construction, he had parked the Audi on the avenue, lucking into a spot where he'd be able see it. The car looked fine from his seventh-floor perch, the alarm wasn't his, but he could have done without his cardboard box reflecting in the storefront window across the street. Security had weaved the flaps shut, and only the top of a small bamboo plant jutted from a torn corner. But he knew the contents intimately. Framed photos of Kara, his MBA diploma, a couple of airport business books, and a half-empty bottle of Johnny Walker Blue kept on hand for toasting new deals.

He wasn't so naive as to think he'd spend his whole career with one firm. After all, he was only twenty-nine. But he never thought the end would come like this. So soon. Over something so avoidable. He sat in his car for hours that afternoon, forehead on the steering wheel, wishing for a do-over, a chance to rewind time. Most of all, he yearned for an escape from having to tell his wife.

As the day's events played in his mind, Kara approached on the sidewalk below. She did a double-take, as if his early arrival home was so unfathomable she refused to recognize their own car.

Even in Seattle there's not that many RS 5s.

Edward watched her stare at the telltale box, saw the slump in her posture, the reach for her phone. He backed away as she looked upward, forgetting the tinted glass was all but impossible to see through from outside, especially with the lights off. Down the hall, his phone vibrated inside his jacket pocket, the silk doing little to cushion it against the hardwood floor.

Anxiety slipped the map from his grasp, spiriting it beneath the couch where all but Oceania fell claim to the dust-bunnies and darkness. The smiley face stared at him, his dismissal of her dream visible in the scars of its creased face.

She didn't deserve that.

Edward snatched the map from the floor as the phone ceased vibrating behind him. *She'll be home any minute.* His breathing quickened, jolted by the surge of an idea, a way out.

Rolling the map as he went, he ran to the kitchen and yanked open the refrigerator. Shifting aside milk, jelly, and a palette of condiments, he unbarricaded a bottle of champagne from the back corner, silently thanking his father for instilling in him the value of being prepared for an unplanned celebration.

He plucked champagne flutes from a cabinet and hurried to the door where he arranged them just so atop a cedar console. He studied the scene from all angles, even stooping low to imagine the effect from Kara's height as she entered. Above the table hung a painting of an orca leaping through a field of stars—a Wyland original. His first bonus check. Edward adjusted the gallery lighting so it twinkled against the crystal stemware.

Am I really doing this?

What choice did he have? Tell her they'd have to move, that he couldn't afford to keep them in Seattle anymore, that he got himself blacklisted throughout the city's financial community? There was no reason to put her through that when she spent months trying to sell him on the perfect alternative.

The elevator dinged, launching his stomach into a backflip.

His grip on the bottle and map tightened as the key slid into the lock.

How will I pay for it?

The deadbolt turned.

I'll figure it out.

Edward shuffled out of Kara's view as the door opened inward. He counted down from three, giddy with the excitement of his surprise gift. "Butterflies, cover your eyes!"

Kara clutched her chest as her breathing returned to normal. It was one thing not to know why he wasn't at work, it was another for him to be hiding behind the door. *What the hell, Edward.* She bent to pick up her dropped keys. "You're home." It came out more statement than question.

"Long story. Why didn't you cover your eyes?"

She raised her hands in answer. They held a gym bag, purse, keys, and an envelope she'd somehow forgotten about in the commotion. "You didn't give me any time," she said. Then, noticing the map—*her* map—and the champagne, asked, "What's all this?"

"This," he said, grinning like a schoolboy about to receive his first kiss, "is a change of plans."

Her mouth fell open as she processed what she was hearing. Kara spent months asking him to take time off, hoping he'd see how important the trip was to her, practically begging. She tore the map down after the holidays, after diplomatic overtures had failed. She'd been holding a bomb ever since, delaying the inevitable. Now, with her self-imposed deadline having come and gone, he wanted to do it.

Today? You've got to be kidding me, she thought, clutching the envelope, dumbstruck.

"I thought you'd be excited." His smile drooped.

"I … I am," she stammered. "I think. You have to admit, it's a lot to swallow."

"You still want to go, right?"

Did she? It'd be an incredible adventure, a badge she'd wear the rest of her life. But, to Kara, cycling around the world was a means to an end. Her gaze drifted to the map, the promise held within its Sharpie itinerary. The promise of change, of resurrecting the man she married, her best friend and lover. For three years, it'd be just the two of them, reforging their bond against the anvil of the open road. And if her plan didn't succeed, if he returned to his workaholic ways when it was over, she'd at least know she tried.

Kara felt a warmth spread through her, sensed her lips curling on a wave of hope.

"That the mail?" Edward nodded at the envelope, a legal-sized manila job with a string clasp. He turned around to pry loose the cork, his enthusiasm returning.

"Yeah, it's nothing." She seized the opportunity to place it face down on the floor and covered it with her gym bag. She unzipped her softshell jacket and draped it over the top for good measure. The cork exploded from the bottle like a starter's pistol, sending a stampede of questions racing through her mind. She didn't know where to begin. His reversal was as dizzying as it was unlikely.

"I saw the box on the passenger seat." She decided to probe. "What's going on?"

"I'm done. I'm not going back."

"You got your sabbatical? What about the promotion?"

"It's not important," he said, handing her a glass, avoiding eye contact.

The job meant everything to him, and she could tell there was something he wasn't telling her, but wasn't this what she wanted? Absolutely. She brought the glass even with her chin. The bubbles erupted like fireworks, tickling her lips and nose while she thought it over.

Can we afford it?

Probably. Even if it was unpaid leave, they had to have enough saved up.

I'll need to quit my job.

She bounced from contract to contract every year, a glorified, monogamous freelancer. She could leave anytime.

Do I still love him?

She looked up at Edward, pondering the secrets behind his creased brow, recalling the passion they'd shared, convincing herself it could be that way again. Yes. She loved him. Ever since college.

Kara began to nod as she tilted the glass to her lips.

"Not yet. We have to toast."

"Kara Vaughan," he said, taking her hand as he dropped to a knee. "Will you bicycle around the world with me?" She looked past him. Embarrassed, cold feet, nervous? He didn't know. *Say yes. Say yes, dammit.*

"Are you sure it's what you want?"

He rose and stepped toward her, barely restraining his sigh. "I wouldn't be here if it wasn't," he said. "We'll leave next month, take advantage of the low snowfall, and spend the rent deposit on new bikes."

She bit her lower lip and stared at the floor.

"Wasn't this your dream?"

She nodded. "It was."

"So, let's do it."

"Are you sure we can afford it?"

"It'll work out," he said, knowing she relied on him to mind their finances. In truth, they spent as much as he earned. The rent, his car, the furniture. He had no idea how much he owed, only what his credit limits were. He figured there was enough for a year or two on the road if they were frugal.

He was tired of waiting. He cupped his hand under her chin and raised it, locking eyes with hers. "Say yes."

Her hesitation faded into a fit of nervous laughter. "Yes," she shouted, clinking her glass with his. "One-hundred percent, yes!"

Edward downed his champagne in a heavy gulp and wrapped his arms around his wife, squeezing her tight, knowing he'd dodged a bullet.

And as Kara squeezed him back, spasming with joy against his chest, a blinding flash of light flooded the apartment. Bathing him from all sides, it washed over him like a wave, immersing him in an otherworldly glow. It was fleeting, silent, and when he realized that Kara hadn't sensed it, he began to doubt its occurrence. But what he couldn't deny was the brilliance of the shade. He'd only seen it once before, in Kara's paintings. *Cerulean Blue*, she called it. *Latin for the heavens*.

Chapter 2

THURSDAY, FEBRUARY 12 — FLORENCE, ITALY

Alessio woke gasping for breath as an ethereal blue flash gave way to darkness. His naked skin crackled with static, shocking him as he huddled in confusion. The fading echoes of a swooshing sound rippled outward across the room, barely audible over his panting. The noise reminded him of a gas lamp catching flame, yet he felt as if he had splashed into existence, like a coin flipped into a fountain.

He had fallen, he was sure of it, and was confident this was no dream, but a quick check of his limbs and head revealed no bruises or scrapes. Alessio shivered in the unexpected cold and groped for his quilt, only to feel the vacant softness of a bare, unfamiliar mattress beneath him. The bed felt of neither horsehair nor straw.

He puzzled over this detail as his pulse beat the drums of his temples in the pitch-black surroundings. He noticed the air was scented with the tang of grapefruit and bergamot, far sweeter than the baser odors of his humble home. *Dove sono?*, he thought, wondering where he was.

Spinning his feet to the cold brick floor, Alessio dropped his head into his hands, puzzled and scared. He pressed his fists against his face, causing black and yellow spots to dance before his eyes like drops of watercolor on a fresh canvas. *Pensa, Alessio, pensa.*

A reddish glow caught his attention as his vision adjusted. Light in the shape of numerals. Alessio recoiled, instinctively making the sign of the cross as he withdrew.

When the strange light refused to be blinked away, he reached for the object. He marveled as the faintest vibration hummed within, a wisp of mechanical life. But it was the mysterious red light that gripped his attention. The four digits, split by a colon, appeared to report the time. When the fourth digit flashed, he began counting. He nearly reached sixty and smiled at his own cleverness when the digit jumped again: 03:25.

That it was the middle of the night was no surprise, but the timepiece was unlike any he'd seen. He turned it around, looking for hands and a dial, only to realize it also appeared to report the month and day.

"Febbraio dodicesimo?" he said in disbelief, so distracted by the suggestion of it being winter that he unintentionally slipped into Italian. *"Ma come?"* he said, wondering how it could be February 12 when it was only August yesterday? He returned the odd clock to the table and slumped on the bed, feeling unmoored.

But there was more. Beneath the fright and mystery lay a palpable sense of loss, of heartache. His chest hitched as if something—some*one*—he loved was gone and never coming back.

The sorrow squeezing him from within intensified with a distracting familiarity. But why? Alessio could remember committing no mortal sin, no infidelity for which he must atone, no abandonment inflicted.

Not recently, he knew.

He winced at the thought, realizing the feeling was reminiscent of a pain he weathered so many years ago. Before his retreat into celibacy. But why should the pain be fresh? He hadn't thought of *her* in twenty years.

Alessio stood, conflicted, wondering where he was if not in his home on Malta. Searching the shadows, he stepped gingerly toward the window, trimmed in a faint strip of moonlight, and was promptly snared by linens piled on the floor. He wrapped the sheets around his waist for warmth and pawed against the louvers, but could find no way to open the interior shutters.

A pang shot through him as the dread of being trapped pierced his sanity. Trailing his hand along the wall for balance, Alessio explored the darkness. Stepping slowly, one hand on the wall, the other clawing the air in front of him, he advanced. Something moved beneath his finger, a toggle of sorts. Instantly, light was everywhere. He clamped a hand over his mouth and suppressed the urge to scream as a beacon in the ceiling bathed the room in a light far whiter and brighter than any he'd thought possible.

He leaned forward, tilting his head to better view the room's arched ceiling. It was a curved expanse he had seen many times before, but couldn't remember where.

Alessio ran his hand through his hair and paused, his eyes went wide in amazement. He clutched his wavy black locks, realizing it reached his shoulders, a length he hadn't maintained since his last voyage to …

"It cannot be," he whispered in his native English, as memories of the apartment came rushing back. "How can I have returned?"

It was so much cleaner than how he remembered. The furniture and decorations were foreign to him, but there was no mistaking the brick floor and tunnel-shaped ceiling of the small studio. Even the wooden door looked similar.

Once his eyes adjusted to the brightness, he took inventory of the room's alien contents. On a table sat a large, black, rectangular mirror that revealed only a faint reflection. Beside it, a box with green, blinking lights.

Alessio spotted a journal atop the kitchen table and rushed to it, hoping it would reveal a clue. The pages felt odd to the touch, like everything else in the room, and contained messages in numerous languages: Italian, of course, but also French and several in English. He tried reading one written in Italian, but the penmanship proved too careless. On the next page was an entry printed in English block lettering.

We had a wonderful time in your studio. We always dreamed of visiting Italy, and your apartment was the perfect place to make our dreams come true. What a fantastic location! Though we wish our trip wasn't so short, we will remember this week forever. Thank you so much!

Regards,

Katrina and Alan,
Pennsylvania, USA

Alessio stared at the signature, repeating the words. It made no sense. Nobody would cross the ocean from America for just seven days.

Turning the guestbook's pages in slow, steady turns, Alessio surveyed myriad vacation memories. Messages written in a flowing script that defied the borders of pre-ruled paper; illegible notes scrawled in looping letters and punctuated by more exclamation marks than he'd seen in his entire life. Every page contained a six-digit date, or so it seemed, but the dates made no sense, as each ended in /13 or /14.

He shook his head as he tried to make sense of it all. Depending on the weather, it had taken him as many as five days to travel by steamer from Malta, and then another full day along rutted roads from Livorno.

He recalled reading about a railway built shortly after his last visit. The Duke of Lucca was said to have constructed it between his city and Pisa in 1846. Surely more lines had followed, perhaps even connecting to Florence. "Or Milan," he said aloud as he came to the final entry in the book.

It was written by an Italian couple from that northern city. They had spent over a month in the apartment and filled the page with affections for their *casa lontano da casa.* A wistful smile tugged at his lips. It had been his home away from home, too.

He read on, trying not to think of the pain that concluded that period in his life, but he was brought to a halt at the bottom of the page. There, beneath their signature, printed in large letters and adorned with curlicues and stars, was a final celebratory remark:

BUON FELIZ 2015!!!

Alessio stared wide-eyed at the page as his entire body tensed, save for his hands, which now trembled uncontrollably. He dropped into the spindle-backed chair, knocking an empty bowl aside. He refused to believe it. It was utter insanity. "This can't be real!" he yelled.

He leapt to his feet and dashed throughout the apartment, from corner to corner, yanking open drawers, tugging on handles. The anxiety he woke with moments ago was a spring breeze compared to the tornado now swirling within him. Kitchen utensils spilled to the floor, plates and mixing bowls rattled on shelves, but nothing rescued him from his nightmare.

Gasping for air and soaked in sweat, he pulled upon the handle of a large, metal chest and startled as a light blinked on. Inside were several food items: a container of tomato paste, an onion, and a glass bowl with three eggs. Alessio reached toward the source of the light and noticed the air inside the box was cooler. He closed and opened the door twice more, in quick fashion, giggling nervously despite his fear as the light flicked on each time. He closed the door for good, nodding his head in approval.

Inside a closet he found a large blanket and threw it onto the bed. Tangled within was a pair of the thickest, softest cotton pants he'd ever felt. He pulled them on, in awe of the waistband's strange elasticity, and noticed that his legs looked thinner, more muscular. His skin was smoother too, devoid of the wrinkles and veins.

Younger? It had to be a trick of his imagination or some satanic sorcery. *This cannot be real!*

He resumed his survey of the apartment, flicking switches, pushing buttons, and twisting the faucets. Each new marvel hammered his nerves, playing an out-of-tune harbinger of his descent into lunacy. Yet, the room was safe. A grace he clung to.

From across the apartment, he eyed the windows. *Not yet*, he thought, stalling. Hoping he'd wake before seeing what he feared most.

Alessio noticed an envelope upon a table near the door marked *Spese di Pulizia*. The cleaning fee. Inside he found several coins (not one a Tuscan Florin), along with a handful of notes, each a different color and denomination. The slippery papers bore an outline of the European continent and a blue rectangle with numerous yellow stars in a circle. Studying the currency, Alessio recalled the American flag and wondered if Europe had become a single country called Euro.

He smiled nervously and stuffed the envelope of money into his waistband, then looked across to the window and took a deep breath. Now or never.

Alessio was a step from the shuttered windows when a high-pitched mechanical scream shattered the silence of the night, sending him scampering onto the bed in absolute panic. Tugging the blanket over his head, he balled his quivering body and began to pray, barely able to hold his palms together, fighting the need to vomit.

The noise faded into the night, its echoes dying out long before his pleas for salvation gave way to sleep.

"What have I done to deserve this, oh Lord? Why must I now suffer your wrath when the sins of the past were not my doing?"

Chapter 3

MONDAY, MARCH 30 — WHITEFISH, MONTANA, USA

Six weeks passed since Edward was fired. The first month had been easy, consumed in a dizzying blur of shopping spree and fire sale. He and Kara spent their days collecting the necessary touring gear, the nights shrinking their lives into a pint-sized storage locker. But as the departure date approached, and the last of their furniture was hauled away by Craigslist bargain-hunters, the reality of their undertaking sharpened, becoming piercing, inoculating Edward against Kara's enthusiasm.

It wasn't only that he never wanted to bicycle around the world; he knew he wasn't meant to. Trips like this were the domain of societal outcasts and runaways, college grads warding off their ascent into adulthood, and professional grifters and fundraisers touring the world in the name of the cause du jour.

If his opinion might ever change, it wouldn't be while pedaling through the snow-spackled ski town of Whitefish, eight-hundred miles east of Seattle, on a road lined with sprawling estates. Warmth and comfort mocked him from all directions, reminding him of the life he lost. To his right, a modern mansion containing a forest's worth of timber, an acre of glass. The kind of home that made it all worthwhile. Through a soaring window he saw an upstairs loft lined with books. *Perfect for her art studio*, he thought before turning away, his teeth clenched in resignation.

Edward tugged his fleece headband down, brushed off the map case, and carefully wiped the frost encasing the flimsy mirror on his helmet, lest it fall off again. "So this is why everyone keeps telling us we're two months early," he said aloud, his voice no match for the spattering snow beneath his tires.

He sighed. It wasn't the jealous sigh of a middle-aged man who never was, but of the promising young phenom aware he pried open the shell only to fumble away the pearl.

The blare of a horn jolted him from his reverie, causing him to jerk the handlebars. He had drifted to the center of the lane—car country—and now fought his overcorrection. He wrestled the bike, willing the tires to regain their grip, as a hulking Range Rover streaked past, dousing his rain pants in murky slush.

No, this wasn't how he drew it up in business school. Back before the job at Madsen Ventures. Before Kara.

Edward glanced at the mirror out the corner of his eye. There she was, her orange jacket a distant spot of sunshine in a monochromatic landscape. He was leading, but he'd follow her anywhere. His breath whistled as it escaped his chapped lips. *Even around the world?*

The chain skipped as he eased his pedaling and shifted into a lower gear. He twisted the shifter back and looked over his right hip as he coaxed the chain higher. The derailleur pushed the links across the snow-packed cassette, but they found no purchase. The sprockets were barely visible, their teeth no more useful than those of an infant. He'd have to leave it in the lone clean gear, the one he'd been using since the weather turned.

"Hey there, speedy, finally decided to wait for me?" Kara's voice rescued him from the monotony of his thoughts.

"Oh, hey. You caught up," he said glancing back. "How are you handling the snow?"

"It's not too bad, actually. The tires are great."

"Yeah, Schwalbes are heavy, but they're worth it. Any problems shifting?"

"A little. The chain skips, but nothing serious."

Edward moved his left hand to his hip—an old steadying maneuver he retained from his racing days—and turned to face his wife. Her yellow handlebar bag and panniers were spackled white and her gloves were soaked, but even through the gauzy curtain of flurries he could see her smile and a few curly tendrils of hair sticking out beneath her helmet. Two weeks in and he still couldn't get used to the purple highlights. "Are you sure you're okay riding in this?"

"I am," she said, blinking away a flake that sailed into her eye. "But so much for making it across the mountains without it snowing."

"In March, too," he added. "What were we thinking?"

Kara broke into laughter, her face shining with a joy he wasn't yet used to seeing so routinely. Edward turned at the sound of an oncoming car and settled into a steady rhythm, his mind quieted.

The road was a cotton-blanketed ribbon of asphalt laid amongst a black forest of Douglas firs and slumbering aspen. The effect was one of a narrow trench cleaved into a plateau of treetops, and Edward imagined the two cyclists mere drifters along a paved stream at the bottom of an inescapable gorge. Out in the distance, the steel-blue silhouette of the Rocky Mountains loomed. It was his first time to Montana, but Edward couldn't shake the feeling that he'd been here before. Not in a goose-bumpy déjà vu kind of way, but something deeper. Like a faded memory, played in reverse.

It was the way he felt the first time he met Kara, and still felt, to this day, when the light hit her in a certain way. Reflections from an unknown life.

The forest blocked the northerly wind, save for when a homeowner had cleared a few acres. Twice, Edward heard Kara yelp as the wind gusted across a meadow and slammed into their bikes.

"Lean into the wind," Edward hollered over his shoulder.

"Can't hear you," she yelled back, her voice muffled by the wind.

Edward pointed ahead. His stomach had been growling for several miles and they were overdue for a snack break.

He leaned his bicycle against a large, brown sign warning visitors to BE BEAR AWARE and rubbed warmth into his hands, arching his back to stretch. The relief felt in that fleeting moment after stepping off his fully loaded torture machine was one of the highlights of his day.

Kara propped her bike against his and stepped through the snow-fringed grass to get a better look at the map on his handlebar bag. "About fifteen miles to Glacier?" she asked.

"Yeah, that sounds right."

"That puts us around here somewhere," she said, pointing.

Edward didn't see where she pointed on the map, his concentration focused on opening the Cordura pouch hanging from her bike. The barrel lock holding the pull cord was proving too tricky to squeeze with his insulated paws.

"There's nothing in there."

"Are you serious? We're out of snacks?"

"I told you this morning we had to stock up on granola bars when we got food. I ate the last one earlier."

He leaned over Kara's shoulder to study the map and traced his finger along a black squiggle of a line, pausing at an intersection, turning north, then jumping south to the spot marked Columbia Falls. "Shit." It was barely a whisper, but she had to have heard it. "Sorry," he added softly.

"Did we miss the turn?"

He sucked his teeth and nodded. He'd been caught daydreaming before, but never someplace so remote, with so few options for food.

"I knew we should have gotten groceries in Whitefish," she said.

"I know." It had been his decision to try to beat the storm.

Edward estimated they missed the turn by eight miles. And if there was one thing Kara hated, it was backtracking. She'd no sooner turn the car around to see if they left the iron plugged in than double-back sixteen miles round-trip on a bicycle. Least of all in the snow. *Shit, indeed.*

"We'll have to hope there's something open in West Glacier then."

Edward shook his head.

"There's got to be at least a visitor's center or gas station. It's a National Park."

"It's the off-season," he countered.

"*Something* will be open."

"No, there won't," he said, his voice raising. "I checked before we left. There were only two places to get groceries, and West Glacier wasn't one of them. Listen, I'm sorry, it's totally my fault, but we need to turn around. We're completely out of food."

Kara mumbled something about needing a map of her own as she walked away with her bike. His stomach growled and, when he looked up, Kara was already straddling her bike, out beyond the sign, facing east.

"We shouldn't split up," she said, "but I'm not riding back to town."

"So you're okay going hungry tonight?"

"I'm not convinced we'll have to."

Glancing at the bear warning, he jerked his bike away from the sign's green metal posts and threw his right leg over the seat. He wasn't about to abandon her in the wild. "So never mind the research I've done—"

"You can tell me 'I told you so' all night if we go hungry, but it'll work out, trust me." Kara clipped into her pedals and started down the road.

He wanted to admire her optimism, her faith in the universe being on her side. But his was an apple that fell from a far more cautious tree.

Edward pushed off and accelerated, sprinting out of the saddle, his grip tight as he strained to catch up to her. Tucked into Kara's slipstream—what little there was at twelve miles per hour—he pedaled on in silence as the passing miles wore down the tread of his frustration. Ahead, the road curved toward a metal bridge spanning the Flathead River.

The clouds parted and a fleeting ray of sunshine offered a touch of warmth as they crossed the converted trestle. Despite his hunger and longing for home—and work—Edward found something magical in crossing borders and rivers by bicycle. They had cycled into their third state since leaving home and now, with the icy waters of the Flathead flowing beneath them, they were crossing another major river.

The road soon joined U.S. 2 outside the city limits. Edward had replayed the day in his mind on a loop since realizing his mistake. Not only had they not passed any stores since leaving Whitefish, but they'd seen few cars on the road. And not a single RV.

Every lodge, outfitter, and campground lining the highway into the gateway town of West Glacier was shuttered. And none looked to be opening any time soon, either. Billboards showcasing majestic snow-capped mountains, advertisements for inns and guide services, offered a glimpse of the alpine views that lay hidden behind the returning clouds and gray pall that cloaked the town.

It appeared as if all of western Montana was hibernating along with the bears. All except for two hungry cyclists stopping for the night.

A shuttered convenience store opposite the park entrance provided the *I told you so* Edward didn't have the heart to utter. The snow had stopped, but evidence of a wicked winter lay everywhere, piled in drifts that tickled the eaves of the chestnut-stained parkitecture.

Edward and Kara pedaled along the tranquil, forest-lined entrance road, past snowbound cabins tucked amongst conifers. Glacier National Park was on both their bucket lists, but March was no time to explore the park by bike; they needed a place to camp, nothing more.

The pay station's gates were raised, the ticket booth empty. Edward coasted past the self-pay kiosks.

"You forgot to pay."

Edward sighed and looped back in Kara's direction, unsurprised to see she had stopped. "Ignore it. Ranger will probably wonder who the sucker was that paid to enter a closed park."

"The park's not closed," Kara said, palm up, motioning at the gates.

"We pay taxes."

"Don't be like that. You know I hate it when people say things like that."

"What? We do. A lot of money, I might add." Experience taught Edward to expect a lecture, but Kara merely shook her head and opened her wallet.

"Do you have a five?"

"No," he said without checking.

"Then I'll leave a twenty." Kara wrote the word BIKES across the fee envelope and slid it into the iron ranger.

"You sure you don't want to shovel the walk or clean some bathrooms too?" He kept his tone light, but knew they were spending nearly eighty dollars a day. A rate that would quickly challenge his ability to meet the monthly minimums on their credit cards.

"Don't mock me when I'm hungry." She punched his arm as she pushed past with her bike. "Wise-ass."

Edward rubbed his arm, feigning injury, then cycled after her.

Neither was surprised to find Apgar Campground gated, the loop buried. Pushing their ninety-pound touring bikes around the barrier through hub-deep snow held little appeal. "Let's search for a clear spot by the lake," Edward suggested.

They soon arrived at a picnic area on Lake McDonald's southern shore. Thanks to the peculiarities of the wind and a grouping of trees, there was a patch of clear ground large enough to fit their tent. Edward jumped off his bike, thrilled at their luck. "We can set the tent up right here," he said, swinging his arms to illustrate the orientation, "and put our heads at this end, where it's a little higher."

"Next to the NO CAMPING sign?" Kara asked, her eyebrows raised.

"Golly Ranger, we got here after dark and didn't see the sign," he said, affecting his best aw-shucks drawl.

"And if the Ranger comes before sunset?"

"Then we'll ask him where he'd like us to go. Geez. The park's covered in snow and we're the only ones here. Nobody's gonna care where we camp."

Kara shifted her gaze and bit her lower lip in silent protest.

Edward was normally a stickler for rules, but even he knew when to put common sense above blind obedience. He turned to his bike, unhooked the duffel bag that rode behind the seat, and slammed it onto a picnic table. Grabbing it by the sides, he shoved it back and forth, plowing snow off the table and launching crystalline clouds into the air. He turned his attention to the bench nearest him just as Kara grabbed his wrist. He turned to face her, his jaw set.

"I'm sorry," she said. "Really. This is a great site."

His glare persisted.

"I should have listened to you about the stores. I screwed up."

His stomach rumbled, but he held quiet. Did she have any idea the seriousness of their situation? Did it ever occur to her what would happen if a storm rolled in, trapping them for days without food?

He swallowed his thoughts as her hazel eyes stared upward at him, glistening, melting his anger. She leaned forward, inviting a kiss.

"We forgot something," she said, wrapping her arms around him. Edward and Kara embraced, his helmeted head tilted atop hers, her cheek nuzzled against his frost-covered jacket. They held one another, motionless, silent, as they had done every afternoon since leaving home. The ritual was borne from the joy and excitement of heading out to see the world, at least for Kara. For Edward, it was grounding, a tether to the life they left behind.

"You rode great today," he said, holding her by the arms.

"I learned from the best." She kissed him again. They smiled, eyes locked, and nodded gently in unison. The nod was the truth. Their nod was the mutual understanding that things would be hard and they'd disagree and they'd get angry and curse, but all would be forgiven. *Always.*

Edward and Kara unloaded the bicycles in silence, each stacking their four panniers, duffel bags, and handlebar bags at opposite ends of the picnic table. Twelve bags in total: six yellow, six red. The tent went up in a flash of practiced choreography, with the granite-on-titanium hammering of the tent stakes providing accompaniment. Kara emptied her duffel, tossing the sleeping bags, air mattresses, and inflatable pillows willy-nilly into the tent. The stuffed Sasquatch she acquired halfway across Washington went in last.

They each grabbed a water bottle (the temperature had mercifully stayed above freezing) and stripped down alongside the picnic table. Edward shed his jacket, wool jersey, and base layer and braced for the assault to come. Armed with a few drops of eucalyptus soap and a washcloth no softer than a pumice stone, he scrubbed the sweat from his reddening gooseflesh as fast he could. With his upper body clean enough, he tugged on a reasonably fresh shirt and a blue fleece sweater. His spiky brown hair would have to wait for a shower.

He stripped off his rain pants and tights while standing barefoot atop a pair of sneakers, then held his breath as he peeled the chamois undershorts from his saddle sores. The pain was brief, but excruciating. It was their sixteenth day on the road, and judging by the high-pitched *ow-ow-ow* coming from Kara, he wasn't alone in his suffering. Kara, wearing only the bra she sometimes slept in, offered him a compassionate look and a packet of disposable wet wipes.

He finished getting dressed and assured Kara they would be fine; they'd callous over eventually. Besides, they had more pressing concerns. "Why don't you find us more water while I check the bags for food? There's gotta be at least a packet of instant soup or hot cocoa mix in there somewhere."

Kara, clad in yoga pants and a pink puffy jacket, pulled a paisley Buff over her head. Edward watched her leave, appreciating the effect two weeks of cycling had on her figure.

Solitude was a rarity on the trip, and he cherished this part of the day, when he was alone to focus on dinner. He had always enjoyed cooking—it was the one trait he inherited from his mother. And, after so many nights stuck working long hours, he was happy to be able to cook for Kara again. But this was nothing like home.

He emptied the pannier containing their kitchen. Pickings were slim. There was a bag of spices, condiment packets, a pouch of dried fruit that felt as hard as the rock he used on the tent stakes, and a bag of Twizzlers with only two pieces left. He grabbed the cookware and felt something shift inside. Puzzled, he undid the clasp and was happy to find a small bag of instant rice. "Well, hello, Uncle Ben, what are you doing in there?"

Kara returned as he finished laying out their foldable dinner bowls and sporks. "Good news! The bathroom down the road is open. Flushing toilets and all the tap water we can use," she said, setting a full dromedary bag and unused water filter on the table.

"Now I don't feel so bad about the twenty bucks," he said with a wink. "Dinner's about ready."

"You found food?"

"Better."

Kara shot him a curious glance, then tilted her head. "Do I smell chicken?"

"Please sit, madam," he said, ushering her to the other side of the picnic table. "Tonight you shall enjoy a private waterside dining experience guaranteed to warm your senses. Close your eyes and imagine the islands. Smell the salt breeze and envision a heaping plate of jerk chicken, rice, and the sweetest plantains this side of the Caribbean."

"That sounds lovely—"

"Don't speak. Just embrace the image and savor the aroma." Edward spooned the food using a measuring cup as a ladle. It plopped into the bowls in a crude fashion. "Ready?"

Kara nodded, her lips a playful smile.

"Voila!"

She stared in disgust.

"Oh, come on," Edward said. "Try it."

Kara dipped her spork into the bowl. She swallowed without chewing and looked as though gagging was inevitable.

"I told you to use your imagination. I found some instant rice and mixed it with bouillon and the dried bananas from your trail mix."

Kara eyed the meal, her face twisted in disgust.

"I also added some jerk seasoning—I think it was from that spice set your boss gave us before we left."

"It's positively awful, but thanks?" she said, her voice rising with incredulity.

"I know it is. I tasted it before you got back. I almost retched."

Kara made a show of chewing it fully, not unlike a cow with its cud, and burst into laughter as soon as she swallowed.

Edward returned her gaze as she wiped her mouth with the back of her hand. "This is fun," she said.

"The dinner?"

"No. The food is awful. I mean all of *this*," she said, sweeping her hand at the mountain-ringed lakeside. "I love being out here. I love that this is our life."

Edward took a deep breath and shifted in his seat. "A lot of people would say we're crazy."

"Let 'em."

"What if I was one of them?"

"You think this is crazy?" she asked, her smile fading.

Edward twirled his utensil in the mush, wishing he hadn't said anything. The trip wasn't just crazy, it was stupid. They sold their clothes and furniture, she quit her job, and their credit cards were going to be maxed out by the time they got home, wherever that would be. Worse still, he'd be lucky to find another job in venture capital anywhere, let alone in Seattle, after what he pulled.

"Earth to Ed," she said, snapping her fingers. "I'm serious. Do you think we're being crazy?"

Edward blinked to. He wanted to deflect. To tell her she was the crazy one, for leaving him alone with the bag of Twizzlers. But he didn't have it in him to fake an attempt at humor. He turned his attention back to the rice, not wanting to ruin her moment.

Chapter 4

TUESDAY, MARCH 31 — GLACIER NATIONAL PARK,
MONTANA, USA

Edward was jolted awake as a bough-full of melting snow bombarded the rainfly. The one-two assault continued as the tent's sunlit yellow interior irradiated his freshly opened eyes. Edward moaned and squeezed them shut in defense.

"Rise and shine, sleepy head."

He rolled over and saw Kara lying on her side, arm bent, head resting on her hand. She'd been watching him sleep. "It's beautiful out today. Not a cloud in the sky."

"You up long?"

"Since sunrise. I had to pee."

"I didn't hear you get up."

"You were out cold. I got dressed and boiled water for coffee. We can heap some sugar in for calories."

Edward's stomach growled. She giggled then leaned in and kissed him quickly on the lips. "Get changed. We should break camp early in case the ranger comes."

His reluctance to leave the warmth of his sleeping bag was no match for Kara's insistence on getting the day started. She unzipped the inner and outer tent doors and bounded from her sleeping bag and through the vestibule in a single move, leaving the doors open to the frigid air. Edward watched in awe, wondering when—or if—her excitement would ever wane.

Not much later, with the gear packed and the panniers strapped to the bikes, Edward spread the map on the picnic table as Kara placed her travel mug on a corner, weighting it against a rising breeze.

"Here's where that convenience store outside the park is." He pointed to an intersection on the map then traced his finger southward along the highway. "And here's the Continental Divide. It's about forty miles and three thousand feet of climbing to the top of Marias Pass—"

"That doesn't sound so bad," Kara interrupted.

"No, except that it's mostly flat for the first twenty miles."

"Oh."

"We'll get a nice warm-up before the climbing begins, but it gets steep near the top. Good news is, it's all downhill from there."

Kara dragged her finger along a different route, one that switchbacked across the park to the northeast. "And no chance of going through the park?" she asked, with a pinch of disappointment.

"Not without a snowmobile and a death wish."

"Yeah. That's what I thought."

"We'll come back," he assured her.

Ten miles down the road, Kara still seemed disappointed. She knew Glacier's famous Going-to-the-Sun Road would be snowbound until June, but the reality must not have settled in until that morning, while they were packing to leave barely fourteen hours after arriving.

Edward pedaled on, thinking about the other places she was looking forward to visiting: New York City, Spain, and New Zealand, to name a few. He would have loved to have seen more of the park too, but what could he do? It was still March, if only for a day. No matter how many lines they drew across a map, they couldn't see everything.

He shrugged it off. One minute you're in a funk, the next you're on top of the world. That's bicycle travel in a nutshell, he thought: The highs were higher and the lows were lower.

Three years was too long to be traveling if they were going to beat themselves up every time things didn't go to plan. But were they really going to be on the road that long? That was longer than it took to earn his MBA, longer than he dated Kara.

The sound of tires peeling off the wet asphalt intensified as Edward's mind swam in a whirlpool of dizzying thoughts, sending his legs on spin-cycle. Ever faster round and round, the pedals turned the wheels, grabbing the meltwater sheeting across the road, and flinging it against his fenders. It was the nature of cycling to have your emotions dictate the pace.

The road curved away, revealing a driveway. Hidden behind the snow bank halfway up the mountain was a bar and grill. A neon sign signaled it was open. He brought the bike to a stop and pumped his arms in Kara's direction. "Food," he yelled, ringing the bicycle bell. She leaped from the saddle and closed the gap in no time.

The two hurried down the stairs to the basement tavern, their handlebar bags clutched tightly with their passports and other valuables inside. The place was empty except for the lone server who met them at the counter with a pair of menus and an offer of coffee. "I'll take one of everything," Edward said, scanning the menu.

"I need something to warm me up," Kara said. "If only we didn't have another two-thousand feet to climb."

They ordered grilled ham and cheese sandwiches and tomato soup as another couple took a pair of stools at the far end of the counter.

"Hiya, Bill," the man said, waving to the server. The diner was a big guy in blue jeans, a flannel shirt, a navy quilted vest, and a face nearly as puffy. He turned to Edward and Kara and asked if they owned the bikes outside. "Well, one of them knocked over the fence out there."

Edward pulled on his jacket and ran outside to see the damage. The fence, little more than cinder blocks with some wooden beams run through the holes, was no match for the weight of their touring equipment. He moved both bikes to a snow bank closer to the door and took a moment to lock them together.

Back inside, the man chuckled as Edward apologized. "Ah, Billy don't mind. He's just happy to see some folks in here this time of year—ain't that right, Bill?" The thin-faced server grunted his acknowledgment as he ladled the steaming soup. The man continued: "We see a lot of cyclists up here during summer. Mainly the ones too scared to climb the road in the park, but I've never seen any this time of year." He turned to the woman next to him. "They've got to be two or three months early, right?"

"Yeah, June at the earliest," the woman said, peering around her companion as her stringy hair brushed the counter.

"So we've heard," Kara said under her breath.

Edward was slurping his third spoonful of soup when the man spoke again. "So, you two headed across the country with all that gear?"

Hesitating, Edward hoped Kara would field the man's question, but she stayed mum. *So much for a hot lunch.* "We're actually headed around the world," Edward admitted, hoping an avalanche of questions wouldn't soon follow.

Bill placed a pair of Bloody Marys in front of the couple and asked if they wanted the usual. "It's why we're here. Best prime rib in Montana," the man shouted in Edward's direction.

"Don't tease me like that. We still got another forty miles to ride today. I can't have that sitting in my stomach." Edward turned to Kara. "Unless you want to split one."

"We shouldn't. We'll get a big meal tomorrow night in Cut Bank."

"Cut Bank, you say?" the man asked.

"Yep. East Glacier tonight and then up through Browning tomorrow. We're gonna follow the High Line across Montana to North Dakota."

"You two better be careful going through Browning. That's Blackfoot rez." He turned to the woman. "What day is today?"

Edward couldn't hear her response.

"Good," the man said. "You don't want to be anywhere near Browning on payday. Every week they're staggering all over the street, drunk as hell after getting their checks. Nah, you won't catch me up there. I fuel up in East Glacier if I'm headed that way, and I don't stop till I'm at least to Cut Bank."

The server approached with their sandwiches. Edward reached for his before the plate hit the counter and promptly took a bite.

"You don't ride at night, do you?"

Edward made a show of chewing his food while holding a finger up until he swallowed. "No, we stick to daylight whenever possible."

"That's good. Those Indians get real rowdy after dark. Don't matter what day of the week it is. Drinking and fighting every night. Would hate to see you two get caught up in that."

Kara stared ahead, ignoring her food. Edward knew that look; she wouldn't stay quiet for long. He placed his hand on her thigh. "Ignore him," he whispered.

"Lemme tell you what you ought to do. Make a right onto the Heart Butte Cutoff road before East Glacier. Take that down to Heart Butte and then angle back up to Highway 2, out past that drunken hellhole."

Kara leaned in to Edward and not-quite-whispered, "Racist much?"

"Excuse me, miss." The man raised his voice. "If you've got something to say …"

Edward squeezed Kara's leg, a silent plea for her to let it drop.

The woman leaned forward to talk past the men to Kara. "Honey, that ain't being racist. That's being a realist. And excuse us for trying to be helpful. These folks ain't like the ones you got in Seattle. They don't have you rich city folks filling their slot machines for 'em."

Kara chomped a large bite of her sandwich and stared straight ahead, showing every indication she was going to swallow her reply.

Relieved, Edward turned to face the couple with a placating smile and a look that confessed his embarrassment. "I'm sure you're right, ma'am, and we appreciate the warning. It's too bad every tribe can't be as fortunate."

The server slid the check to Edward. "When you're ready."

Edward and Kara finished their lunch in silence.

Outside, Edward unlocked the bikes and rolled the smaller of the two to Kara, eying her as she took it.

"What?" she demanded.

"You know what."

"That guy was a jerk."

"Yeah, he was. But you can't go around calling people racists. And how'd he know we were from Seattle anyway?"

"They asked while you were outside," she said, reattaching her bag.

"And you couldn't wait to show them your bleeding heart ... We don't know anything about Browning. For all we know, it might really be dangerous and maybe—"

"Okay, okay, I get it. Let's just go," Kara said.

"Hold on. What do you want to do?"

"I'm not going to be scared in my own country, if that's what you're asking."

"What happened to being more careful?" As he spoke, an icicle the length of a broadsword broke free from the eave and sliced the snow bank inches from where the bikes had been leaning.

Kara glanced from the hole to her husband. "Maybe we both oughta be more careful."

"Which way do you want to go?"

"The way we planned," she said, matter-of-factly. "I'm serious. We can't be detouring all over the place every time someone says we should, least of all a couple of indigenous-hating hicks."

He knew she was right in a practical sense. Still, it would fall on him to keep her safe if things got rough.

"We're in Montana, Ed. What do you think people will say when we tell them we're headed to Turkey? Or Uzbekistan?" Kara pedaled off, leaving her words ringing in Edward's head while a sour taste built in his mouth. *Uzbekistan? Where the hell's that?*

The road continued its ascent to Marias Pass for twenty miles, each one steeper than the last, but no harder to pedal thanks to a stiffening tailwind. The higher they climbed, the faster they went. Edward yipped and hollered in delight as an invisible hand pushed against his back and his jacket billowed in front, its collar tickling his chin. The map case flipped forward on its button snaps, pinned upside-down by the wind, as if some invisible wanderer were studying its reverse side.

To rider's left, Precambrian pyramids floating atop snow-covered slopes marked the park's southern boundary. The exposed cliffs were too steep to hold the snow that now spun and danced in miniature vortices all around them. The aspens and pine growing near the highway were stunted, bushy tufts of green prairie-dogging on a wintry field.

Edward stopped his bike near the sign marking the Continental Divide (elevation 5,216 feet) to soak in the vista—and the moment. He swayed side to side, west to east, east to west, in an effort to stay warm as Kara took photos. "The spine of North America," he intoned while teeter-tottering atop that invisible blade that split families of raindrops in two, sending half to the Pacific, the rest to the Atlantic.

It was the fourth mountain pass they'd crested, but this one carried a significance the others hadn't. To descend its eastern flank, to roll with the wind, was to commit to the trip.

He and Kara celebrated the milestone with a high five and a hug, but without shelter from the bone-chilling wind, she didn't loiter. He watched her go then gazed back over his shoulder, a pensive look to the Pacific Northwest—toward home, the life he knew, the dreams he harbored.

"Come on, Ed!" she yelled over her shoulder.

Edward struggled to swallow the lump in his throat as his fear rooted him in place. He wanted to call her back, to retract everything he'd done, the mistakes he made. Every last bit of the past two months. Longer if it's what she wanted. But that was impossible. In faith, his option was singular: he must follow. If he couldn't hold onto the life he promised her, he had to at least give her this trip she cherished. No matter the sacrifice.

The descent to the Great Plains wasn't long, and the tailwind propelled them to speeds exceeding forty miles per hour. Edward flew past Kara in a tucked position, spurring his two-wheeled steed ever faster, the wind whipping at his face, watering his eyes. Down they plummeted mile after gleeful mile until, all at once, everything changed.

The mountains flanking the highway terminated abruptly and, like bullets from a barrel, they were shot onto a sea of undulating dirt-covered hills stretching to the horizon. No more snow, no more pines, no more Rocky Mountains. There was only a road gently wending its way downward across a khaki-colored, hazy expanse of near nothingness.

Edward sat upright on the leather saddle, feeling smaller than ever before, a mere blip on a landscape that spread to infinity. Yet despite it being so unlike anywhere he had ever been, he felt an element of homecoming, as if he expected to find a part of himself left behind. It was the same feeling he got when stepping from the ferry onto Vashon Island, outside Seattle, where his parents still lived in his childhood home.

He coasted into town, passing the recommended detour without a glance, and stopped at the first motel he encountered. He recognized nothing, yet he slipped into the alien environment as one does a favorite sweater after an Indian summer.

Edward sat quietly during breakfast, picking at a ragged cuticle. He'd started chewing his nails again.

Kara thumbed through a tourist brochure about a Native American museum in Browning. She wanted to go, it was on the way, but he was against prolonging their stay on the reservation, given the warning they had received. Prime Rib Guy was a bigoted jerk, of that there was no doubt, but even the most tired stereotypes often walked with a bounce of truth in their step. He wouldn't say anything to Kara—no sense starting off the day with an argument—but it was best to get through town early, he reasoned. If there were any drunks, they'd probably still be sleeping it off.

The ride to Browning was only thirteen miles, but spring in the High Plains doesn't abide the calendar. The grit carried on yesterday's wind now mixed with soggy snowfall, caking the roads, their bicycles, and outerwear in sandy slush. That it was April Fool's Day wasn't lost on Edward as they pedaled into the storm. *This is how people win a Darwin Award*, he thought as they cycled past the last ramshackle house in East Glacier. Once out of town, as visibility diminished on the open road, his sense of having been there before intensified.

Fortunately, traffic wasn't an issue. Every passing car held its line, following the tire tracks carved before it. The drivers didn't move over to give them any extra room but drove in a straight line, which was all Edward could ask for. He glanced in the mirror and spotted Kara right behind him, her head tilted down to keep the snow from her eyes. "We should have brought ski goggles," he yelled to Kara, but she didn't respond.

By the time Browning came into view, Edward had changed his mind about the museum. The storm was intensifying and they needed a place to warm up. Any trouble-making locals be damned.

Edward tugged on the door. The lock yielded a millimeter, at most, before the heavy steel panel with its narrow, wired glass security window thudded against the deadbolt. The interior was dark and the sign said weekends only, but he tried again anyway. Twice.

"Closed," he said, descending the stairs.

Kara shook her head sullenly. "Dammit, Montana."

"Two months—"

"Don't say it," she interrupted. "We're early. I know." Kara wheeled her bike around and pointed up the road. "There's a taco place. Let's warm up there."

They racked the bikes against a signpost and ran the locks through the wheels and frames. The restaurant was similar to a Taco Bell, right down to the menu and signage, only slightly off. Like an identical twin that walked with a limp and stuttered.

Edward arranged their dripping-wet gloves, headbands, and jackets across the chairs of an unused table and slid into a nearby booth, his back to the door so he could see the bikes outside. Kara returned a few minutes later with two cups of coffee, chicken quesadillas, and an order of something called Mexi-Rolls. Taquitos in plain-speak.

He was blowing the steam off his coffee when he heard voices and the stomping of boots behind him. Kara flicked her chin toward the door as four haggard-looking locals entered. Each was dressed in multiple layers of plaid flannel, work boots, dungarees, knit cap, and gloves. Edward suspected they had spent the entire winter in those same outfits. Their hair—inky, wet, and stringy—draped over their shoulders. One by one they leaned large, wooden sticks against the doorjamb, alongside the height marker security strip.

Edward and Kara exchanged a cautious glance as metal chairs were dragged screeching across the tile floor.

Two of the men stared as Edward sipped his coffee. Lowering his gaze, Edward noticed plastic bags—poor man's water proofing—protruding from their scuffed, life-beaten boots. Wetness dripped from their heavy denim, leaving Edward feeling self-conscious in his Gore-Tex excess.

"You two like riding in the snow?"

Edward looked up as Kara turned around. The foursome, a woman and three men, one with a cloudy eye, stared back. Edward had no idea which had spoken. Was he supposed to answer? Did he need to? *Do we like riding in the snow?*

"Not really," he said, trying to make eye contact with the whole group at once, "but it's not so bad as long as it doesn't get too deep. One or two inches is okay; more than that and it gets difficult." He talked fast; their attention waned.

"Where you from?"

Kara's eyebrows arched halfway to her hairline as she grinned across the table. "Looks like another cold lunch for you," she whispered.

"Seattle."

"Nice," the woman said. "Got a cousin who moved there. Works with computers. Maybe you know him." She spoke with a confidence that belied her soft, curious face.

Edward was struck by her complexion, her tawny skin hosted the worst acne he'd ever seen on an adult. Still, he couldn't help but wonder if she was putting him on. "Maybe. It's not that big of a city," he offered, attempting to be polite.

"It's bigger than Browning," she said, as her companions snickered and shook their heads.

Kara placed a Mexi-Roll onto Edward's quesadilla wrapper and turned in her seat to take over conversation duty. He listened as she gently ribbed one of the men about his NFL allegiances—he was wearing a Minnesota Vikings cap. It was one of those pointless common-ground conversations strangers cling to when compelled to chat. Something Edward's Wisconsin-raised wife was far better at than he. Still, he didn't like the way they were looking at them, their constant glances outside, the size of the sticks leaning against the door. *Were they scoping out our bikes?*

Beneath the table, Edward tapped Kara's ankle with his shoe to get her attention before rising to clear the table. "We should get going."

He didn't want to look scared, and he would have liked to enjoy his coffee once it cooled, but he didn't like the ragtag bunch watching his every move.

Kara rolled her eyes. "They're *finnnne*," she mouthed, silently.

Maybe so, but Edward didn't want to take any chances. "I'll deal with the trash," he said, collecting the food wrappers. "You get our stuff. I'll meet you at the bikes."

Kara clearly thought he was overreacting, but rose to collect their outerwear.

Outside, Edward undid the locks then knelt to retie his shoelace as a motley collection of dogs approached. Two had obvious wounds and matted fur. One hopped on three feet. The tail of another was half gone. Edward startled and nearly tipped over when Kara thrust the damp winter wear at him and bent to pet the dogs.

"These yours?" she asked the locals who followed, each grabbing their stick on the way out.

"Kind of," the woman replied. "They follow us so we feed them."

"The sticks are for the others," Vikings Cap explained, leaning against his knotty staff. "Always some rez dogs running around, biting people."

The men circled around the bikes and ran their hands along the seats, squeezed the brakes, and rang the bells. The guy with one good eye attempted to pick up Edward's bike. The front wheel lifted two inches off the ground then fell to the cement with a thud. He shook his head and backed away whistling. Edward had seen that reaction before and couldn't help smiling with pride, despite wishing he'd left the bikes locked.

"Nice bikes. How much you pay for 'em?" Vikings fan asked.

Edward snapped in his direction.

This was exactly why they shouldn't have stopped, why they should have taken the detour. They were exactly where they were told not to go, and surrounded by four locals stinking of rain and sweat and dog—and stale beer. The bikes were their most valuable possessions. They cost thousands each, and carried as much in clothes and camping gear. Gear that was their *home*. Edward's chest tightened as he thought of the junkies in Seattle who fed their addiction by pawning stolen bicycles. These four weren't junkies though, he hoped.

"Oh, not much. They were a gift from my grandmother," Kara lied, stepping between them. "They're more sentimental than anything."

The men nodded in appreciation and backed away.

Kara ruffled the gimpy dog's fur before straddling her bike. She cast Edward a disappointed look as she pulled on her helmet. "Lighten up."

The storm dissolved as fast as it had risen. Highway 2, desert dry and arrow straight, glimmered in the afternoon sun. Big Sky Country stretched to infinity.

The bicycles hummed. Edward pedaled casually in his tallest gearing as a rising tailwind lent a hand. Over two hundred fifty pounds of man, bicycle, and gear cruising at thirty miles per hour; it was rarely this easy. He unzipped his jacket, pushed his sunglasses higher on his nose, and cranked along, bolt upright in the saddle with his arms stretched wide, basking in midday euphoria. Takeoff. In his mirror, the snow-capped peaks of the Front Range shrank into memory.

"Downhill to the Mississippi," Edward said, as Kara pulled alongside him on the wide shoulder.

She shook her head, smirking. "Yeah, right. It's never 'all downhill from here.'"

He laughed. "Spoken like a true cyclist."

Kara carefully withdrew her camera and pointed it at Edward as he rode hands-free. "Slow down, I'll get some video," she said, pulling in front of him for an action shot.

"Look," he yelled, pointing. Eighty yards to their right and closing fast, was a herd of wild horses at full gallop. At least twenty, all but three were burnt umber with a black mane, the others white with chestnut markings. The horses turned near the highway and sprinted alongside Edward and Kara, keeping pace with only a rusty barbed-wire fence between them.

Up ahead, set back from the highway, slumped a gray, weather-beaten structure. He thought it might be an old cabin from frontier days, but soon realized it was probably for livestock. A shelter left to rot in the elements, standing only by the grace of rust and gravity.

The horses, running not quite single-file, and kicking up tufts of golden weeds and grass, veered toward the structure.

"This is amazing!" Kara hollered.

The camera swung from her wrist as she grabbed two handfuls of brake and skid the bike to an abrupt stop. If not for Edward's quick reflexes, he would have ridden right into her. He yelped in surprise as Kara raised the camera and focused on getting her shot.

She panned as the horses galloped straight toward the dilapidated structure. With the Rocky Mountains in the background and a solitary contrail texturing the cold steel blue of the sky, it would be a hell of a photo.

"Keep going. Almost," Kara whispered, urging the horses into a better composition.

The lead horse squealed and cut hard from the barn, sliding on its front hooves while digging for traction in the loose soil. The others squatted and slid, narrowly avoiding a pileup. The trailing horses changed course, cutting the corner as if sensing danger, but never stopped. Edward watched as the herd disappeared into the horizon behind a cloud of dust.

"Aww, why'd they turn? That was gonna be a great shot," Kara said, dropping her arms to her side. "Something scared them."

"Think it was the barn?"

Kara shrugged. She raised the camera, zoomed in, and took several more photos. Edward approached, straddling his bike, and looked over her shoulder as she magnified the images on the screen.

"Wait, go back. What was that?"

Kara zoomed in further on the barn's opening. "Is that …"

"It can't be."

"I think I see a face."

"Hold my bike," Edward said. He dismounted and ducked between the strands of the barbed-wire fence, then ran across the hummocky field toward the shelter, a blend of fear and curiosity spurring him on.

The stench of rancid meat intensified as he neared the shelter. He zipped up his jacket, tucked his face inside the collar to filter the smell.

In the corner of the three-sided shelter, atop a scratchy bed of grass dried into a rotten brown, lay the remains of a man, naked aside for some cellophane tied around his waist. An empty bag of Cool Ranch Doritos, fashioned into a loincloth of sorts, was held in place by grass twine.

Edward gagged, then took a hesitant step closer. The man's skin had frosted over, turning blue in spots. His eyes were sunken and elbows frozen in place at hard angles across his chest, hands burrowed in his armpits. Only his stomach appeared bloated. *The winter cold must have slowed the decomposition*, Edward thought. Metallic green flies perched atop the face.

That the man was dead was not surprising. Nobody could survive a night out in this weather clothed, let alone naked. What Edward found most astonishing was the man himself. He appeared to be at least six feet tall, and those parts of him not blue were deep bronze in color. The man was broad-chested and lean, despite his distended stomach. Even in death, his limbs appeared taught and rope-like under the blotchy skin. He had very little body hair, but a tuft of stubble on the chin and a head full of shimmering black silk that disappeared beneath his shoulders.

Edward trembled, nauseated by the sight and the smell. He had never seen a corpse before. There was no telling how long the body had been there, but he was thankful for the refrigerating benefits of winter.

In the distance, Kara's voice called to him, but he couldn't pry his eyes from the body.

Edward inched closer and saw the toes, black as night, poking from a layer of straw. All nine of them.

The missing digit, an oblong hunk of charcoal flesh, lay several inches away.

Edward convulsed as the revolting stench brought his lunch to a boil. He doubled over and vomited onto the untamed grass of the makeshift morgue. As he wiped his mouth, he saw Kara waving near the fence. He took a final glance at the body then sprinted back to her.

"Took you long enough. What were you doing?"

"There's a body. A Blackfoot," he said, panting. "Must have died from hypothermia. Frostbite all over."

"So close to the road?"

"He's naked."

"What? All the way out here?"

"I can take that," Edward said, grabbing his bike by the handlebar and seat.

"You think somebody dumped him on the side of the road?"

He had no idea how the man got there. "He had a Doritos bag tied around his waist with grass from the field. Nice twine, too. Like he had made it before."

"If he was sober enough to get crafty, you'd think he would have flagged down a car."

"That's what I thought at first, but there's something else. You're going to think I'm crazy, but he looks …" Edward looked back to the shelter, carving his thoughts into something that wouldn't sound crazy. "Never mind. It doesn't make any sense."

Kara cocked her head. "Looks like what, Edward?"

"Like the real deal. I mean, he doesn't look like any of the Native Americans I've ever seen. Not modern ones, at least." He said it flatly, as if coming clean from a horrible deceit. "He's not watered down."

"What?" she said, her arms akimbo.

"He looks like he fell out of one of the dioramas in those Ben Stiller museum movies, like a drawing from a history book."

Edward matched Kara's stare as she scrutinized him.

"I've got to see this," Kara said.

"No, you don't. It's bad. It's starting to smell. I threw up. Kara, just no."

"You're telling me there's a guy over there who looks like he fell out of the history books, I'm taking a look."

Edward grabbed her by the wrist, "No." It came out more stern than he'd intended. "You're gonna have nightmares."

Kara's eyes dropped to the hand holding her in place. "That bad?"

Edward nodded.

"Okay, but we have to tell someone."

Edward looked away.

"We have to at least let the police know he's there," Kara repeated.

"Or maybe we call someone from the tribe. Or a historian."

"And tell them what, Ed? That you found the body of a time-traveling native? I know you're shaken up, but there are plenty of pure bloods still around, especially out west."

"So you just think—"

"I don't know what to think," she said, cutting him off. "Wait here."

Edward watched her approach the road, waving her arms overhead. Several truckers passed, ignoring her, but eventually a pickup truck filled with welding equipment pulled over. The driver lowered the passenger-side window and asked if they needed help.

"We're fine, but there's a dead man in the barn over there. We were taking photos of the horses and spotted it on the screen," Kara explained. "My husband said he's practically frozen solid."

"Noooooo shit? Well that's a new one. Ya think he's homeless?"

"Maybe. Probably. I don't know. He's naked, though."

"In this weather? *Sheeeeeiiit.*"

"We don't have a phone and were hoping you could call 911 for us."

"Yeah, sure. I'll give the sheriff a call after I take a look. You two headed to Cut Bank?"

Kara gave the man their names and told him the motel where they'd be staying in case the sheriff had any questions. The man nodded and pulled the truck further onto the shoulder, hazard lights blinking.

Edward watched the man head for the barn, then yanked his bike in the direction of Cut Bank. He threw a leg over the saddle and glared at Kara. "Still think I should lighten up? That everything always works out? Tell it to the guy who froze to death."

Chapter 5

MONDAY, APRIL 6 — CIRCLE, MONTANA, USA

The temperature plummeted as winter dug in for its final stand. Bundled against the frigid air by day and forced to forego camping in favor of heated motels at night, Edward and Kara paralleled the Canadian border eastward through a string of no-light depot towns left to fade into history with barely a tub of Skippy on their store shelves. Diesel locomotives rendered the High Line's old coal-and-water stops obsolete and the wheat industry swept the landscape clean, depositing people and places into larger piles with names like Glasgow, Inverness, and Zurich. Not one showed a whiff of the splendor suggested by its European name.

They had the wind at their back and flat roads ahead. Each day's sixty miles went by in a blur of blue skies and golden fields. Trains, one hundred thirteen cars long (or was it one hundred twelve?) were the only distraction, oil-filled eels racing across a calm sea.

Thoughts of the peculiar Blackfoot body retreated from Edward's mind, the image shrinking in the mirror of his consciousness with each passing mile. Kara hadn't mentioned it since the night after they found him, and even then only to express surprise that the sheriff never called.

Five days and three hundred thirty miles later, Edward led the way south from Wolf Point, across the Missouri River, and into a raging headwind—no good fortune lasts forever. Barbed-wire fences lined the sides of State Route 13, ensuring nobody strayed onto the lolling waves of tilled wheat fields. Thousands of sun-burnt, amber acres of winter grain stretched uninterrupted in every direction, the expansive western edge of the good ol' American breadbasket.

There was no escaping the monotony.

Edward folded himself as small as he could while pedaling into the wind, encouraging Kara to imitate his time-trialist posture. She wasn't comfortable drafting, but she needed to keep her front tire inches from his rear if they were to maintain their pace, sluggish as it was.

"Want me to take a pull?" she asked, yelling over the wind.

Yes, he did, but shook his head no. He wanted to be done. Warm. Having Kara lead would only slow them further—she being too weak to battle the wind, too petite to block it.

Edward rode on, head down, staring at the odometer, watching as the mileage ticked by with agonizing lethargy. They had their chance to stop early in the day, to cut their losses and hope for a tailwind tomorrow. But no. The woman running the last motel they had seen, overstuffed in her mismatched tracksuit, ruined that option. Unwilling to budge from her recliner until a *Price is Right* commercial break, she had a room available, then asked why they were cycling in the cold. "You lose your license?" she said with unmerited disdain.

Kara laughed. "Not at all. We're cycling around the world. Left Seattle three weeks ago."

The woman scoffed as she straightened, then stared from Edward to Kara, her eyes drawn into pinpricks of blackness. "What are you, a couple of trust-fund babies?" She said it with such venom, even Edward felt the sting.

Kara spluttered an indecipherable blend of denial and anger, the hurt burning in her surprised face. She had grown sensitive to anything concerning her upbringing, the sacrifices her parents made to send her to college, her lack of contact with them. Her leg twitched beside him. "Come on. We're not staying here," she said, yanking open the door and nearly knocking the little bell above it from its hook.

Edward shook his head at the woman. "On second thought, the tent will be just fine tonight." He followed Kara out the door into the frigid, gusting emptiness of eastern Montana.

The map hinted at a town—a flea speck of a dot—but he was determined to reach it. And soon. It was midday, their water was turning slushy in their bottles, and the wind was cutting him like a scalpel.

The bleach white steeple of a countryside chapel soon rose above the horizon. It was the first structure he'd seen in over twenty miles since the motel. A fertilizer depot sat opposite the church, a barn lurked in the distance.

Edward felt his heart sink at the absence of a diner or store. He needed shelter. Gesturing for Kara to slow down, he rode up the driveway of the chapel, right to the front door flush with the asphalt, and gave it a tug. It didn't budge.

"So much for warming up inside," Kara said. Her face melted in pity as she sensed his discomfort when he turned. "How bad is it?"

"Bad. Can't feel my fingers," he said, shivering, "and my feet are frozen solid."

"Let's go around back, out of the wind."

They pushed their bikes to the leeward side of the chapel and leaned them against the peeling paint. Edward flopped to the grass and drew his knees to his chest. He wrapped his arms around his legs and rocked, trying to generate warmth.

"Do me a favor," he said. "Get my bag of winter gear."

Kara retrieved the orange stuff sack and gave it a squeeze. "You should be wearing your mountaineering socks."

Edward shot her a look. "What do you think I'm wearing? The wind cuts right through the shoes."

"Too bad we don't have any of those plastic baggies like the guys in Browning," Kara said, positive, as usual.

Edward's mind galloped twenty miles east of Browning, to the body. All alone in that field, naked, the cold piercing him, turning him black, knuckle by knuckle. Edward was neither naked nor alone, but he wrapped himself in the other man's desperation.

"I need to put the sock liners on," he said, trying to untie his laces. It was no use. His numb fingers were on strike. "Can you help?" he asked, his frustration rising.

Kara squatted at Edward's feet, tossed her cycling gloves to the ground, and deftly untied his laces and eased the shoes off, her Wisconsin upbringing having left her impervious to the cold. His feet warmed in the exposed air as blood returned to his toes. He tugged the Gore-Tex socks on over the thick wool and asked Kara to retie the shoes loosely.

"I've never seen you like this. You look miserable," she said.

Edward opened his mouth to speak, then looked away. He stared at the dancing grass until his eyes went cross, wondering if he was really built for this.

He wanted to confide the truth, only he didn't know what that was anymore. Should he tell her he never truly wanted to do this trip? That he enjoyed being on the bike every day, but spent most of those hours struggling—and failing—to not think about the home and career they left behind? The earnings he suspected would one day be needed to provide for her parents, assuming they ended their estrangement. Was he miserable? Yes, today he was.

"It's the wind. It's beating me down, that's all."

She looked at him with such tremendous sympathy, it was as if she personally took the blame for the wind. Her eyes fluttered, half-closed, as she kissed him on the cheek. "You can do this."

He nodded, despite his misgivings.

The remaining twenty-five miles to the town of Circle were grueling, but they made it before sunset. With ten miles to go and Edward's strength all but depleted, Kara pulled around him, patted her hip as if calling a dog to heel, and accelerated. She didn't just hold his pace, but quickened it. And he warmed in her draft.

Kara led the way to a motel off the highway that blended Old West ruggedness with Victorian fragility. Crushed velvet and lace lined the lobby, while wispy pastel cameos of the town's elders, framed in gold-leafed ovals, adorned the walls. It reminded Edward of an old-timey train car, the kind the Carnegies or Rockefellers might have sipped a brandy in. The thought warmed him, body and soul.

Edward paid in cash, no need to see the room. He'd have slept in a Burger King to escape the cold.

The clerk slid the room key across the counter. Its large, plastic keychain was good for a free drink at the local American Legion.

Kara smiled as she dangled it like a charm. "Thirsty?"

That night, after showering and a quick dinner in their motel room, they went to the American Legion. Edward hesitated before ringing the doorbell, believing it a private club for veterans. "You sure we're allowed in?"

She waved the chunk of plastic in front of him and grinned. "According to the magic key we are."

He made a face, unconvinced.

"It's gonna be fine. You're a conversation chameleon, I've seen you work a room."

"A chameleon in civvy clothing. Look at us," he said, stepping back for the full effect. They didn't pack much for going out and each wore their lone pair of tan hiking pants, gingham ExOfficio button-down, and soft-shell Patagonia jacket. As if it wasn't bad enough that he was about to lead his young, attractive wife into a veteran's bar in eastern Montana, he looked like he stepped straight out of an REI catalog. "We look ridiculous."

"You're overreacting. At least our jackets aren't matchy-matchy."

Sticking out would be bad enough, but there was more. It didn't matter how much of a guy's guy you were, being the one non-military guy in a room full of vets was emasculating. Dressing up in yuppie hiking gear only made it worse.

Edward swallowed his insecurities and rang the bell. He felt the security camera judging him unworthy, just as his active-duty cousins did during family gatherings. He averted its gaze as Kara smiled upward at the lens.

The door buzzed and a small light flashed green. Kara pulled the door open. "Ready to make some friends?"

Her smile comforted and frightened him in equal measure, all love and trust. Trust in the world around her, that wherever she went only good would follow and, if not, that Edward would keep her safe. Could he? Her beauty never failed to turn heads when they went out, but he didn't worry about other men in Seattle. Most were too shy to make a move, and the few who did backed off when they saw the ring. But here? He wasn't so sure.

Edward stopped the door with his foot and put a hand on her shoulder. "Be careful, okay."

"We'll be fine," she said, then pecked him on the lips. "Besides, I've got you to defend me from any grabby jarheads, right?"

The forgotten stench of the nightclub trifecta hit him instantly: equal parts spilled beer, cigarette smoke, and Lysol. His eyes adjusted to the dim lighting as he followed Kara to the bar, wondering how long it'd been since he was someplace that allowed smoking indoors. They claimed two empty stools at the far end, alone.

Edward had no idea of the town's population, but figured at least half its residents were present, keeping the two bartenders busy. Couples tearing through a small mountain range of pull tabs lined the rest of the bar. Elsewhere, wind-burned ranchers played darts and shot pool to a cacophony of high fives and trash talk, while their kids circled around pitchers of soda and bowls of popcorn. Everyone seemed to know everyone. And above the conversation and cracking of billiard balls was the elevator soundtrack of a television tuned to The Weather Channel. *Local on the 8s* reported what they already knew: it was damn cold outside.

The faux brick wall behind the laminated bar was plastered with beer advertisements, shelves displayed a collection of dust-covered domestic beer bottles, and a menu tempted the inebriated with frozen pizzas unlikely to be mistaken for delivery.

A thin man in his fifties approached. He wore a striped, wrinkled dress shirt with a bar rag draped over his shoulder, and a smile that betrayed his nicotine-stained teeth. "How can I help you two?"

Kara slapped the plastic keychain on the bar. "I was told this gets us a couple of free drinks."

"It does, but you gotta buy the first round. Second round's on the house."

Edward scanned the taps and thought better of it. "I'll have a Beam and Coke."

"Make that two," Kara added.

"Coming right up."

Edward couldn't conceal his surprise. "No cosmo?"

"I figured I'd tone down the whole city slicker thing since you're worried about us fitting in."

"That'll be four dollars," the bartender said and slid the two highballs toward them.

"Each?"

"Total."

"My kind of bar." Edward gave him a five and left the dollar as a tip.

The man turned on the television nearest them and clicked through the channels. "Let me know if anything catches your eye."

"Ooh, the Mariners are on," Kara said, as a baseball stadium flashed on the screen. "Must be the home opener." She jumped her stool forward and rested her chin atop her pyramided elbows, eager to watch.

A female bartender, chewing gum and possessing a surly demeanor, eventually came over to check on them. Kara showed her the room key and ordered another round as Edward added three dollars to the earlier tip.

Kara waited for the drinks then asked: "Can you maybe turn up the volume on the baseball game and mute the weather report? Our team's playing."

Had a record been playing, it wouldn't have merely skipped. It would have kicked aside the needle and hurled itself across the room. Edward felt the glare of everyone within earshot.

"Honey, there ain't nothin' more important to the folks in these parts than the weather. And certainly not some ballgame." She wiped the bar where the drinks had been sweating and leaned closer, lowering her voice. "Don't get me wrong, I don't like listening to it all day either, but that TV has been playing The Weather Channel nonstop ever since the cable man first came to town. And it ain't gonna stop 'cause some out-of-towners want to watch men play with a ball and scratch themselves."

Edward fought to conceal his amusement as Kara looked on in frozen surprise.

"Holler if you want another round," she said, leaving them.

"What. Was. That?" Kara asked, in cartoonish shock.

"That was all hope of you fitting in going right out the window. Might as well order that cosmo, princess." Edward laughed and wrapped his arm around his wife. He took a long pull from his drink and settled into the stool as the stress of the day melted in bourbon warmth. In silence, the red-carpet player introductions wrapped up and the team took the field.

An empty Bud Chelada can soon appeared in front of Edward. "Excuse my reach," a deep voice said. Then louder, "Two more, Sally." Edward turned and came face-to-chest with a man who appeared to be a third again his size in every dimension. The landscape's alkaline scent perfumed his mustard-colored Carhartt jacket, the size of a billboard. Edward straightened atop the stool.

"You two Mariners fans?"

"Yeah. From Seattle," Edward said.

"What brings you this way?"

Edward leaned aside as the man reached for his drinks. "We're biking across the country." It was easier for acquaintances to swallow this nugget of information than the whole menu of their itinerary.

"No kidding. Well, welcome to Circle. I'm Ricky."

"I'm Edward and this," he said, getting her attention, "is my wife Kara."

Ricky nodded and smiled. "Nice to meet you, Ed," he said, shaking his hand.

"It's Edward."

Ricky shot him a puzzled look.

"You'll have to excuse my husband, he's a bit formal," Kara said, elbowing Edward in the side.

"Hey, no worries. Anyway, that's my family over there by the pinball machine, and this big slab of beef is my buddy Matt." Ricky wrapped his arm around the shoulders of a man that could have been his twin. The four exchanged pleasantries as Ricky passed Matt the other can and said, "We've been standing all day. Let's grab a table. Come tell us about your trip." Then, to Matt, "These two are biking across the country."

"Wow. You riding Harleys or a Goldwing?"

"No, no. Bicycles. Pedal power," Edward said, smiling as he and Kara followed the men to a table.

"You okay?" Kara whispered to Edward.

"Better than okay," he said, swirling his drink. It wasn't just the alcohol though, but the vibe. He didn't know what to expect before they entered, but family-friendly wasn't it.

Kara draped her jacket over the back of a chair facing the television.

"So, bicycles huh?" Matt asked.

"We're headed around the world," Kara said without looking, the response automatic.

"We left Seattle three weeks ago," Edward added.

"You two biked across the Rockies this time of year? That's crazy." Matt's disbelief seemed genuine.

Kara, taking advantage of a commercial break, explained their route across the northern United States and their plan to cross into Canada at Lake Superior. Having recited the same description a dozen times in as many days, Edward played with the stir straw in his glass and looked around, barely paying attention.

Matt spoke up: "I haven't heard of half the towns you mentioned, but—and I hope this ain't being rude—what are you doing for money?"

"Yeah, that's what I'm wondering. You look pretty young. Are y'all working while you travel?" Ricky asked.

"You tell them," Edward said to Kara as he grabbed their empty glasses and stood. He gestured at the men's beer cans, asking silently if they needed refills. They declined. At the bar, Edward ordered two more Beam and Cokes, then, because he couldn't remember if they said yes, ordered two additional Bud Cheladas for his new friends. And since the booze was cheap, he tossed back a shot of Jameson before returning with the drinks.

"Thanks for the beers. Kara was saying the trip was all her idea at first and you didn't want to do it." That was Matt. Or Ricky. Edward had forgotten who was who.

Kara interjected, "*Butttt*, then he surprised me. I came home from work one day in February and he was waiting for me with a bottle of Veuve Clicquot and a poster-sized map of the world. We left a month later," she said, beaming.

"Verve click-what?"

"Oh, sorry. It's champagne," Kara said. Then, tilting her glass at Edward, "He was practically raised on the stuff." Everyone laughed. Even Edward.

"So what changed your mind, you win the lottery or something?" Ricky (or Matt) asked.

Edward took another sip and glanced over the ice cubes. Kara gazed back with pride, clearly loving the attention, but he sensed she too was curious.

He hiccuped. "No lottery. Actually, kind of the opposite. I was in VC, venture capital. I'm not sure what you guys know about the VC world—"

"Nothing, except you probably make more money than we do driving combines," one of them said, clinking his beer can with the other.

"Yeah, that's probably true. Well, we're like angel investors. Start-ups come to us for money and guidance, and we help them grow. A little seed money, a little nurturing. Profit."

"Sounds like farming," one of the guys said with a laugh, "Minus the profit part." The other snorted.

"So I was working eighty, sometimes a hundred hours a week," Edward continued, noticing that both Ricky and Matt turned to Kara when he said this. She nodded, sullenly, confirming the veracity of Edward's statement. It was a look he was all too familiar with.

"I was in line to get promoted to Principal—that's like Junior Partner. And then the owner of the firm, Ron Mad*sen*—" Edward said the name with such vitriol he earned a startled look from Kara. "He called me into his office to tell me they were going in a different direction. Tells me my career's just beginning, that I should be patient. Then he says they're going to promote this other bastard instead. I doubled the guy's revenue two years in a row and *he* gets promoted."

"Huh," one said.

"You don't say," the other added with fading interest.

"Wait a second. Did you quit?" Kara asked, setting her glass down. "You never told me any of this." Matt and Ricky exchanged curious glances, as if a surprise plot twist had been revealed for their entertainment. Mischievous smiles crept across their faces.

Edward cleared his throat as a drop of sweat ran the length of his chest, leaving a trail of nervousness streaked behind it. He stood and grabbed the back of the chair.

"No. No. Well, not exactly," he admitted, his thoughts drifting back to the day he was fired. Edward's knuckles turned white as he clutched the chair back, straining against the pressure he'd been living under. He needed a release. For two months, he'd been silently battling constant regret, the worry that Kara would leave him if he couldn't maintain the lifestyle she'd been accustomed to, the shame of having never told her what really happened.

The room spun as he sucked the last vestiges of bourbon from the ice in his glass. He bit down on a cube. He wanted more. Needed it. But even drunk in a bar serving two-dollar wells, he knew they didn't have money to burn. It was this awareness that pushed him over the edge, the stinging slap of reality reminding him that his top shelf days were over.

"All those hours. All that money for the company?" He was gaining steam. "Still young? Be patient? Fuck him!" he yelled, shoving the chair against the table, causing one of the cans to tip, spilling a slick of tomato-stained beer.

"Whoa, whoa, easy." Matt (or Ricky) leaped from his chair and clamped a meaty hand on Edward's shoulder as the other reminded him there were kids present.

"Sorry. Sorry."

"So you quit," Kara spat, now standing, her hands on her hips. "I thought you took a sabbatical."

"I never said that."

"Well, you sure as hell didn't correct me." She glared at him, her eyes were bulging, unblinking.

He had to come clean. The realization struck him with a thwack, like a cartoon character stepping on a rake.

He couldn't look in her direction. "I lost my shit. I went nuts."

Kara yanked his arm, spinning him to face her. "What are you saying? What'd you do?"

Edward's chest heaved as he sipped tiny breaths of air, drawing courage from the barroom vapors. "I cursed Ron up and down and—" he explained, glancing back to the guys, "I never swear. I don't."

Kara nodded.

"I got so worked up, though … There was this autographed baseball on his bookshelf—" Edward pointed at the TV just as the camera zoomed in on the pitcher, "Signed by that guy right there. Felix. And I wound up and threw it at him, display case and all. I missed him, but the ball flew out of the case and went straight through the window. It was one of those old wavy windows in Pioneer Square, and, well, the ball was from Felix's perfect game. Thing was probably worth thousands."

There was a brief pause of astonishment before Matt and Ricky burst into a fit of laughter. They held onto one another for balance as they doubled over in hysterics.

Edward's stomach knotted as Kara's sobering gaze wrung the energy from him, leaving him unable to withstand the shame washing over him. "I don't know who packed up the box," he said. "Security threw me out before I had a chance to do it."

Kara stared at him, her almond-shaped eyes pulled into walnuts, her head shaking in disbelief. Her face twitched, seeming to oscillate between confusion, hurt, and fury.

Across the table, Ricky and Matt reenacted the office scene in Vaudevillian theatrics. Two corn-bred giants performing wild, leg-kicking wind-ups, delivering empty-handed fastballs.

Edward fought every desire to look away, to order another drink, or even retreat to the motel, but he didn't. He deserved whatever he had coming and wasn't too drunk to know it. He let his temper get the better of him, jeopardizing their future, and doubted he'd be able to find work in Seattle again. The VC world was small and Ron was a big fish.

Kara swallowed twice and ran her tongue across her lips. When she spoke, her voice was faint, scratchy, as if she had to drag the words out of her. "So, if you had gotten the promotion, we wouldn't be here right now?"

"No, I can explain—"

"You didn't really want to take this trip, did you?"

"Kara, no, it's ... it's not like that," he said. But wasn't it? He'd never taken the idea seriously. It wasn't until he was alone in the apartment, drowning in self-pity like some unemployed loser, that her suggestion became his lifeline. The champagne, a nice touch when she got home. It was easier to let her think whatever she wanted. "We would have done it, just not right away. Maybe once I made Senior Partner."

Kara stepped to him, challenging his desire to retreat. "You don't even know why I wanted to take this trip, do you?"

Edward slumped into the chair and avoided her glare, afraid to guess wrong.

"Send Ron my thanks." Kara snatched her jacket and barged past Ricky and Matt on her way out the door.

Ricky and Matt pulled their seats closer, flanking Edward. Once the silence had downshifted from awkward to unnecessary, and perhaps in an effort to distract him from the fact that his wife had stormed out, taking the motel key with her, the men engaged him with questions about camping gear and bicycles. Edward's responses were light on details, his attention never straying from the cocktail napkins he was tearing into confetti.

"So, you packing?" Ricky asked.

"What?" Edward replied, not understanding the question.

"A gun. You got a gun, right?"

Edward repeated the word until it sank in. "Nah, I'm not much of a gun guy. Besides, we're headed into Canada in a few weeks and then over to Europe. You can't carry a gun around with you outside the States."

"Aren't you worried about protecting your wife?" Ricky asked. Edward remembered the mustard Carhartt was Ricky's, the drama having sobered him.

"From what? People bike across the country all the time. The only thing cyclists ever talk about is how nice people are, especially here in America."

Ricky made a face like he had smelled something awful. "People are always getting shot, don't you watch the news?" he asked.

"That stuff is rare," Edward said, earning him polite head shaking. "Besides, we've got pepper spray. Though that's mostly for dogs."

"One of those keychain things women keep in their purse?" Matt chortled. "Yeah, that might help against a dog, but what if somebody tries to rob you—or worse?"

Ricky leaned closer, his eyebrows raised. "You ought to at least get yourself a big ol' can of hornet spray. That shit can stop a man twenty feet out."

"You don't say." Edward's interest fizzled. He needed to leave. If for no other reason, than to escape the litany of unsolicited advice. "We're really just worried about dogs and cars. I swear."

"Suit yourself," Matt said before heading to the men's room. When he returned, he took the seat next to Ricky. Conversation shifted to hunting stories and tales from the wheat fields, leaving Edward isolated with his thoughts.

He waited as long as he figured it would take Kara to get back to the room, to calm down. Would she let him in? He could only hope.

Edward rose to leave and thanked Ricky and Matt for the company. The two wished him good luck with the missus, a glint of humor in their looks.

Ricky hollered across the room as Edward reached the exit, "Get a gun!"

"Dogs and cars," Edward yelled back, "Nothing but dogs and cars."

Chapter 6

TUESDAY, APRIL 14 — JAMESTOWN, NORTH
DAKOTA, USA

Kara woke to warm breath on her face and the sense that the tent had shrunk in the night. It was Edward leaning over her, smiling brightly. She blinked the sleep away and tried remembering where they were as he brushed the hair from her brow and kissed her forehead. His lips glanced her nose then landed tenderly on her mouth, lingering, his eyes closed.

"Happy anniversary, my love." His face hovered an inch from hers, his breath minty.

Eight days had passed since the incident at the American Legion, six since Kara had ceased giving him the silent treatment. She hadn't forgiven him, not completely. Rather, she ran out of the energy required to ignore a husband with whom she spent every moment of every day. Unlike at home, where she could retreat to her studio, slamming the door behind her, bicycle touring forced compromise, or at least a ceasefire. A tent was too small a battlefield for open hostilities.

She fought to stifle a yawn as a cowbell clanged in the distance. Closer, the sound of flags snapping in the morning breeze. The fairgrounds, she realized, recalling the colorful pennants atop the wash house. "Happy anniversary to you, too." She reached between them, tugged at the zipper on her sleeping bag, and peeled the top flap back, an open invitation.

His eyes flickered with flirtatious excitement as he rolled onto his side, his hand on her belly. "I've got a surprise. Hurry up and get dressed."

"Can't it wait?" Kara grabbed his wrist and pulled him near. It had been too long.

He let out a faint groan, as if the temptation was a test of will against which he had taken an oath. "I'm already dressed. I got up early. But tonight …"

Rejected, Kara raised her hand and turned away, waving at the air where her mouth had been as he moved in for another kiss. "I haven't brushed yet," she said.

"Since when has that stopped us?" He scooted closer.

Suspecting he might be willing to ignore his policy on their anniversary, she pulled the top of her long underwear off. To hell with subtlety. Kara closed her eyes and leaned back, propped on her elbows in anticipation of his caress.

With the force of a feather, he traced her profile. From her forehead, he dragged his finger over her nose, her chin, and down the length of her throat. His touch rose and fell as she gulped for air, her throat choked with passion. She arched her back ever higher as he descended along her torso, plummeting between her breasts toward her belly button. He didn't detour, he didn't rush. Unlike her heart, which now fluttered like a hummingbird.

He dipped his finger beneath the waistband of the full-length silk underwear and slid it back and forth across the trim of her bikini briefs. She breathed deep and arched higher still as she raised her pelvis off the crinkly sleeping pad. Another invitation. Her muscles tightened as he traced ticklish figure eights across the satin triangle. She willed him to go further, lower.

Beyond their nylon cocoon, a tractor rumbled to life on the featureless landscape. But inside the tent, it was the luxury of a palace and she was the queen to be worshiped.

A soft breeze on her face. She felt him leaning over her now like a parachute holding her in suspended anticipation. She licked her lips, he blew them cool. The elastic stretched and snapped audibly against her waist as he yanked his hand away. He patted her on the stomach twice, pecked her lips with his, and rolled away. "Not in the tent."

Kara's eyes flashed open as she jerked upright, the blood of her passion now boiling with rejection. His words were a bucket of ice water and the chill stung. "This tent is our *home*, Ed."

"Don't be mad. I just wanted to give you a little taste of what's to come later," he said, squeezing her shoulder and offering a seductive look that came off as trying too hard. "Don't be long. I've got something for you."

Kara balled her hands into fists and stared at the ceiling after he left. *You've got to be kidding me!* She went along with his no-sex-in-the-tent rule in the mountains; she knew bears were attracted to the pheromones. But halfway across North Dakota? "We're not in bear country anymore, ya know," she yelled through the zippered-shut door.

Outside the tent, she heard pots rattling, the stove being lit. She sighed and changed into the day's clothes, pulling on the same pants and jersey she had worn previously, except for a clean chamois. In no mood for breakfast, she stuffed the sleeping bags into their sacks, punching them into submission, causing a downy feather to float an escape.

She took her irritation out on the sleeping pads next, forcibly squeezing the air out of them and, in so doing, her frustration gradually softened into understanding. Edward was always generous around special occasions. Her family used to think it was his way of showing off; her friends thought it an admission of his guilt, of acknowledging how little he was there for her, but Kara knew him best. He truly loved buying her things. And he gave with such enthusiasm. She'd never forget their first anniversary, when he insisted she open her present a week early because he couldn't wait to see the look on her face. She knew there'd be no Tiffany earrings this year, but she was curious.

Nature's call eventually spurred Kara from the tent, but heeding it would wait.

Edward called out to her as she unzipped the tent, "Butterflies."

"Cover your eyes," she said, groaning, wishing she never told him about this childhood memory. When Kara was young, her mom would hook her thumbs and flutter her palms like butterfly wings coming in for a landing, alighting on Kara's face and covering her eyes for whatever surprise laid in store. Kara obliged, begrudgingly, and exited the tent with her eyes shut.

"Liftoff," Edward called back, giving her the signal to look.

Her bike was propped against a tree, a small wicker basket lashed to its handlebars. Inside the basket was a bouquet of daffodils, her favorite. Petals of yellow, orange, and white invited her to begin the day anew. She covered her mouth in surprise. He had a way of leaving her speechless, for better, for worse.

Edward approached hesitantly with a mug of coffee and kissed her on the cheek.

"When did you …"

"I saw them in the market yesterday and thought of you. A dozen flowers for the six years of our *two*-getherness," he said, emphasizing the pun. Kara groaned at the awfulness of his joke, as she had done throughout their marriage. "You can toss the basket away tomorrow if you'd like, but I thought you might enjoy having something colorful to look at while you rode. I'll carry milady's handlebar bag today," he said, bowing low and sweeping his arm in the direction of the picnic table, where fresh fruit and oatmeal awaited her.

She had wanted to stay mad, to let him know how much it hurt to get spurned on their anniversary (not to mention how stupid she thought his rule was), but he made it impossible. So he didn't want to have sex in the tent, was that so bad? While she was laying there, gritting her teeth, he had arranged breakfast, made coffee, and somehow found a way to surprise her with a basket of flowers. And what did she do for him besides show him her boobs? If anyone had a right to be upset, it was Edward. But he wouldn't be, and she loved that about him.

Back on the bike, Kara battled to dislodge the doubts that had wedged in her mind. A task most unsuitable for the contemplative nature of the open road.

Thoughts concerning their dwindling sex life returned as they pedaled eastward across the rolling hills of central North Dakota. Despite her attempts at justifying it, she struggled to understand how they could spend twenty-four hours a day together, yet have sex so infrequently—only once since Idaho, by her count. Kara knew the fiery passion of a college romance couldn't last forever, but she expected the flames to burn longer than this. She had a million questions running through her mind, but the one she tried hardest to ignore shouted the loudest: Was he not attracted to her?

No, that wasn't it. The lack of sex was something new. It's the trip. He was mad about the bike tour. *He resents me*, she thought.

With her wrists getting sore, she balanced her forearms on the handlebars in an aerodynamic position, her face inches above the flowers. Her handlebar bag, tucked beneath a cargo net on the rear of Edward's bicycle, was a bike length in front of her, its empty map case reflecting a dancing square of sunshine on his back, spotlighting the leading man in her life as her legs turned the cranks on autopilot, as they had for a thousand miles.

She recalled the night at the American Legion, as she did every day since learning he'd been fired. She never saw Edward look as angry as he did when telling that story. But amidst all that rage, she saw disappointment and shame. And something else. Longing. But they were a month into a multi-year dream adventure. What else did he want?

A purpose, she posited, before snickering at the thought. *How about saving your marriage? That enough purpose for you?*

The ease at which the sarcastic retort came to mind unsettled her. Worse still, it reminded her of the divorce papers squirreled inside a suitcase at a Seattle storage unit, a short flight away.

Kara hated these imaginary back-and-forths, not only for stealing her from the moment at hand, but for the insecurity they suggested. Was she really so fragile as to require make-believe arguments, constructed solely to guarantee herself the winning riposte?

Maybe if he didn't lie …

Yes. There was that. Did he not trust her? Was he worried about the money? What kind of person gets fired from their job and doesn't tell their wife?

What kind of wife doesn't ask?

He said he was only one or two promotions from being set for life. She tried envisioning the humiliation he endured while getting escorted out, the pain he felt when being told he wouldn't get the promotion. The job was everything to him. And she didn't demand an explanation? He told her not to worry about it, and she was all too happy to oblige. She could blame it on the excitement of the moment or the endless list of preparations they had to make, but the truth was, she didn't care about the why and the how. They were spared.

For now …

She shook the thought from her mind and focused on the scenery. The landscape looked different from the saddle of a bicycle. It was quieter for one, and bigger. In it, she felt no larger than an ant blazing a path across an empty swimming pool. But the map's white space wasn't empty. It was miles of lightly golden wheat fields stretching beyond sight, its shimmering color reminding her of the champagne they drank in celebration of their decision. She sure didn't see that coming.

Kara had spent the prior months hoping things would change, to see if his long hours and weekends spent in the office would end. They hadn't. Enough was enough, she was through with the meals for one and going stag to her friends' art exhibits. It was like being single, minus the jealousy of her married friends. And spring was coming. And with it the invitations to go camping. They were Edward's friends, once upon a time. Now they were hers alone. But it wasn't just mutual friends on those trips, there were always newcomers. Brothers and friends-of-friends whose eyes would eventually settle on hers, outdoor action heroes who either didn't look for a ring or didn't care. Campouts were no place for a lonely woman who wasn't single. She learned that lesson the hard way.

She dreaded what was sure to be one of the worst moments in her young life, the night she'd ask for a divorce. But while she spent the afternoon psyching herself up to do what she knew had to be done, he was waiting for her, eager to make her dream come true.

And now they were living it, their bodies in a constant state of motion, churning through the miles, making their way across North America.

Edward swerved to avoid a pothole without warning and Kara, riding close behind, hit it square on. She had no time to react. Her forearms slipped forward off their perch atop the grips and her face dove into the daffodils, narrowly missing the handlebar with her chin. Only the weight of the bike and her momentum kept her upright. Her yelp was muffled by the flowers tickling her nose and lips and the wind, the constant wind. Kara couldn't remember ever noticing a daffodil's fragrance before, as it's so faint, but she never had her face buried in them either. The petals were soft, the scent ever delicate but concentrating with each breath, masking the earthy smell of the harvest land.

Nobody would have gone through this trouble except him, she thought. It was his way of saying he loved her, that he was sorry for lying. Little did he know, it was she who should be begging forgiveness.

Chapter 7

Edward left Kara to lock the bikes while he went inside the café. His frozen fingers struggled to grip the doorknob, but two hands eventually proved capable of what one wasn't. Inside, with his back to the other customers, he grimaced as he strained to undo the buckle on his bicycle helmet. Rainwater sluiced from his pants and jacket, and each clumsy effort wrung ever more water from his gloves onto the frayed carpet. He fought to hold back tears as he bit the middle finger of his glove and slowly worked a single grease-stained hand free.

Unseasonable cold, pouring rain, and three flat tires—all on the rear wheels—turned a hard day masochistic. Three times they had to unload panniers so he could flip a bike upside down. Three times he slipped the wheel and accompanying gears out of the filthy chain to replace the tube. The first flat was an annoyance; the third had him questioning God.

His pruned, colorless fingers—those that weren't smeared black—were locked into an open fist, as if still clutching the handlebars. The bell above the door jingled as Kara entered.

"Oh, you poor thing, let me get that." Kara, adding to the puddle at their feet, unclasped his helmet and unzipped the front of his jacket. "Turn around."

He lowered his head to avoid the inevitable stares as she tugged his rain jacket off from behind. In that moment, he felt as helpless and embarrassed as a schoolboy who needed his mommy to dress him, and he knew he looked every bit as weak. He would never wish to see Kara in pain, but would it kill her to admit she got cold too?

His teeth chattered as he shivered, while his fingers burned. The controlled climate of the diner was a blast furnace, thawing him from a deep freeze and torturing him with a pin-pricked itchiness.

He composed himself the best he could as Kara hung their dripping jackets and helmets on a coat rack. He trailed behind as she led the way to the table furthest from the drafty door. The diner was a country time capsule of simplicity. An array of scratched wooden tables and spindle-backed chairs awaited working-class families willing to gather in an undecorated, fluorescent-lit box of a room to chow hearty, home-style food. The sauce and butter smells reminded him of his annual trips to visit Kara's family in Wisconsin.

A teenage waitress wearing a hockey jersey and a mask of Midwestern politeness approached. She glanced toward the door. A crack formed in her friendly façade, her brow furrowed. Edward could tell she wanted to ask what everyone in the café was wondering: What kind of idiots go cycling on a day like today? He spent all morning asking himself that very question.

Kara ordered for the two of them as Edward blew warmth into his reddening hands and wallowed in his misery. There was talk of meat loaf and bottomless bowls of soup. He didn't care what they had, as long they ate it indoors.

"Soup and coffee is over there. It's self-serve," the waitress said, pointing somewhere.

Edward waited for her to leave before speaking. "I can't keep riding today."

Kara seemed surprised to hear this. "Sure you can. Let's get you warmed up, get some feeling back in your hands, and then we'll leave when you're ready." She offered him a comforting look and added, "With any luck the rain will lighten up."

"And if it doesn't?"

"Don't be so negative—"

"Don't tell me how to feel." He glared at her, aware he was making a scene, and not caring one bit.

Kara opened her mouth to speak, then stood. "I'll get the soup."

Edward chewed on his resentment until Kara returned alongside the waitress. At once, vessels of steaming coffee and soup sat flanking a pool of congealed ketchup, under which, he assumed, was a slab of meat loaf.

Kara stared across the table at Edward as he ate. He was miserable, and he could tell that she knew it. *Why won't she acknowledge it?* Ever since leaving Seattle, he's wanted nothing more than for her to admit the trip was a bad idea and that she wanted to head home. Today, he'd settle for her conceding that it was really cold. When she unleashed a lengthy sigh and shifted her gaze to the ceiling, he thought she just might relent.

"Hang in there, okay? I know you've got another twenty miles in you."

His head dropped. Edward knew right then that there was no getting out of this, nor was there anything to say. Nothing was going to convince Kara that bicycling around the world was anything but a terrific idea. His only out was to admit they had no savings, only debt—that he had nothing to show for his years at Madsen Ventures. But she couldn't know that now, if ever. With any luck, he'd figure something out before they got home, pull some strings.

"I know you've dealt with worse weather than this," she said, alluding to the adventures he used to take with friends back home. Total suffer-fests, he called them, regaling her with tales of his wilderness exploits. If she wasn't allowing him to give up easily, he had only himself to blame.

"It's not just the weather. I miss it."

"Miss what? Seattle?" she asked, confused.

"Work."

"We've got our whole lives to worry about work. I thought you agreed."

"But we don't," he said, dropping his spoon into the bowl, splashing ruby red broth onto the table. "I'll be thirty in a few months. These are the most critical years for career advancement—"

"Ed—"

"Don't 'Ed' me. You don't get it."

"What I get is that you worry about money too much. Instead of being mad you lost your job, why can't you just be happy to spend more time with me?"

He almost interrupted her to say that one of them had to worry about money. As a freelance artist, she couldn't even afford his car payment, but he caught himself. She had him. To say anything more, to even attempt explaining that the two weren't mutually exclusive, that he could enjoy spending time with her but *also* worry about work, would only shift the argument into a fight. And what good would that do? Instead, he turned his frustration against the smothered meat loaf, chopping it into six massive bites, devouring it.

Kara watched him, ignoring her food, until the steam ceased rising from her bowl. "People reinvent themselves all the time, Ed. Now it's your turn. You can go on feeling sorry for yourself about losing your job or you can embrace being on a journey of a lifetime." She paused then added softly, "With me."

Did she really think it was that simple? That he'd be able to find work in Seattle after they returned? And what if he didn't want to reinvent himself? He didn't go to business school just to change careers before he was thirty. These thoughts ran through Edward's mind in the span of a sigh, but he kept quiet. He wanted both, to make her happy *and* return to the way things were. But until he figured out how to do that, there was no point in saying anything at all.

Standing outside the café an hour and three bowls of tomato soup later, the rain continued to fall. Edward was warmer, and his gloves, which were now merely damp, felt surprisingly comfortable as he worked each finger into the clumsy inner linings. No part of him wanted to ride the next twenty miles, but he knew a hotel suite was waiting for him at the end. Not to mention a night on the town in Fargo, the biggest city since leaving Seattle five weeks earlier.

The rain never let up, but the southerly wind that blew across their path all morning ultimately aided them as the final ten miles stretched in a northeasterly direction. It was all Edward needed to put himself in a better mood.

They had reservations at a shiny new business hotel on the west edge of town, situated amongst a sprawling mass of recent development. Condos spread out in every direction, presumably a result of all the oil money that flowed into the state's coffers a few years earlier. Edward couldn't help but wonder how many stood vacant now that the boom turned to bust.

Edward sheepishly apologized to the receptionist for how wet their bikes and panniers were as they wheeled them into the lobby, trailing inky smears of filth behind them in figure eights. But that Midwestern friendliness revealed itself once again. Towels were presented in a flash, drips mopped up, and all assurances made that it was really nothing at all.

He was showered, warm, and relaxing in a plush cotton robe atop an oversized sectional an hour later. It was his first taste of luxury in over a month. "Hey look, we've got cable again!" Edward hadn't seen a proper television since they left. And by that, he meant high definition.

"Ugh, it's been so nice without it," Kara hollered back from the bathroom, where she was washing their jerseys in the sink.

Edward rolled his eyes, but realized she may have a point after clicking through dozens of channels worth of mindless programming. He left it tuned to a local news station in hopes of catching the next day's weather forecast.

He skimmed a visitor's magazine as the reporter ran through the day's top stories. There was mention of a robbery and some local flooding. Edward's mind wandered at mention of the Minnesota Wild hockey team; it hadn't occurred to him before then how few professional sports teams there were in the Midwest. None in the Dakotas, Wyoming, Nebraska, Idaho …

Edward snapped to attention upon hearing the anchorman segue into a story which, he promised, was quite unusual, as if overhearing a spicy secret from a neighboring table in a restaurant.

"Authorities in Montana remain puzzled over the identity of a man discovered naked in an abandoned barn two weeks ago."

Edward leaned forward on the sofa, his eyes wide.

"Neither the Montana state records office nor the Bureau of Indian Affairs were able to match the deceased's fingerprints or dental records."

"Kara, get in here quick!"

"Officials from the nearby Blackfoot Reservation have been brought in, as well as anthropologists from a local university, to study the unusual corpse."

"Kara, you gotta hear this."

"What is it? I'm kind of busy," she yelled from the bathroom.

"It's about that body we found."

"One source, speaking on the condition of anonymity, said that— now listen to this—the body contains the physiological hallmarks of a Plains Indian from over seven hundred years ago, and that the university

is preparing to commission a full autopsy and DNA testing should no next of kin be identified."

"Are they talking about the Blackfoot?" Kara asked, now standing beside him.

Edward nodded and held his finger up; he'd fill her in during a commercial.

"The body was found naked in a dilapidated barn near Highway 2, with several pieces of stray litter tied around its waist. A railroad worker from Billings is credited with its discovery. Authorities believe the victim died to due to exposure sometime in February."

"Figures," Edward said, nonplussed.

"He probably thought there'd be some kind of reward."

"Maybe. Or just lazy reporting."

"I can't believe he'd been laying there since before we even left on our trip," said Kara, worrying a still-sudsy jersey in her hands.

It was as if she had read his mind. And by the sounds of it, Edward wasn't the only one whose life went to shit two months ago. He gazed to the window, hoping something would distract him from the memory of the frozen, partially bloated body.

"I wasn't kidding when I told you the guy looked like he was right out of the history books. He looked like he was in his twenties, but ancient."

Chapter 8

THURSDAY, APRIL 23 — DETROIT LAKES,
MINNESOTA, USA

Edward let out a low whistle as they walked their bikes up the driveway
of a sprawling lakefront home, complete with twin cedar columns and
a dizzying array of eaves and gables. "Are you sure this is the right
address?"

"Yep. Nice place, huh?"

"I'll say. Reminds me of my parent's home, only bigger."

Kara had arranged for them to be hosted through a hospitality
network that catered to cyclists. This was their first time staying with
strangers and, by the looks of it, wealthy ones at that. Edward assumed
the only people using the site were younger couch-surfing types with
messy apartments, offering little more than a hot shower and a spot on
the floor to throw their sleeping bags, but this was more dream home
than crash pad.

They laid their bikes on the driveway, no longer worried about
every scuff and scrape their panniers received, and rang the doorbell.
An opulent chime echoed beyond the door. Edward scrunched his
face and sniffed the air. "Do I stink?"

"No more than usual," Kara said.

"Point taken." They spent all day cycling, of course he smelled. He brushed the grime from his clothing and, while looking in his helmet's mirror, licked his fingers and rubbed away the white crystals beneath his eyes.

Kara laughed. "You're acting like you're going on a first date. Relax."

Edward felt the heat rise in his cheeks. She was right, the couple was probably used to hosting cyclists far dirtier and sweatier than they were, especially come summertime. But it wasn't every day he showed up on a stranger's doorstep hungry, tired, and looking like he had just biked sixty miles. Which reminded him ...

"Come here," he said, pulling Kara in for their daily post-ride hug. "Great riding today."

"You too." She squeezed him tight and, when she stepped back, her face shone with childish exuberance. "Minnesota. I can't believe we're already halfway across North America."

He nodded, a proud smile on his lips. "Hell of an accomplishment." He kissed her briefly then rang the doorbell again. "What're their names again?"

"Brenda and Tom O'Donnell."

"And they live here year-round?" Edward asked, raising his eyebrows. Many of the smaller lakes they pedaled past on their way in from Fargo were still frozen, all of them ringed by snowbound aluminum rowboats staked upside down in the yards of homes whose windows were clad in plastic sheeting. Boat trailers, chained to trees like forgotten dogs, dotted the area. "Every other house looks like it's still hibernating."

"Brenda said something about flying in from Minneapolis. It wasn't clear in the email."

"Flying in to host us? That's nuts."

Kara shrugged.

Edward saw movement through the door's beveled window and attempted to drill the couple's names into his memory. "Brenda blender, Tom turtle, Brenda blender, Tom turtle—"

"Blender?" Kara interrupted, barely restraining her laughter.

"It rhymes. Sort of." Edward repeated the pattern under his breath until he heard the deadbolt unlock.

A petite woman stood before them, wearing a flower print apron over a turquoise sweater and pleated corduroy pants. Laugh lines suggested she was in her mid-fifties. She clasped her hands beneath her chin. "Hellooooo," she said, stretching the word, "Welcome to Minnesota." She spread her arms as if taking in a niece she had only seen in photos. "You must be Kara. I'm so glad you could make it. And no rain today. How wonderful."

"Thanks so much for hosting us," Kara said, bulging her eyes at Edward as she hugged Brenda hello.

"You must be freezing. Let's get your bikes into the garage and get you warmed up. I can't believe you two are—"

A slam echoed from down the hall, stealing Brenda's words. Then, a gruff voice shouted, "I don't give a damn if he ..." before trailing off into silence.

Brenda's hand moved to her mouth in shock. "I'm, I'm," she stammered. "Please excuse me. I'm so sorry." The heavy door clicked shut behind her, stranding the cyclists outside, stunned.

"What was that about?" Kara asked, her voice low.

A child of a fist-slammer, Edward knew the sound all too well. And if the man behind it was anything like Edward's father, his temper would be simmering all night. "We should go."

"Where? We can't just leave."

"It's not a good time—"

The door swung open before Edward could finish his thought. Brenda had returned, flush in the cheeks, a timid smile on her lips. "I'm so sorry about that. Can we start over?"

"Absolutely," Kara said.

Brenda nodded and stepped forward as if to hug her again, then turned. "You must be Eddie." She took Edward's hand in hers, shaking it vigorously.

"It's Edward. Nice meeting you, Brenda. Thank you so much for agreeing to host us tonight."

"Oh, pish," she said, dismissing his gratitude with a wave of her hand. "We're happy you could make it. Tom's on a call, but should finish up soon. I'll show you around."

There was no leaving now. The rules of polite society had snared them. He was resigned to the hope that Brenda's warmth could coax an evening of good behavior out of her husband.

Brenda opened the garage using a keypad beside the middle garage door. "Don't mind the Moggie, just lean your bikes over by the workbench." The door rose panel by panel, slowly revealing an uncovered Morgan convertible with deep crimson paint and black leather interior. Edward's face reflected back from the glimmering hood.

He stared at the slanted vents on the Morgan's lengthy hood and saw only the cranberry shutters of his childhood home. But he wasn't home. He was halfway across North America, just like Kara said. They were finally amongst the great northern forests after weeks of farmland, but the wintering hardwoods, as leafless as they appeared lifeless, had him missing the year-round color of the Evergreen State. As did the flatness of the landscape. He soon felt Kara alongside him, motioning his bicycle forward, whispering something in his ear. "I'm fine," he said, guessing a response to a question he didn't hear.

Being careful not to bump the walls with their dirty bags (and happy to leave the camping gear on the bikes), they followed Brenda on a brief tour of the house, thankful for access to a laundry room.

The tour ended in an undecorated guest room. The only furniture was a mattress on a bare metal frame and a fancy doll, whose face would have been at home in an '80s horror movie. The gaudy floral comforter provided the only splash of color. That such a house would offer such spartan accommodations for houseguests struck Edward as odd.

"I hope you don't mind. The bed's only a full."

"It's perfect," Kara said, rubbing her hands mischievously in Edward's direction. "Someone won't be able to avoid cuddling tonight."

Brenda laughed and touched them both on the wrist. "You two are cute." Her hands lingered and Edward caught a glimmer of melancholy in her eyes. Brenda shook free of whatever thought had gripped her and forced a smile. "Tom likes to eat early, so come down as soon as you're ready. And don't forget to bring your appetite."

Showered and dressed in their lone off-the-bike outfits, Edward and Kara found Brenda in the kitchen, clutching a fistful of uncooked linguine before a six-burner stove. Over her shoulder, through the window, a floatplane bobbed alongside a dock in the evening light.

Holy shit, they really did fly out to host us.

"This is for you," Kara said, presenting a bottle of table wine Edward had forgotten they bought. It was his idea not to show up empty-handed, but upon seeing this place he wished he had splurged on a nicer label—or that Kara had left the convenience store swill in the pannier.

"Oh, you shouldn't have," Brenda said. She glanced briefly at the wine, thanked them, and then tucked it behind a small collection of designer olive oils and vinegars, hiding it from view like a museum curator might a child's finger painting.

Figures. In their effort not to be rude, they wound up looking cheap. A sin Edward found far worse.

"Your house is beautiful," Kara said, seemingly oblivious to their faux pas.

"Thanks. We don't get out here as often as I'd like, what with the long winters and—oh, I think I hear Tom coming."

A door swung open from down the hall and the large figure of Tom O'Donnell stepped out, wearing dark blue jeans, a collared shirt, and flannel slippers. Tom strode down the hall, his cheeks flush above his graying beard, his feet thudding against the polished hardwood with each step. Brenda, at ease a moment earlier, now appeared flustered as she introduced her husband.

Echoes of his father's temper tantrums ricocheted between Edward's ears as he looked at Tom. Through the din of his memory, Edward heard his mother imploring him to be on his best behavior and he straightened his back instinctively.

Tom gave Kara's hand a brief shake, meeting the minimum requirements of politeness, then gripped Edward's hand with a firmness the younger man found challenging. "Nice meeting you, Edward," he said, staring at him. Edward tried his hardest not to blink or look away and committed himself to not ending the handshake first.

Satisfied, Tom released his grip, looked from Edward to Kara, then sighed in a theatrical huff. "Brenda, why do our cyclists not have any beers yet?" Tom gave Edward a look, the feigned exasperation of a husband who thinks he has to do everything himself.

Brenda knitted her brow as she searched for a response, then noticed the pasta water boiling over. "Okay, everyone out of the kitchen. Scoot. Dinner's almost ready," she said, scurrying to the stove, where she twisted the burner to low.

"What can I do to help?" Kara asked.

"Brenda's got it under control. You two come sit."

"Are you sure, because I can—"

"Just listen to Tom, dear."

Kara looked to Edward, who shrugged and followed his host to the dining room where a live edge table sat beneath a wagon wheel chandelier in a cavernous room. The table was set with what Edward's mother would have called *the good china*.

Edward pulled the chair out for Kara, then took the seat opposite her and draped a cloth napkin on his lap. Tom took his seat at the far end of the eight-person table, beyond the empty chairs near Edward and Kara. Edward felt the arrangement, especially once Brenda took her seat at the end nearest them, would be that of a private dinner for three—with the head of household observing from a safe distance.

It wasn't long before Kara urged Edward with her eyes to break the silence. But he was spared when Brenda backed her way through the swinging door, carrying a heaping platter of chicken and linguine, along with a bottle of wine tucked under her arm. "I hope you're hungry," she said in a sing-song voice.

The steam rising from the chicken scented the room with lemon pepper and fresh herbs. Capers dotted the plate and sent Edward's mouth watering as Brenda piled a heaping portion of protein and carbs on his plate. Still, he couldn't help but wonder where the beer was as they clinked wine glasses, toasting his and Kara's progress across the country.

"So, tell us about this trip you're on," Brenda said.

It was Kara's turn. "Well, we left Seattle in early March and are heading across the U.S. and Canada to New York City. From there, we'll fly to London, spend some time in the UK, and then make our way south across Western Europe, and over the Pyrenees to Spain. After Madrid and Seville, we'll cross the Strait to Morocco and—"

"From there we'll head east to Greece and across Central Asia to China," Edward interrupted. "We'll probably visit New Zealand on our way home." He could sense Tom's interest fading and chose to spare his hosts from Kara's impromptu geography lesson before she began naming every village they'd pedal through along the way.

"You forgot South America," Kara said before turning to Brenda. "There's no way we're going to miss Patagonia."

"We'll see," Edward said, in a tone more dismissive than he intended, earning him a silent rebuke from Kara. *Shit.*

"Well, that sounds amazing," Brenda said, before taking a lengthy sip of wine. "Don't you think so, Tom?"

"Aye-up." Tom looked unconvinced, distracted even. Like a man chewing not only on his meal, but on a question he was biding his time to ask.

"The whole trip should take two to three years," Kara said. "But what about you two? Do you cycle much?"

"Oh, no," Brenda said, shaking her head as Tom grunted a supercilious laugh. "My niece cycled down the California coast and raved about the nice people she met through the hospitality network. I was worried about inviting strangers into our home, but she convinced me we didn't have to worry about any axe murderers."

Kara laughed. "Ed's mom said the same thing when I told her about staying with strangers."

Brenda patted Kara's elbow. "We don't get to host as often as I'd like …" she said before taking another sip of wine. She dabbed the corners of her mouth with her napkin and then, with a dreamy sigh, said, "I just think what you two are doing is so inspiring."

Quiet settled over the room as conversation yielded to hunger and silent thought, leaving Brenda's comment unaddressed. It never occurred to Edward that what they were doing was inspirational. Impulsive, certainly. And unorthodox. But inspiring? Across the table, Kara sat, biting her lower lip, smiling demurely at her plate, twirling the linguine with her fork. Edward could tell Brenda's comment made her day.

"Enough quiet. I want to hear how you two met," Brenda said, breaking the silence while crossing her fork and knife on her plate.

A different question for a change, Edward thought. *About time.*

"We met in college," Kara began, after clearing her throat. "I was a senior and was assigned a semester-long project with some business students and engineers.

"Ooh, lemme guess, Edward, you were one of the engineers, weren't you?"

"Actually, I was in my final year of business school. I got my MBA that summer."

"Did you hear that, Tom? Edward's got an MBA"

"Aye-up."

"Tom owns an investment firm in Minneapolis. Most of his employees went to business school."

Edward nodded and arched his eyebrows, impressed. He hoped showing the proper level of awe would conceal the pang of jealousy he felt. *Hence the second home and private plane*, he thought.

"Brenda, would you let her finish?" Tom motioned his meaty hand at Kara, palm up. "Please, Kara, continue."

"Well, so, yeah … Edward was also on this project. He was one of the two B-school students. And normally, well, I guess I didn't really know many business majors, but Edward was so friendly. And really respectful of everyone's work. *Annnd* he was really cute."

Brenda giggled. "She's right, Edward, you are handsome."

Edward looked to the chandelier as he felt himself blushing.

"Brenda." Tom barked her name in an exasperated tone. Brenda quieted and poured herself another glass of wine, subtly shaking her head.

Kara's eyes searched the room before she continued hesitantly, "I guess I had a bit of an inferiority complex about being an art major—God knows the engineers hardly cared at all what I had to say—but Edward treated everyone in the group as equals."

Kara stabbed a piece of chicken with her fork and smiled at Edward as she lifted it to her mouth, her nose crinkling, eyes sparkling. It was the smile he fell in love with all those years ago. "Kara had this way about her that attracted me. To be honest, I knew it the first time we met—"

"We both did," Kara mumbled, covering her full mouth with a hand. Edward felt a foot brush slowly against his ankle and extended his leg to invite more of Kara's flirting, relieved she had seemed to forget his South America comment.

"It sounds like love at first sight. That's so sweet," Brenda said. "So tell us about your first date. I bet you took her someplace romantic, didn't you Edward?"

"I'd like to think so," Edward said, then gestured to Kara with his chin. "You tell it."

"Oh gosh, okay. It was really sweet, actually. He called me up the night before our date and said to be ready by six."

"A little early for dinner, Edward, don'tcha think?" Brenda said.

"Oh, no, not for dinner," Kara corrected her. "He picked me up at six in the morning."

"What? Edward!" Brenda startled.

Tom harrumphed from the far end of the table as Edward grinned and leaned back in his chair.

"He knew I was a Midwest girl. I'm from northern Wisconsin—"

"Really, I would have never guessed. What happened to your accent?" Brenda asked.

Kara shrugged sheepishly, before continuing. "He knew I hadn't gotten off campus much since moving to Seattle. So he planned this whole day on Orcas Island for me; it's this beautiful island off the coast of Washington." Kara took a sip of wine before regaling the O'Donnells with a play-by-play of their first date.

Edward didn't need to hear Kara's recollection. He'd forever remember the sight of the wind whipping her sun dress around her tanned legs as she hugged herself warm on the ferry deck. And how the late morning sun reflected from her sunglasses as she stood, her mouth agape, atop the lookout tower on Mount Constitution, two thousand feet above a sea dotted with forested islands. After lunch they strolled galleries of Northwest art. He watched, mesmerized by her grace, as she admired the delicate works. And it was there, in front of a woodblock print of the island's namesake whales, where his heart raced as he raised his trembling hand to reach for hers. He treasured the softness that gripped him in return, the tender silkiness of her lips as she kissed his cheek, thanking him for a lovely day.

In his mind they were still walking the narrow beach, hand in hand, the salt of the sea and sweetness of her perfume colliding on every breath.

"We didn't get back to campus until two in the morning," Kara said, her voice floating across the sea of the dining room table to Edward, plucking him from his island memory. "By the end of the date, I felt I had known him forever."

"Oh, that's wonderful," Brenda said, a glimmer of moisture in her eyes.

"Well done, Edward," Tom said in a familiar, patronizing tone.

Edward accepted the compliments with a smile, still replaying the memory of that first kiss in the gallery. Then he said, "It's no Picasso, but I kind of preferred the whales."

Kara gave him a confused look that quickly broke into warm realization. She tilted her head to the side, her face wide with surprise. "You remembered?"

"I actually went back to buy the print a few months later—I was going to surprise you with it when you moved in—but it had sold."

"I had no idea," Kara said, melting. "That's so sweet."

Edward gazed at her, shouting his love for her with his eyes.

"What was that about Picasso?" Tom asked, deflating the moment.

"Oh," Edward started, dazed. "Umm. Kara's a big Picasso fan."

"I can't wait to visit Spain," Kara said. "There's a Picasso Museum in Barcelona."

"And Madrid. To see *Guernica*, right?" Edward asked.

Kara's jaw dropped. "When did you learn about *Guernica*?"

Edward flashed his eyebrows and winked. "I'm full of surprises."

"Well, I don't know much about art, but I imagine you'll visit Florence too," Brenda said, swirling the wine in her glass as she spoke.

"Maybe. I'm not that into the Renaissance," Kara replied somewhat absently, still staring at Edward, shaking her head as if she couldn't believe he'd shown an interest in her passion.

"Well, the only Florence I know is the one in Kansas. Unless you include that lady from *The Brady Bunch*," Tom said. "Brenda, how about serving dessert?"

Brenda's eyes closed softly and she inverted her glass, sending a mighty pour of Chardonnay straight down her throat. When she stood, Kara rose too. "I'll help."

The ladies were barely out of sight before Tom leaned back and crossed his leg. With an elbow on the chair's arm, he pointed, jabbing in Edward's direction as he spoke. "I'm curious—and I know it's rude, but I'm gonna ask anyway—but you're what, thirty? What possesses a fellow your age to take three years off from his career to travel?"

Edward swallowed his mouth dry as Tom's tone caught him off guard. It was the practiced blend of a father's condescension and disapproval. He'd heard it before, but never from a stranger. He felt the hairs on his neck vibrate as a chill swept over him.

"No, I don't mind," he lied, "And I'm twenty-nine, so you're close. To be perfectly honest, I found myself between jobs a bit unexpectedly and, knowing that this was something that Kara wanted to do for a long while, we decided it was either now or never."

"Sure, sure, but aren't you worried about having to jump back in after being out so long? Doesn't it feel a little reckless for someone your age?"

"Well, there's that but …" Edward paused to take a sip from his glass, to calm his nerves. He fidgeted as two months of anxiety raced through his mind and sweat beaded on his chest.

Edward wished he could tell Tom that his company was holding his job for him and that everything would be okay, but he couldn't. Tom was right. Edward was scared to death about not being able to find a job when they got home, that his peers were going to climb right past him, and that he'd miss his window and be stuck in associate hell for the rest of his life while everyone around him made partner.

From beyond the door, Kara's laughter penetrated the room, reminding Edward of what he stood to lose most. Would she still love him if his career plateaued?

To hell with thinking about all of that now. It was bad enough he spent half the time on the bike trying to fend off these same worries. *And what the hell's with this guy anyway? He thinks because he feeds me he can ask anything he wants about my private affairs?* No. Not today. Edward sat taller in his seat.

"I have confidence in myself and what I've accomplished. I trust it'll work out," Edward said matter-of-factly, trying to end the conversation. He took another quick sip of his wine, slurping the remaining drops. Through the empty glass, he could see Tom eying him from the end of the table.

"What'll work out?" Brenda asked, coming through the door, an apple pie in her hands. Kara followed with a tray of coffee mugs.

Edward and Tom exchanged a glance, but neither spoke.

"Suit yourself," Brenda said with a shrug and began serving the pie.

Edward ate his dessert without speaking, feeling his armor cracking under the strain of Tom's glare, while Kara and Brenda rattled on like old friends till the coffee went cold.

Tom stood abruptly. "Edward, why don't we take a drink outside while the gals clean up from dinner? I can use some fresh air."

Edward took a deep breath and nodded, knowing he had no choice but to go.

Kara backed through the swinging door to the kitchen, humming, her arms loaded with cinnamon-streaked plates. Empty mugs dangled from her left hand while wine glasses clinked against one another, wedged between the fingers of her other. "Where would you like them?" Brenda did a double-take upon seeing her. "Oh heavens, you didn't have to carry them all at once." She swung the faucet to fill the other side of the sink, then rushed to unload Kara's arms onto the butcher block island.

Kara followed her to the sink as the lights outside by the dock blinked on. *Tom must want to show Edward his plane,* she thought. After more than a month of traveling alone with Edward, side-by-side, twenty-four hours a day, Kara was happy to have some female companionship. Even if it meant doing dishes.

"I wash, you dry?" Brenda proposed, extending a dishtowel.

"After you did all the cooking? It's the least I can do." Kara plucked the towel from Brenda's yellow-gloved hand and twirled it as she waited to dry the first glass. "I think you've spoiled us for our future home stays."

Brenda stared at the dishwater as her smile wavered. "You're welcome back anytime. I try to spend most of my summers out here. It makes it easier."

Kara sensed resignation in Brenda's voice and aimed to keep the conversation light. "It's great that Tom can work remotely. I bet it's hard for him to focus with the lake outside. Does he fish?"

"He flies out on weekends when he can. He works so much during the week I hardly ever see him anyway."

"I'm sorry," Kara said, her voice a whisper as delicate as the soap bubbles. They had only just met, but Kara felt an instant kinship with this woman.

Brenda's brow furrowed as she straightened her posture. "Our house back in Minneapolis is bigger, and there's a lake there too, but I'm happier here."

Kara couldn't imagine needing one house this big, let alone a second even larger. She'd never understand what the point of being rich was if you never had the time to enjoy it. Still, she knew Brenda's predicament well. "Edward was always working too. Long nights. Weekends. It's hard sometimes," she said, resting her hand on Brenda's arm.

"It is, but I keep telling myself it'll be worth it once he retires." Brenda dunked a plate in the hot water and handed it to Kara. "You kids are smart not to wait till it's too late to take your bike trip. Tom says we'll do plenty of traveling in retirement, but," she said, her voice cracking as she continued, "between you and me, I wonder if we'll even make it to then."

Kara stretched an arm around Brenda in an awkward hug and rubbed her shoulder. How many nights had Kara spent alone, biting her lip just like Brenda did now, fighting back tears, wondering when she'd cease coming second to Edward's career? She felt Brenda slump under her arm and fished for something to say, but the only words she found were an echo of Brenda's.

Smart not to wait till it's too late …

Maybe Edward wouldn't have agreed to do the bicycle tour if he hadn't been fired, but he was. It *wasn't* too late. Kara felt her face flush as tears of happiness welled in her eyes. *Not for me.*

Brenda cleared her throat and forced a laugh. "Look at me being silly." She shook out her arms, as if flicking the unwanted emotions from her fingertips. "I really shouldn't drink so much," she said, blushing.

"Are you okay?" Kara asked, feeling her own tears on the verge of spilling.

"I'm fine," Brenda said, "But, oh my. What's wrong?"

Kara laughed and wiped her eye. "A little too happy from the wine, I guess."

"I'd be happy too if I had a husband showing me the world."

Edward followed Tom toward the dock, swirling a glass of Lagavulin only four years younger than himself. He had no idea why Tom wanted to go outside to talk, or why he had made a point of saying the whiskey was only for special occasions—right before pouring two generous portions—but he wasn't about to object. He could do without the cigar smoke though, which now trailed behind Tom like the exhaust of a locomotive.

Tom's broad silhouette came to a stop near the floatplane, its frost-covered wings sparkling in the moonlight. "Got this baby back in 1981, right before Cessna stopped making them. Damn shame."

Edward nodded, feigning agreement. The plane, white with red stripes, looked the same as any other floatplane Edward had ever seen. He'd never ridden in one, but they were a common sight in Seattle. The tourists loved them.

"Yeah, used to be half the homes on this lake had a Cessna 180 docked outside. Hold this a second, will you?" Tom handed Edward the cigar then opened the plane's door. He climbed from the metal step above the pontoon onto the seat, resting his glass on the cockpit dash.

Edward held the cigar at arm's length, trying to keep clear of the smoke, else the stench would permeate his entire wardrobe when he packed in the morning. He looked to see what Tom was doing in the plane, but averted his eyes as Tom's expansive behind, protruding from the open door, wiggled and shook as he rummaged for something behind the pilot's seat.

"Ah, here it is," Tom said, straightening atop the seat. "Edward, do you know why we flew out here to host you and Kara tonight?"

"Actually, no. I figured it was a coincidence. Maybe you were coming out to clean up after winter." Edward realized how silly that sounded as soon as he said it. Even by moonlight, he could see that most of the yards still had patches of snow sharing space with buried picnic tables and tarp-covered vehicles.

Tom spun his feet to the step, grabbed hold of the wing support, and swung himself down onto the dock with a grace that belied his hulking size. "Brenda will probably do a bit of tidying up tomorrow, but do I really look like the kind of guy who would fly across the state so my wife can make dinner for some hippies on a bike tour?"

Edward laughed to deflect his nervousness. Tom was intimidating, and certainly a bit gruff, but there was a secret only now surfacing. And Edward felt a trap forming around him.

"We flew out here because of this," he said, trading Edward a dog-eared magazine for the cigar.

Edward's body tensed as he recognized it immediately. Not only was there a copy of the Northwest Business Review in every bathroom stall at his old office, but there was no mistaking the issue. It was the journal's bi-annual "Thirty Under Thirty" issue. He smiled as he shook his head slowly in amazement.

"I thought you'd recognize it. I would too if I were number five on the list. Very impressive, Edward."

"I don't understand. How'd you know that was me?" Edward asked, his brow crinkled.

"Brenda showed me your profile photo on that cycling website the other day—Kara's email damn near had her singing for joy—and there you were smiling back at me from the computer screen. And it wasn't the first time I heard your name this month."

"I don't follow," Edward admitted. He took a sip of the Scotch, hoping the peaty warmth would calm his nerves.

"Sounds like you put on quite a show in Ron Madsen's office," Tom said as he tipped his glass with a wry smile.

Tom's words landed like an uppercut to the gut. Edward choked on his whiskey, scorching his nasal passages with the firewater as his throat lurched in humiliation. *What are the odds?*

"I've known Ron for years," Tom said. "Met him at a conference a while back. We keep it strictly business. We're not golf buddies and our wives don't play bridge together, but we usually get together once or twice a year to talk shop. I put my contacts in touch with him when they're looking for some seed money and he encourages your wealthy Seattle clients to invest with my firm in Minneapolis. High-net-worth individuals only," he added, sneering as he took another puff from his cigar.

Edward felt frozen in place and stared at the magazine, a blank look on his face. "I used to wonder how we'd end up shepherding startups from the Midwest."

"Now you know. But the problem I'm having is that the new money, the geeks behind the apps with the eight and nine figure valuations, they're clueless when it comes to investing. And, worse still, they're chicken-shit. They're so damn scared of losing their money, they won't accept any risk, least of all from a bunch of guys that remind them of their fathers. They don't trust us. We don't speak their language. Ron's always been able to send me the C-suite guys, but they're getting old. They want income, not growth. And my revenues are drying up. I need young blood. Guys your age."

"I know the kind you're talking about. I've handled the VC for a few of them. They're good guys, just a bit cautious," he said, thinking about his own reservations with the stock market. To men like Tom, every bubble that burst was nothing but an opportunity to buy low. But to those growing up in a post-Enron world, every day seemed to bring with it a new crisis. "Why tell me this? I mean, you said it yourself, I don't work for Ron anymore."

"No, you don't. I know that. You're just out there riding your bike, not a care in the world."

"Well, I—"

"Let me ask you something, Ed—I can call you Ed, right?"

Edward nodded without hesitation, too anxious to hear where Tom was steering the conversation to insist on being called by his given name.

"Does your back ever hurt hunched over those handlebars all day?"

"Sometimes. You get used to it," he said, unsure what Tom was getting at.

Tom stiffened. "Well I got a pain in my back too. And I think you're the perfect one to straighten it."

Edward took an instinctive step back. Everything about Tom overwhelmed him—his brusque manner, his size, his age—but he was intrigued. *He wants my contacts.* But at what cost? His gaze wandered from the floatplane to the other houses around the lake. Million dollar vacation homes, the kind of luxury he always dreamed of providing for Kara, and each probably belonging to a guy just like Tom.

Edward took a deep breath and turned to face him. "I'm listening."

Inside the kitchen, Kara reached for a mug to dry and caught Brenda staring at her bracelet. She angled her arm for Brenda to get a better look.

"Oh, that's pretty. Is that from that bead place in the malls?"

"Yeah, Pandora. Edward picked it up for me before the trip." Kara turned the leather bracelet so the glass beads bunched together atop her wrist. "He knew I felt awful about storing my engagement ring in a safe deposit box so he got me this. One bead for each of the continents we plan to visit."

"That's sweet. So what country are you most excited about seeing?"

"Oh, that's easy. Definitely Spain."

"Picasso, right?"

"He's part of it. But I've always wanted to visit Seville and the Andalusia region. I can't wait to see the Flamenco dancers and the white villages. And the olive groves—I love olives," she said.

"Don't forget the tapas!"

"And the wine!"

"Cheers to that," Brenda said, clinking the sudsy coffee mug she was washing with the one Kara was drying.

"I can't wait," Kara said, thinking about the coming months. "And I've heard it's easy to find good camping in Spain."

"So, you don't mind camping?"

"Not at all. I love waking up in the outdoors." Kara looked out the window toward the lake, admiring the reflection of the moon on the water.

"Well, you're young. You'll be wanting a hotel once you're my age."

"Edward already does. I think he's convinced that I'm some sort of princess. Fancy cars and a big house. I don't know where he gets it. To be honest, I'll take a bus and a burrito over a limo and lobster any day."

Brenda laughed. "So, what about Edward? Where's he looking forward to going?"

"I'm not really sure. Probably Scotland. He loves whiskey."

"Oh, Tom's the same way. The only place I've ever heard him say he wanted to go was Ireland. For the whiskey, of course." Brenda rolled her eyes and the two laughed.

"Too funny! They're all the same, aren't they?"

"They really are. But it looks like you've got yourself a good one." Brenda smiled at Kara and yanked the plug from the sink. "I'm glad you emailed us. Tonight was fun."

"It really was." Kara gave Brenda a brief hug and repeated her earlier thanks. She was appreciative of the hospitality, of course, but as she lost herself in her thoughts, she realized she was thankful for so much more.

Kara had finally forgiven herself. She was through feeling guilty for planning to divorce Edward. For weeks her chest would tighten every time she saw him, every time someone asked about him. And then the trip started and she felt even worse for being … *No, Kara, you're not going to beat yourself up over that anymore.*

A spark jumped along her spine, plucking her vertebrae like harp strings.

Poor Brenda, alone in this kitchen all summer long. Kara turned away as a guilty smile played on her lips. Thanks to Brenda, Kara now knew that everything she felt these past months was perfectly normal. Healthy even. Brenda was a glimpse of the future she avoided. All the years of coming in second were over. *I won.*

When Kara turned around, she saw Brenda's eyes were pink and watery. The two were the same, but headed in different directions, and Kara sensed they both knew it.

Brenda took a deep, sniffly breath in through her nose as her lips tugged at the corners in a wide smile. "Let's go sit in the den and wait for the men. I want to hear more about you and Edward. It's not every day I get to meet a couple of soul mates."

Edward stood on the dock, swirling the black granite cubes around his empty highball glass as he listened to Tom's proposal, trying to not let his enthusiasm show. But each word sounded better than the last and, well, he never had much of a poker face in the first place.

"I'll set you up with an office in Seattle and match your previous salary to start. Bonuses are based on the assets you gather."

"Net deposits? Not performance?"

"Well, yeah. Haven't you been listening? I've got programs that read the charts. I'm not hiring you for your investment knowledge. It's your Rolodex I want."

Edward squinted in Tom's direction, puzzled at the reference.

"Oh, for chrissake, your contact list."

Edward laughed while nodding his understanding, then erased his smirk. *Careful, keep it professional.* How could he be this lucky? Every day another sixty miles in the saddle and not a step closer to getting back to work. It was driving him mad. And then this. The one couple in western Minnesota available to host them, and the guy turns out to be a veritable Willy Wonka. A job in private wealth management was the holy grail of finance jobs: reduced hours, big money. *And a corner office with my own support staff!*

"I don't know what to say. Thank you."

"Say yes."

"Yes," Edward said smiling. "I'm definitely interested. But are you sure you can wait for us to finish our trip?"

Tom's entire body stiffened. "Who said anything about waiting?"

"Well ... I thought—"

"That's too long to be out of the game. You'll be worthless to me. Your contacts won't even remember who you are, and they sure as hell won't trust a guy who goes gallivanting around the world for three years. No, you need to start next month."

Edward's knees buckled as his billowing sails fell slack, the wind stolen. The dock was steady, the lake calm, but his head swam with growing nausea.

"I ..." Edward began, then turned toward the house. Through the kitchen window, illuminated by a golden square of light, he saw Kara, laughing. Nearly two months spent battling the cold and the wind and wishing he had kept his damn mouth shut and never lost his job. And now all he could think about was the smile on Kara's face every morning when they started pedaling. There wasn't a person anywhere in the world happier in that moment than she was. He picked at a cuticle as he watched her, not noticing until he felt the sting of the cold air on the torn skin.

"What's it going to be, Edward?"

He turned to face Tom. "I, I can't. This bicycle trip means everything to Kara." Edward closed his eyes and sighed.

"Forget the damn bikes! You'll have enough money to see the world by yacht," Tom said, dotting his exclamation with a thrust of his cigar. "I'm offering you the chance of a lifetime. You think there are going to be any doors open to you in Seattle after what you pulled? It's not exactly Wall Street, you know, where people expect you to act like an asshole from time to time."

"I know. I can't. She'd never forgive me," he said, his chin falling.

"Uh-huh. Had a feeling you might say that, especially once I saw you two completing each other's sentences at dinner." Tom ran his hand along the side of the floatplane and strode past Edward, shaking his head.

Edward kicked at a pile of ropes and searched the water for his reflection. Looking back from the moonlit ripples was a memory of his eight-year-old self, the birthday boy stood up by his father, a marketing executive overseeing the Windows 95 launch. Young Edward had fled to the solitude of the dock behind his family home on Vashon Island after his father called to say he had to work late. Again. And there he stayed, toeing a rope intertwined with sun-baked kelp, his face burning with disappointment and resentment, until his father came home to retrieve him.

He could still remember his father slowly setting his leather briefcase down on the grass before walking out onto the dock. Rather than an apology, or a present, or even a hello, his father offered advice.

"Do you remember what you ate for your seventh birthday?" his father asked.

He shook his head, sniffling.

"Do you remember the trip to Disney?"

Young Edward nodded while wiping his nose with his shirtsleeve.

"And the trip to Whistler?"

He nodded again, recalling the fond memories of that winter's ski trip to Canada.

His father knelt, grasping his son by the shoulders, holding him at arm's length, face to face. It was hard to look his dad in the eyes—it still was, even to this day—but he didn't dare look away. "Whistler, Disney, this house on the water," his father said, gesturing out over Puget Sound, "Those are the things you're going to remember when you're my age. Not whether I was home for dinner or what we ate on your birthday. It's why I work the hours I do, Ed. It's so you and your mom never have to want for anything. So I can be the provider I promised to be when I married your mom. Does that make sense?"

Edward scrunched his face, trying to understand.

The boy who would grow up to earn his MBA and be managing multi-million dollar accounts by the time he was 26 said it did, even if it would take years for it to sink in.

The dock tilted as Tom approached. He looked three inches taller than he was a minute prior. Edward lifted the glass to his mouth and tongued the stone cubes, searching for a drop of whiskey.

"I'm not a guy who makes many mistakes in life, Edward. Know why that is? I see the icebergs coming and correct course before it's too late. And that's what I'm trying to do here. There's not a soul who works for me who isn't at least forty-five. Most are pushing sixty. And it's not by coincidence. I've heard too many damn horror stories about these so-called Millennials. About how soft they are, how they think they know everything but are too damn afraid to make a decision. People say they have no concept of business hours, they want to wear goddamn flip-flops in the office and ride scooters in the hallways. And then you give them these things and they come back asking for a mental health day because their pussy hurts."

Edward snickered. How many times had he heard this same rant before? Another self-important Baby Boomer thinking he's the only one who ever logged a full day's work.

"I offered you that job because I need the company to get younger. I need guys who the new money can relate to; guys who know what the hell Snapchat and Insta-whatever is and don't need to take a pill to screw their wives. I thought you were who I was looking for."

Edward felt himself scowling and tried to interrupt, but Tom continued, seemingly unperturbed.

"I'm not even sure I'm talking to the right person. The Edward Vaughan I thought was coming to dinner was the one Ron Madsen used to rave about. Ron said you had my work ethic."

Edward's eyes widened with shock. Ron wasn't known to give compliments. "I'm him. It's just that now's not the right time." Edward raised the magazine still in his hand, "But I am this guy."

Tom grimaced and rubbed the back of his neck as he turned away, lost in his own thoughts.

Edward knew he should be pleased. That Tom was selling past the close was terrific. Nevertheless, he felt a dread knifing toward him from across the lake, like the dorsal of a shark set to swallow him whole.

Tom spun to face him with a mischievous twinkle in his eyes. "So you're really that guy?"

"I am."

"Prove it. How about we play a game. A contest. You like games, Ed?"

"Sometimes," Edward said, clearing his throat.

"I think you're going to like this one. I just thought of it. We both want you to work for me, right?"

Edward bobbed his head in a noncommittal manner.

"But you've got this bike trip in the way. And that's going to take how long?"

"Two or three years, depending on the route Kara wants to take."

"What if it was the route *you* wanted to take?"

"I don't follow," Edward said, wrinkling his brow.

"I'm willing to hold that job for you, but only if you can prove you have what it takes. That you're a man who knows what's right for his future—his family's future—and can put this fool's errand in its proper slot."

"I can't—"

"Let me finish, Edward. I don't tolerate being interrupted. I'm proposing a contest. Continue with the bike trip. Give that pretty wife of yours her dream vacation, but hurry the damn thing along. Get back to Seattle and be ready to start six months from today. Enjoy the spring and summer, then get the hell back to work. You do that and I'll make you a very wealthy man."

Edward was speechless, the roller-coaster of the past few minutes taking his breath yet again. He could only stand there, staring, expecting to hear it was all a joke. Tom arched his eyebrows twice as he took a puff on his cigar.

Edward's mind was off and running. He could envision the map on which they plotted their route. So much north-and-south. So much zigzagging. If they straightened it out, maybe took a train across China and increased their daily mileage, it could work. But Kara. She'd never go for it. Never in a thousand lifetimes.

"What's it going to be, Edward? Mind giving me an answer? It's getting cold out here."

Edward snapped to, caught off-guard by Tom's impatience, but confident. "Can I sleep on it? It's a great offer, but I need to think about it. I need to talk with Kara—"

"What's to think about?" Tom demanded, striding closer.

He stalled as his mind reeled and Tom breathed down at him, glaring, blowing smoke in his face.

Edward retreated a step and looked down as his feet bumped the rope, reminding him again of his father's words. *Like I promised when I married your mom.*

"I need an answer now, Ed. I'm flying back first thing in the morning."

Edward realized he'd be able to retire early, they'd never have to want for anything. Kara would never have to work again. They could start a family, get a house on the water just like the one he grew up in. Their vacations would be second to none.

"Okay, Okay," Edward said, practically panting as his stomach twisted itself into knots. "Six months," he agreed.

"Excellent," Tom said, clapping him on the shoulder. "Around the world and ready to work on October 23rd."

Edward knew perfectly what agreeing to a six-month timeline meant, but Tom's verbal announcement of the date landed like a sledge to the midsection, crushing that part of him that was excited moments ago. With a hand on the plane for balance and his voice cracking as he spoke, Edward called after Tom. "You need to promise me something."

"What's that?" Tom didn't turn to face him.

"My wife can't know."

PART TWO

Chapter 9

THURSDAY, FEBRUARY 12 — FLORENCE, ITALY

Hours after his sudden appearance in Florence, and still hoping it was all a hallucination, Alessio found himself pondering the younger man staring back at him in the washroom mirror as he smoothed the wrinkles from a forgotten, olive-colored shirt. His chest and shoulders were broad, their muscles not yet repackaged as the older man's flab he'd grown accustomed to in his later years. His jaw was angular, neck taut, and his hair thicker, wavier than he was accustomed to. He swept his hands through his hair, smiling at the way his biceps flexed, and watched as the strands cascaded between his fingers—just as he had done with Sylvia's hair in this very apartment.

But Sylvia was in the past and he was somehow, inexplicably, in the future.

Alessio slumped against the sink, hands clutching the basin, his head hanging, tugged by the lead sinker of his discomfiting memories. It had taken years to get over the rejection, to cease writing her, and to forfeit any attempts to win her hand. Swearing off future trips to Florence, he retreated to his home in Malta, to his ever-hardening heart and isolation, eking out an existence off his savings after surrendering the trade that cost him his one true love.

The more he thought about it—about *her*—the easier it became to accept being young in the future than how he grew old in the past.

Now he was back in Florence. Whether through divine intervention or perhaps only in a dream, he didn't know. A thought came to him as he tried to work out his new age: Maybe he had come back at thirty-three, resurrected just like Jesus Christ. Alessio laughed, forgiving himself the blasphemous thought. He turned to the side and lifted the hem of the shirt as he sucked in his stomach, listening to its rumbling. *I'm going to be as thin as Jesus, too, if I don't get something to eat.*

Alessio had been sneaking longer and longer glances out the window throughout the morning, marveling at the brightly lit shops, the colorful horseless carriages, and the array of black ropes strung between the buildings. The shock of the world outside the window had worn off, but it had taken him all morning to amass the courage it would take to venture out.

Having already tested the key he found while mining the apartment for clues, he braced himself for mockery and the filth of public roads as he stepped beyond the threshold, barefoot and disheveled.

He descended the wide granite steps to the first floor. It was dark but the hall lights blinked on as he reached the landing. "*Chi è la?*" he whispered, afraid. Nobody answered. *More sorcery,* he thought. A pair of floppy brown leather boots sat on a mat outside a door. He hesitated, then dashed on tipped toes, swiped the boots, and disappeared down the stairs to the ground floor. The shoes were at least two sizes too large but better than nothing.

Alessio steeled himself against the fear of the unknown lurking beyond the massive doors at the end of the hall. Self-preservation implored him to stay sheltered; the need for food drove him out. It had been years since his last visit to Florence, and he would need to reorient himself. He paused, eyes closed, visualizing his route when the door swung open, striking him in the shoulder, and nearly knocking him over.

"*Mi dispiace,*" apologized a man entering. Alessio slipped past without eye contact, flushed from his burrow like a frightened rabbit. For all the changes that had taken place since his last visit in 1845, it was the cleanliness that proved most shocking. Alessio walked the center of the pedestrian street, marveling at the stonework sparkling underfoot and the scent of focaccia, not filth, which perfumed the air. Though the incessant whine of the motorized velocipedes was a nuisance, he found it far less offensive than the rivers of horse piss that soaked the cobbles only yesterday.

He turned quickly onto Via dei Calzaiuoli, the district's main thoroughfare, and retraced the route he long ago walked each day on his rounds, while acquiring art for his gallery in Malta. This would take him to the center of Florence and Piazza del Duomo. There, in the shadow of the city's famed cathedral, rising like the North Star above the skyline, he hoped to gain his bearings.

He walked at a pace that belied his excitement, taking time to read the multicolored signs, struck dumb by the plethora of gelaterias and boutiques lining the road. But it was the scents that nearly waylaid him. From every bar wafted the intoxicating scent of espresso mingling with that of a warm *cornetto*. His stomach rumbled with approval, demanding he give in to the temptation. *Not yet. I'll eat only after I visit the cathedral.*

"Mamma mia." Alessio crossed himself and approached a poster inside a store window nearest the piazza. The woman in the photo, revealing expanses of lightly tanned skin in a provocative pose, was the most sexually arresting sight he'd ever seen. Clad only in a miniscule black lace chemise and matching pantalettes, she peered over her shoulder at him, one hand dangling near her inner thigh, the other brushing back her hair, her arm squeezing her décolletage as she twisted in his direction. She stared at him, inviting him to come closer. Alessio darted his eyes left and right, expecting others to be as startled by the sight as he was. But nobody seemed to notice. Or care.

Inside the shop's window, a phalanx of headless mannequins displayed a rainbow of string-like garments cleaving unnaturally sculpted backsides. Alessio felt a stir in his groin and dropped his hands to shield his growing erection, shamed by the reflection of the cathedral in the window. He squeezed his eyes shut, but a kaleidoscope of vibrant satin pinwheeled in his memory.

Alessio was no stranger to the female form. He'd undressed women in the slatted light of a midday rendezvous, felt their warmth, nuzzled at their bosom through the night, but he never knew one to possess such revealing lingerie or the ardor to flaunt it so publicly. Memories of his prior loves coalesced in a single image of a woman leaning out from behind a door, the top two hooks of her corset undone, a seductive smile playing on her lips. Sylvia.

He shook free of the vision as two women exited the store with shopping bags, laughing, leaning into one another conspiratorially. He wanted to lash out, to shame them for patronizing a business that would endorse such a sinful display of flesh so close to the Lord's home, in the shadow of the Baptistry of St. John no less. But he was paralyzed, frozen by the woman nearest him, as her eyes locked briefly on his. Entranced by the sway of her hips, his mind filled with images of the lacy intimates he imagined lay hidden beneath her woolen skirt.

Watching them disappear into the crowd, Alessio struggled to recall the last time he was aroused. He had grown so old in Malta, he couldn't remember.

He bolted for the piazza, averting his eyes from any and all women that crossed his path. The massive cathedral's polychromatic facade, installed in the intervening years, distracted him from his lust. Like most Florentines of his era, he thought the Duomo was destined to remain unfinished forever. Maybe one hundred seventy years really had passed. What else had changed in his absence?

Outside the cathedral, hundreds of tourists willing to brave the winter season posed for what he could only guess were photographs, while dark-skinned Africans hawked dazzling toys flung into the air. Others shouldered bags of silver canes shouting "Selfie stick! Selfie stick!" Alessio squeezed the envelope of cash in his waistband and reminded himself to keep his head down to avoid attention.

He took a seat on the aged cathedral steps, shadowed by the towering steeple above him, relishing in a dose of the familiar. He needed food—that had to come first—and proper trousers and stockings. A jacket too. Though it was unseasonably warm for February, he knew the Tuscan nights could remain cold for months to come. *Months?* How long was he going to be stuck here? He didn't know, but thought it best to be prepared.

Alessio craned his neck, taking in the cathedral soaring above him, as he struggled to recall the trade districts of Florence. The shops on Via dei Calzaiuoli were no place for paupers. He needed an alternative.

Mercato Vecchio. Of course! The goods were much less expensive there.

Zigzagging south toward the river, he took a meandering route that led through Piazza de Cimatori. There, to his pleasant surprise, a kiosk was selling one of his favorite sandwiches, the *lampredotto panini*. Relishing a taste of something familiar, he ordered one of the peasant sandwiches from the proprietor who appeared to be of Persian descent. His mouth watered at the sight of the simmering tripe being heaped onto the roll. Unsure what language the man spoke, Alessio gestured for him to dunk the bread in the broth and then pointed to the pot of green sauce. It wouldn't be a lampredotto without the salsa verde.

"Vino?"

"Yes. Si," Alessio corrected himself.

"Ah, English?"

He nodded, taking a bite of the sandwich and instinctively bending forward so it wouldn't drip on his shirt. Out the corner of his eye, he could see the man staring at him as he poured the wine.

"Let me ask. Why you dressed like that?" Then, with a smirk, "Your lady kick you out?"

Alessio wiped his mouth with the back of his hand, taken aback. "It's a long story. I'm on my way to Mercato Vecchio to buy some new trousers right now."

"Mercato Vecchio? There's no such place. Central Market, maybe?"

That's impossible, Alessio thought. "No, Mercato Vecchio. Near the ghetto." Alessio took the small glass of wine and nearly dropped it when the clear material flexed in his grasp.

"My friend, there is no such place. Go to Central Market. Inside is just food, but the tents outside sell clothes. Very cheap. Good choice. Very cheap." The man wiped his hands on his apron. "That will be five euros."

"Is this market outside the city walls?"

"Walls? Florence has no walls," the man said, mocking Alessio's ignorance with his eyes. "Central Market is in the biggest building in San Lorenzo. You can't miss it. Been there a hundred years."

Alessio's hand began to tremble. No walls? No Mercato Vecchio? The notions were preposterous, yet the man did not seem to be passing fraudulent information. The morsel of confidence gained by the familiar sandwich had vanished. Alessio took the wine in his left hand, the steady one, and raised it to his lips. He downed it in a single gulp.

"Ahem," the man said, holding his hand up, five fingers extended wide.

He retrieved his envelope and sheepishly gave the Persian one of the smaller notes. The man thanked him and offered directions, but Alessio scoffed at the help. Things may have changed, but of course he knew where San Lorenzo was. The neighborhood was only a few blocks north of the Duomo. Anyone familiar with the city could find it in their sleep.

But Alessio's nerves frayed with each step as he considered the news. Could Florence exist without walls? What would protect her from invaders? Alessio found himself wishing for someone to ask as he neared the cathedral. Someone he could trust. He paused outside the heavy bronze door nearest the bell tower and considered attending confession, drawn by the organ music heard from within.

But what would he say? Which of his sins were so abhorrent as to justify this miraculous torture? Forgive me Father, for I have awoken in the future? He spat at the absurdity of it while his hand shook, beating thumb and pinky against his thigh like the wings of a game bird. Penance would steady his nerves. It always had in the past. But three Hail Marys and an Our Father weren't going to clothe him. "Maybe tomorrow," he said, turning his back on the church.

Central Market was just as the *trippaio* had said. Dozens of white tents encircled a building the size of a palace. The crowd was suffocating, hundreds of shoppers from all corners of the globe jostled him, squeezing tight to scour the racks and tables for bargains. Leather perfumed the air, mixing with the earthy scents of cheese and aged beef whenever the market's doors opened.

Alessio purchased a pair of trousers as dark as the basalt paving stones of the piazza, a matching canvas jacket, and a gray sweater. He stepped from the makeshift changing room in the tent and modeled his strange new clothes before a full-length mirror strapped to a tent pole. He turned from side to side, admiring the cut of the clothes, flexing his chest and legs, and smiling at his new look. In the mirror he caught the eyes of a woman staring at him. It was the one from the lingerie store.

Has she been following me?

Their eyes locked and Alessio, feeling a surge of his old self fueled by his restored physique and modern clothing, offered a roguish smile. She arched her eyebrows and licked her lips as she held his gaze in the reflection. For the second time in as many hours, Alessio felt a stirring in his loins.

He hesitated—how long had it been?—but the invitation was undeniable, and so he wheeled on her, closing the distance in two strides as his pulse raced, and without hesitation placed one hand on the small of her back, his other behind her head, and he kissed her. The woman resisted, if only for decorum, then matched his dominance, smashing her lips against his with vigor. He released her, ignoring the catcalls of the onlookers, as he planted his lips delicately on her hand, breathing in the scent of her perfume, exhilarated by his own daring.

She soon retreated into the swelling masses of the crowd, their moment consumed in a flash of spontaneous lust. Despite all that might have changed, there was no doubt in Alessio's mind: this was still Florence.

Alessio returned to the apartment, sixty euros lighter, with a bounce in his ill-fitting step and a dormant swagger rekindled. As he licked the residue of the woman's cosmetic from his lips, his thoughts again turned to Sylvia and the glimmer of hope that she had returned to Florence too.

Chapter 10

FRIDAY, APRIL 24 — DETROIT LAKES, MINNESOTA, USA

Kara woke the next morning with pins and needles in her arm. Grimacing with discomfort, she slipped it from beneath Edward's pillow and massaged it. He slept on his side, his back to her. The double bed in the O'Donnell's guest room made for cramped conditions, but she'd never seen him toss and turn like he did that night. Especially not after a long day's ride and an evening of drinks.

She cozied up behind him, welcoming the warmth of his body against her skin, the familiar scent of his hair, and the softness of the linens and comforter enveloping them together. It was a lovely break from their steady diet of sleeping bags and scratchy motel sheets.

Kara dragged the tips of her fingers along his leg and side, back and forth, willing him awake. She dropped her hand over the horizon of his hip and brushed his sex. He didn't flinch.

Nuzzling behind him, her cheek in the reverse nook of his neck, Kara ached with the unfulfilled craving she wore to sleep. He was next to her, body against body, but miles away. Still.

She never thought she'd be the type to have sex in a stranger's house, but last night was different. She nearly tore free of her clothes before the bedroom door shut behind them. And it wasn't just the wine. It was everything: being back in the Midwest, her talks with Brenda, seeing Edward in something other than a fleece sweater for a change. And, of course, the chardonnay. But more than that, it was witnessing the future she narrowly escaped. How could she not feel hot after seeing, in Brenda's loneliness, the life of isolation and boredom from which Edward's firing had saved her? And though she'd never admit it, a part of her wanted to be loud—to celebrate that rescue with wild abandon.

Kara bit her lip as the lingering frustration of the prior night's failed seduction gnawed at her. He'd been distracted before, especially when he was working, but not like this. Through the kissing, fondling, and tickling his disinterest was absolute. Still she pressed on, taking him in her mouth in an ultimate attempt at coaxing him to attention. Yet his body was broke, his blank face a portrait of white space. Only now, in hindsight, did she realize it was the look she expected to see back in February, on the night she planned to ask for a divorce. A chill ran through her and she snuggled up behind him, pressing deeper into his warmth, smothering the memory.

Hoping the night's slumber calmed his troubled mind, she tried again, wrapping her hand around his member and giving him a squeeze. Nothing. She wanted him. Not just inside her, but to be held and kissed. She wanted to plummet asleep spooning on the too-small bed, legs intertwined, their bodies joined like the soul mates Brenda called them.

Kara propped herself against the headboard, adjusting to the dim light, scanning the room for her clothes. "Oh, for chrissake," she said, tossing the comforter aside and striding across the room to snatch her underwear from the head of the porcelain doll staring down from atop the dresser. "Real classy, Kara."

She tugged on her pajamas and pulled open the blinds, illuminating the room in stripes of morning sun. Outside, steam rose from the driveway while the barren trees swayed in a gentle breeze.

A gray squirrel clambered down the side of a tree and hopped from one square of sunshine to the next, staying clear of the tree branch shadows. *Great day for a bike ride.*

Yawning, she found her wristwatch in her handlebar bag and saw they had overslept. "Time to wake up," she said, gently shaking Edward by the shoulder. "It's past eight." When Kara returned from the bathroom, she found him lying on his back, staring at the ceiling. She pulled the covers off him. "Come on. We gotta get moving." She paused, noticing his immobility and remembering how detached he was. Ever since dinner. "Everything okay?"

"Huh? Yeah." Edward rose and looked around the room as if he had never seen it before. "I'm not ready for this," he muttered.

"Want me to ask Brenda if we can stay another day?"

He didn't respond, choosing instead to pull on clean bike shorts and socks.

Kara shrugged and turned to do the same, rummaging through the stuff sack containing her cycling clothes. "Oh, speaking of Brenda, I have to tell you," she lowered her voice before continuing, "That woman is lonely. Lone-*LY.*" She stretched the word for emphasis. "Listening to her is like being stuck in a Dickens story. All I kept thinking was how much I'd hate to become like her. Thank God you're not working for Madsen anymore. I swear it was like talking to the ghost of housewife yet to come."

"Huh."

Kara stiffened and balled a long-sleeved jersey in her hands. "That's all you've got? *Huh?*" she repeated, imitating him.

He looked at her, his face expressionless, almost catatonic. "We should try to get eighty miles in today."

"What?" she demanded.

"Minnesota's flat. Maybe we'll aim for a hundred tomorrow."

"What's gotten into you? We've never ridden more than sixty-five miles, and that was downhill. With a tailwind! Now you want to do a hundred?" She scoffed loudly and watched as Edward transitioned from getting dressed to packing. Only, instead of rolling up his dinner clothes, he collected random items from around the room. She watched as he placed a box of tissues in one bag and her shoes in another.

"Hey space cadet, you gonna steal the towels too?"

Edward snapped to, a small figurine in his hand. He rolled it between his palms as he looked from his panniers to Kara, who now studied him with growing concern.

"Wanna tell me what's on your mind? This isn't like you."

His eyes flashed wide, as if he'd been slapped, then settled on hers. He managed a weak laugh that crept into a smile. "I guess I was just daydreaming about today's ride." He walked around the bed and gave Kara a kiss on the cheek.

Kara returned to her packing, rolling her pajamas with nervous detachment. Something wasn't right. They've had bad days before. Each of them. But he was acting like he'd seen a ghost. Kara hoped a home-cooked breakfast and the responsibilities of navigating the backroads of Minnesota would distract him from whatever was troubling him.

Downstairs, they found the dining room table set for two. Edward placed their panniers against the wall and sat while Kara went in search of their host. Brenda was in the kitchen, filling a carafe of orange juice. "Good morning, Brenda. The pancakes smell wonderful."

"I hope you're hungry. Did you sleep well? I know the bed can be a bit tight, but you two don't look like you mind snuggling." She gave Kara's elbow a squeeze on her way to the dining room.

"You and Tom aren't joining us?" Kara asked, then quickly regretted doing so.

"He flew back earlier. I'm surprised you didn't hear the Cessna." Perhaps reading the apology written on Kara's face, Brenda explained. "I'm going to stay a few days and get the house ready for the summer. I'll fly back from Fargo later in the week if he's too busy to come get me. Tom said he might have a new hire to prepare for."

Kara watched as Brenda winked at Edward as she mentioned Tom's departure. A practiced gesture of spousal support in front of another man, no doubt to ward off sounding ungrateful. Kara knew the move well.

"Enough about that. Sit and enjoy. I've got scrambled eggs coming right up, and there's toast keeping warm in the oven. Help yourself to as much as you want."

Edward remained distant through breakfast and Kara was too focused on filling her stomach to force small talk. After eating, he excused himself to tend to the bikes. It comforted Kara while she cleared the table to know he was outside going through his pre-ride checklist, squeezing the tires and checking the chain and brakes, always making sure her bike was safe.

He probably just needed some food in him. A hundred miles? Kara couldn't help laughing.

With their bags mounted and helmets on, it was time for goodbyes. Brenda went to Edward first, as he was closer, and hugged him farewell. She appeared to linger, leaning in as if whispering something in his ear. But Brenda was moving toward Kara before she could give it much thought. "It's been so nice having you here," Brenda said. "I really hope we see each other again."

Kara echoed the sentiment, recognizing the well-intended, keep-in-touch goodbyes for what they were. Every day she met such nice, generous people, and every day she had to keep moving. She wondered how many new friends she'd meet by the time she got across the country. Or to Europe. Bit players in the story of her trip around the world.

"If you're ever in Seattle, be sure to look us up. We'd love to return the favor one day."

"I'm gonna hold you to it," Brenda said, pulling her in for a hug.

"Guess it's time to hit the road," Kara said, as Edward approached with his bike.

"You mind holding this? I think I left something inside."

Kara watched Edward run back inside, unable to notice the coy smile playing on Brenda's lips.

The door clicked shut behind him and in the empty solitude of the house, Edward felt he could exhale for the first time in hours. He backed against the door, hands on his knees, doubled over, like an Olympic miler finishing on fumes. But the race had only just begun.

The reality of what he'd agreed to hit him on the way to bed last night. The absurdity of his decision, thinking he could rush them through the trip without Kara realizing—or objecting—overwhelmed him. All night he groped in the fog of his mind, searching for a solution, a way to get her on board. It was impossible, he knew; they hadn't been on the road long enough for Kara to entertain any discussion about his career. And she had long since given up believing his promises of reduced hours, more time at home, fewer weekends spent with clients. Of course, it was easy for her to say she cared more about his time than his money while he was clearing twenty thousand a month. What if he couldn't find work after the trip? He couldn't risk it. He had to win the job with Tom—for Kara's sake.

Still, he'd never lied to Kara before. Not directly. It was paralyzing, rendering him unresponsive to Kara's touch—another first. In a way, he was glad Brenda winked at him when she mentioned Tom's new hire, just the jolt he needed to snap him out of his daze. Edward wondered why Tom bothered to tell Brenda anyway, then he remembered why he had come inside. There was a letter for him in Tom's office. He'd better find it before Kara grew suspicious.

Edward pushed open the door to Tom's office and recoiled as the stench of stale cigar smoke accosted him. But his repulsion didn't linger. Despite his unease, Edward felt himself relaxing as he crossed the threshold, a step into his old life. Oversized bookcases lined the walls, filled with leather-bound binders and framed photos of Tom glad-handing a who's who of Fortune 500 executives. Beyond a pair of nailhead armchairs sat an intricately carved desk near a window overlooking the lake. There, on a felt-lined desk blotter, was a bulging envelope bearing Edward's name, propped against an old cell phone.

From the envelope stuffed with cash, he extracted a folded sheet of letterhead with a handwritten note.

Edward,
Call me every Thursday at 10 p.m. Central time. Don't be late!
If I don't answer, leave a message. I want to know your location
and where you're headed next. I'll be tracking your progress.

No excuses!
Tom

PS: Despite my better judgment, I've decided to include a
signing bonus as a show of good faith. Don't make me regret
it! Also, Kara's email mentioned you two not carrying a phone.
This old Blackberry should still work. Get yourself a SIM card
and use it.

Edward rolled his eyes as the letter reminded him of what a jerk he was signing up to work for. Probably no better than his last boss, he thought. He sighed, knowing it came with the territory. At least he'd be working halfway across the country, in his own office, setting his own hours. And the pay would be fantastic. *Speaking of money …*

He stretched the envelope wide and rifled through the cash, quickly counting fifty hundred-dollar bills. Not bad, he thought, given the circumstances, but it didn't change much. If anything, the money was a complication he could do without, another thing needing to be hidden from Kara. He hesitated, then stuffed the envelope of cash into the pocket of his pants, thankful he'd chosen baggy, mountain bike pants over the skin-tight Lycra so many other cyclists wore.

A pit formed in his stomach as he stared at the phone, realizing he didn't know the first thing about SIM cards and international calling. And then there was the issue of time zones. They were headed to Europe. Did Tom really expect him to wake up in the middle of the night to call him? And what if they were out of cell phone range, camping in the mountains? He shook his head, remembering the underlined words: *Don't be late.* "What a pain in the ass," Edward muttered, annoyed he couldn't just email him like a normal human being. "No wonder he can't land any younger clients. The guy's a dinosaur." He checked the letterhead for a phone number and stuffed it in the pocket with the cash.

The friendly jingle of Kara's bicycle bell reminded him he'd better hurry. He dropped the phone into another pocket and quick-stepped out of the office and into the bathroom. There, he flushed the toilet and ran the faucet behind a closed door, pretending to wash his hands as he planned his next move.

Is this really worth it?

He broke into a cold sweat, hating what he knew he'd have to do in order to win the job—and to keep everything a secret from Kara. But what choice did he have? He loved her too much to risk finishing the trip unemployable and bankrupt.

Edward realized he could hide the money in the zippered pocket inside his pannier, where he kept the spare spokes and brake cables. Kara would never look there. As for the phone, he considered pretending it was a gift from Tom and Brenda, but quickly decided it was better to just hide it. Telling her would only invite more questions.

There was no way she would understand what a great opportunity this was for him—for *them.* Even though six months of travel was still more than most people ever experience—equivalent to thirteen years of two-week vacations by his count—he knew it wasn't why they sold their belongings, and it was a far cry from the three-year tour she dreamed of.

Cycling around the world in six months would require an incredible amount of good luck: a complete lack of mechanical problems, good weather, and long days in the saddle. Not to mention a militant approach to route planning. Edward exited the house wondering if it were even possible, but knew he had to try.

He looked at his watch: 9:45 already. *Shit.*

Chapter 11

WEDNESDAY, APRIL 29 — TWO HARBORS,
MINNESOTA, USA

Five eagles—four adults and a mottled juvenile—danced atop the carcass, wings flapping, beaks wide and stained with blood, jostling for their turn at the mangled deer. Edward and Kara watched from afar, their bikes tottering in the center of a desolate highway in northern Minnesota. The spectacle, the latest in a string of delays Edward felt coiling around him, constricted his movement.

His plan to straight-line across Minnesota on a northeasterly heading to Grand Portage and the Canadian border was struck with one setback after another. It all looked so easy on the state's bicycling map. The plan was to pedal east along the Heartland Trail to Grand Rapids, and then northward on the Mesabi Trail, into the green and blue expanse of Paul Bunyan country, where quiet forest roads and lakeside campgrounds promised to make for smooth going.

But spring had yet to thaw those paths. Rather than marching past in a blur, the ubiquitous white birch trees, so stark against the blue sky, crawled by in slow motion as Edward and Kara pushed their bikes through drifts of lingering snow, ice scratching at their panniers. The going was glacial. On the fifth day of a three-day ride, they decided to angle south, to the shores of Lake Superior, and rid themselves of the state's icebox interior.

"I can't believe our national symbol is a filthy scavenger," Kara said from behind her camera.

"I think the word you're looking for is *opportunist*," Edward said, watching an eagle tear free a fresh strip of meat. "It might not be noble, but neither is starving."

"I suppose," Kara said, her face a portrait of disgust. "But roadkill?"

Edward didn't know bald eagles ate carrion either, but why shouldn't they? There was no shame in taking advantage of the blessings strewn across your path, especially when desperate. He considered the alternative—nature demanding the eagles wait till spring to fish their meals from melted lakes—but knew they'd die of starvation if that were the case. No, it was better to take advantage of chance encounters, pride and appearances be damned. The more he pondered the morality of their ways, the less he found himself thinking about the birds.

The eagles took flight as Edward and Kara approached the carcass. He stared into the butchered heap of fur and bone as they rolled past and, in that moment, with the birds carving circles higher and higher in the blue sky above, doubt sank its talons into Edward's mind; he wondered where he and Tom stood upon the food chain.

Edward assuaged himself, confident he and Tom were on the same team, members of an elite flock, believing he wasn't just a passing meal for a shrewd predator. *A teammate with hoops to jump through*, he thought with a sigh. As the miles rolled by and the town of Two Harbors drew near, so did his need to buy a SIM card. Tomorrow was Thursday, and he wasn't about to miss his first call to Tom.

Later that day, the couple descended straight into town. Kara took the lead, pedaling across a sodden field in the shadow of two massive piers, and didn't stop until they were at the shore of Lake Superior. Dumping her bike on the gravel path, Kara ran to the rocky coastline, her arms stretched wide, as if trying to embrace a distant relative.

Edward hesitated. He wanted to join her on the rocks and twirl her around in celebration of their reaching the Great Lakes, but he didn't. He held back, anchored to solid ground, struck by the beauty of the moment. There, on the shore, with half a continent behind them, and concentrated within Kara's effervescent glee, everything was forgotten: the wet feet and frigid toes; the saddle sores; the incessant headwinds; the grease-stained fingers and frustration of flat tires; the hurt feelings and lost tempers. None of it stopped them. Not even his own disinterest. *We're really doing this.*

"You didn't think it'd be this big, did you?" Kara asked, her Midwestern pride beaming as she spun around.

"I guess I never really thought about it." He paused, scanning the mirror-like sweep of blue. "It's just like the ocean."

Kara laughed and skipped the final steps toward Edward, hopping into place, her toes against his toes, her arms around his neck. She smiled at him from mere inches away, and he was struck by how intimate the moment felt, even more than kissing. "And I always thought seeing the Pacific would be more impressive than it really was." She kissed him quickly then stepped beside him, ducking under his arm, and taking his hand in hers.

Edward held his wife tight by the shoulder, proud of them, of her. The odometer hit two thousand miles earlier that afternoon. He hadn't given it much thought at the time, but now, standing at the edge of this ocean of a lake, he could happily drown his thoughts about money and the contest and focus on what they had accomplished. And how much of a team they had become.

As if reading his mind, Kara spoke, her voice contemplative: "We used to go to Copper Harbor every summer, up on the coast. The cabin seemed so far away when I was a kid. It was only a three-hour drive from home, but the minutes passed like hours. My world's gotten so much larger since then. Copper Harbor used to feel as far away as California. Now I know I could have biked there in three days. Two if I was in a hurry."

Knowing what her response would be, he asked anyway, hopeful. "Are you sure you don't want to take the southern route around the lakes? Go through Wisconsin?"

She shook her head. "I'm sure." Her voice barely registered above the cawing of the gulls.

How many times had he sat, gritting his teeth, as her family blamed him for living so far away? About her big city lifestyle? Her work? How many times had Edward offered to fly her parents out to visit, only to have them provide one excuse after another as to why they couldn't come? The truth was, no matter how much the distances shrank for Kara, her world would never again be as small as it was for them. And they resented her for that.

Edward squeezed Kara close, knowing how much was going unsaid, as only a husband would. She wanted that water buffer. That she'd rather chase winter along the longer, Canadian shoreline than go anywhere near her hometown was expected.

Thirteen hours. That's all he had until his first call to Tom, all he could think about as he stared out the window over the toasted horizon of an Egg McMuffin.

At least he was able to get the phone working.

Edward had no idea convenience stores sold phone cards, but life on the road held many lessons. He bought a prepaid SIM card last night, along with microwave popcorn and soda, while Kara was in the shower. To his relief, the clerk helped him activate the account and even called the phone to make sure it worked. Now, all he had to do was find a way to use it without Kara noticing.

Edward took a bite of the sandwich, wondering whether people in this part of the country were truly more helpful or if being on the road for two months rendered him more willing to request assistance. Across from him, Kara scribbled away in her journal with one hand, holding a breakfast burrito like a cigar in the other. He wanted to ask her, but already knew her answer. She'd tell him the world was filled with generous people and that the idea of Midwestern politeness was just a myth perpetuated by coastal homebodies who never went anywhere. He'd heard it before.

That he was pondering the kindness of strangers as a direct result of a lie he was telling his wife wasn't lost on him. And it wasn't one he could cycle away from.

Edward and Kara spent the day pedaling north along the shore of Lake Superior, passing riotous rivers plunging through narrow canyons, swollen with snowmelt and sediment, staining the lake the color of a root beer float. Where the road curved inland, Subarus adorned with whitewater kayaks dotted roadside pullouts, as neoprene-clad action heroes stood nearby, preparing for battle against the rapids.

While crossing one of the numerous mist-shrouded bridges of State Route 61, Kara proposed shortening the day's ride to do some sightseeing. Edward glanced at his watch, now covered in droplets from the billowing mist. Ten hours to the call. Had they covered enough distance this first week? He gave a mental shrug and agreed to Kara's suggestion. His legs felt dead, a shorter day would do him good.

So instead of pushing a full eighty miles to Grand Marais, they halved their goal and took time to visit a pair of state parks along the way. Though hesitant to stray beyond sight of the bikes, Edward let himself be talked into taking a short hike to a waterfall. It felt damn good to get off the bikes and actually see something for a change. That there needed to be a NO SWIMMING sign in front of a raging waterfall had them both laughing, and helped to take Edward's mind off things.

Despite the detours, they arrived at Tettegouche State Park by five o'clock—over five hours till he had to call Tom. Edward paid for a small tent site on the bluff directly overlooking Lake Superior and exited the campground office to find Kara talking with a wisp of a woman whose angular features were a rarity for the region. A small RV was parked near their bicycles, a mural of the Grand Canyon painted along its side.

"This is Ineke," Kara said, barely containing her amusement. "She thought we were German."

"Because I did not think Americans had Ortlieb here," the woman said, gesturing at their panniers. "To travel like this is very German."

Edward chuckled, noting her heavy accent. "Nope. Ortlieb's panniers are real popular here too. Anyway, nice to meet you, I'm Edward." They shook hands. "Are you camping here tonight?"

"Yes, I have a reservation."

"Just you?" Kara asked.

"Yes. For now. I will meet my boyfriend out west in three weeks."

Kara smiled, rolling her bike back and forth in quarter turns.

"Well, it was nice meeting you." Edward waved as he grabbed his bike then turned to Kara. "We've got a walk-in site across the highway."

"Would you like to join me for a beer after you are set up?"

Edward and Kara exchanged a quick glance, then replied in unison, "Absolutely."

Edward led Kara to their campsite across the road, where they pitched their tent within earshot of the waves lapping against the cobbled beach below them. After showering and eating, they stowed their panniers inside the vestibule, double-locked their bikes to the picnic table's metal frame, and carried their folding camp chairs in search of Ineke's campsite. Edward, not about to arrive empty-handed, carried a partially eaten can of BBQ-flavored Pringles.

The wet-wood smell of a campfire made finding her easy. Ineke sat cross-legged on a folding chair, black leggings sticking out from under a tie-dyed flowy skirt, a road atlas on her lap, and a blanket around her shoulders.

"Ah, you came. Welcome." Ineke hopped to her feet and strode toward Kara, planting two quick air-kisses on her cheeks. Edward stared, wide-eyed at Kara, as Ineke repeated the process on him, not knowing which side to turn to, and whether or not to actually kiss her cheek. He was certain he did it wrong and wished Kara, who had spent a semester abroad in Paris, had filled him in on European greetings.

"Sit, sit, I'll get the beers," Ineke said. She disappeared through the RV's screen door and returned seconds later with two bottles of Becks, already opened.

Edward glanced at his watch as he took a drink. It was almost eight.

"Tell me about your trip, are you going far?" Ineke asked.

Edward motioned to Kara. "The floor's yours."

"We're headed around the world," Kara said, opting for the shorthand explanation. "We left Seattle six weeks ago."

"Seattle?" Ineke repeated, her eyes bulging. "Kurt Cobain!"

The comment caught Edward by such surprise he barely avoided showering the women with a mouthful of beer. How long had it been since Cobain died? He couldn't remember, he wasn't even ten years old when it happened.

"So, what about you? Where are you going?" Kara asked, a bit too anxious to be on the listening end for once, Edward thought.

"I rented the RV for three months—my boyfriend is meeting me in Seattle, actually. But I may keep it the whole year. Your country is so big."

"Yeah, tell us about it." Kara said with friendly sarcasm.

"Ah, that's funny. Because of your bicycles."

"I've never met a foreigner touring the U.S. in an RV before. What do you think?" Edward asked.

"I only started in Chicago, but the scenery is so beautiful and the people are much friendlier than I expected. We hear so much about guns, and I know many people in Germany are scared to travel to America, but—"

"Well, we're not carrying one," Edward interrupted. "Chips?" he asked, passing the Pringles.

Ineke peered in the can then passed it to Kara, her lips pursed.

"Not a fan?" Kara asked, tipping a small stack of powder-coated orange chips into her palm.

Ineke scrunched her face up like a ball of aluminum foil and shook her head. "I am having a hard time digesting your American food."

Edward settled in with his beer as the conversation shifted to the state of food in America: the over-priced, low-quality produce, the same restaurants in every town serving greasy, sauce-slathered meals. As a captive member of Kara's congregation, he'd heard her sermon numerous times before.

"The key is to not eat at any restaurants that advertise on television," Kara said.

"But I don't have television."

"Then you have to follow my other rule. Stay away from restaurants near highway exits."

An epidemic. That's what Kara called it the last time they went to visit her family. Her favorite pancake restaurant had gone out of business. Now the only place in town serving breakfast was a Subway. Even Edward had to admit, seeing the town's old-timers squeezed into a yellow laminated booth, solving the world's problems over cups of coffee at a Subway, felt wrong.

"Places like Applebee's and Chili's? They're just McDonald's with waiters," Kara continued.

"Hey, I like McDonald's," Edward teased.

Kara rolled her eyes. "Ignore him."

Ineke laughed, eventually. As if she couldn't decipher Kara's sarcasm. The group stared at the campfire and fell into brief silence, save for the pops and snaps of the embers.

Kara was the first to break the peace. "Tell us more about your trip. How long will you be in the States?"

"I'm on sabbatical for one year."

Edward and Kara recoiled in surprise and offered their congratulations.

"The university where I teach lets us take every fourth year off in exchange for paying less of my salary. So every four years, I travel. This year I'm seeing the United States."

"You get to take every fourth year off?" Edward asked.

Ineke smiled. "Yes."

"But you're not getting paid, right?"

"I still get paid. But instead of collecting all of my paycheck every year, they deduct twenty-five percent and let me take every fourth year off."

"That's amazing." Kara said. "I wish we could do that."

"I don't know. That sounds crazy to me."

"Most professors don't do it," Ineke said. "They think they need the money."

"Don't your colleagues get mad? And what about your students? You must be an adviser to some of them?"

Ineke shrugged. "If they get mad, they never say anything to me."

"But still, what about your responsibilities? Your research?"

"I'm sure she wouldn't do it if it was frowned upon," Kara said, giving him her best *dial it down a notch* look.

Fair enough, he thought. He was drinking her beer, after all. No reason to be rude. "Don't get me wrong, I think it's fantastic," Edward said, slowing his cadence. "I don't think I could do it."

"What about this trip you're on? Isn't cycling around the world going to take you away from your work for several years?"

"This was Kara's idea," he said with a laugh. "I wouldn't be here if I didn't get passed over for a partnership."

One sentence. So concisely worded. So easily avoidable. He knew it before the words ever left his mouth.

"Well," Ineke said, rising from her chair, "I guess Kara should thank your former employer for her good fortune." Edward watched Ineke give Kara a sly, almost pitying glance, her eyebrows raised. And in Kara's return glance, he realized Ineke merely said what Kara had been thinking ever since that night in the American Legion.

Edward finished the night in silence, wishing he could float away in the tendril of smoke rising from the campfire. He listened as Kara and Ineke traded travel dreams and discussed Kara's work as a graphic designer, counting down the minutes to when he'd silently steal out of the tent to use the restroom, the phone tucked in the pocket of his shorts.

Chapter 12

TUESDAY, FEBRUARY 17 — FLORENCE, ITALY

Alessio sat at the table, a forkful of pasta raised to his mouth, when he heard the key slide into the lock. He knew this moment would come. Three days ago, he returned to the apartment and found the bed made and fresh towels in the bathroom. Since then, he slept in his clothes, kept what little money he possessed on his person, and only took his boots off to sleep. He even knocked when returning. Just in case.

The key turned, then stuck. Alessio could hear the key being jiggled, then turning freely in the other direction. He bit down on the bucatini, savoring the taste of the garlic and tomato, and in that fleeting moment that hung between his domestic life and homelessness, he said a silent prayer, thanking God for the days he had in the apartment.

A young couple entered, as tall as trees with hair like corn silk. Matching suitcases trailed behind them on wheels the size of coins. Alessio twirled the pasta on his fork and spoon and took another bite, refusing to leave unfinished what might be his last warm meal. The couple startled, their smiles vanishing from their angular, confused faces. They spoke rapidly, in a guttural language Alessio didn't recognize, but one he pegged as Scandinavian. Maybe Dutch.

He finished the last bites of pasta, brushed his hair behind his ears, and stood.

"*Me scoozy, pour fa four,*" the woman said in mispronounced Italian. "*Me scoozy?*"

Alessio scanned the room to ensure he wasn't about to leave anything behind, then slid the chair under the table.

"Is there a conflict? We have a reservation," the man said in English. "The host said the apartment was ready."

The couple parted as Alessio approached, leaving a current of tension swirling in their wake. Alessio had every intent of walking silently out the door as if the couple wasn't even there, but he couldn't help himself. He turned to the woman and repeated the words *mi scusi* twice, conducting the pronunciation with his hand, an invisible baton clutched between his fingers, rising and falling on each syllable.

He could smell the pizza on her breath.

Alessio reached for the woman's suitcase, holding her gaze, and grasped the handle, his finger brushing hers. He turned and thrust it toward the man, letting go in one swift move. The bag wobbled back and forth as Alessio eyed the taller man. "A gentleman carries his lady's luggage."

Alessio descended the stairs as the couple's awkward laughter faded into his ever-expanding past. At the door, he counted his money. The thirty-five euros were enough for a few meals, but not much else. Though he tried to be frugal, he expected this nightmare to have been over by now. But it had been five days since he awoke in the future, five days without indication he was returning home, to Malta, to the nineteenth century. He needed somewhere to stay long term, maybe a job too.

Alessio knew where to go, but not even the heat of the midday sun could warm him to the idea. He'd find a place to stay in the ghetto. Public decree corralled the city's Jews in a perpetual state of poverty, but there was always room for more. Thieves, prostitutes, and drifters called the area home as well.

With his hands balled inside his jacket pockets, Alessio made his way north along the *via*, then took a deep breath and turned west. The serpentine alleyways of the old quarter felt familiar, but something was amiss. The area had been swept of its filth and poverty. In its place stood clothing boutiques and neon-lit hotels and restaurants bearing Anglicized names.

Alessio couldn't be certain—after all, he hadn't been to Florence since 1845—but he suspected he hadn't gone astray. Nevertheless, not only had the decrepit Mercato Vecchio been erased, but the entire Jewish ghetto along with it.

Alessio's hand trembled as he approached a merchant selling leather bags and journals on the edge of a large square. "Excuse me, what is the name of this *piazza?*"

"*Piazza della Repubblica.*" The man replied without looking up from the flashing device in his hand.

Alessio repeated the name as he scanned his surroundings. The deplorable conditions he expected to find ringed by a haphazard array of plaster-coated tenements were gone. The ramshackle dwellings had been torn down, their foundations leveled to make room for canopied cafés. Palatial buildings now surrounded the square, walling off the area, funneling one's attention to an arch bearing an inscription.

L'ANTICO CENTRO DELLA CITTA
DA SECOLARE SQUALLORE
A VITA NUOVA RESTITUITO

"The ancient center of the city restored from age-old squalor to new life," Alessio read aloud. *Age-old squalor.* The only remnant of the ancient center was the stone Column of Abundance. Alessio didn't so much as sit on the column's base, as much as the stone pedestal caught him as he stumbled backward, the strength gone out of his legs, the oxygen abandoned his head.

Alessio scanned this one-time hovel in disbelief. One hundred seventy years had passed and the only constant was the paving stones. As gray as his mood and loose in their mortar, they wiggled nervously with each footfall, as if they too were trapped out of time, wishing escape.

Tourists shuffled along as old men fed pigeons where urchins once begged. Alessio considered the quiet an affront to the boisterous souls that once called this area home. Across the *piazza*, a red and gold contraption with obscenely painted horses sprang to life. Music echoed across the square as the horses spun gaily round and round, whisking children in circles.

Alessio tensed as he realized the world had moved on, obliterating the memories of the past. Thousands of people had taken shelter here—their singular refuge—and the only acknowledgment of their struggle was a sign commemorating their poverty? "Squalor," he spat. "That's their legacy?"

Infuriated, he swiped at a nearby pile of leaflets, sending them fluttering to the ground. A woman strolling past in a fur coat gave him a disapproving look, and Alessio glowered at her.

A flyer landed faceup between his feet, an advertisement for a nearby hotel with rooms for ninety-nine euros per night. He stared at the impossible price, reminded of his impoverished state, and realized he too had left no mark—or descendants to call upon.

The oblique reminder of his failed love affair stirred up old emotions, like an anchor dragged along the seafloor. He reached for the flyer, an effort to swim free of the murky memories, and chafed upon seeing the hotel named after Michelangelo. For even in the future, there was no escaping the master's shadow.

As a young artist, Alessio struggled to market his own style during a time of the Renaissance's growing popularity. So he took to imitating the styles of Titian and Giotto and, yes, Michelangelo. But this too failed to produce steady income. So he turned to outright forgeries.

When incurable tremors negated his skill with a brush, he transformed his studio into a gallery and made thrice-annual pilgrimages to Italy. His time in Florence had always been short, washing ashore from Malta on business for a month at a time, on the hunt for hidden talent. His years as an art dealer had been profitable, but all-consuming.

Alessio recalled the paintings he had sold and flattered himself, believing he may have imbued those who visited his gallery with some artistic appreciation before returning home to England. Perhaps, some of his earlier, less scrupulous wares had survived the years. He smirked, imagining one of his fakes still hanging in a family estate, proudly shown to guests, passed as an original.

"Tourists could be so gullible," he said, shivering as the statue he sat upon sapped his warmth.

The comment sparked an idea, a path to shelter. Alessio crumpled the leaflet and tossed it into the rising wind, knowing he had to act before nightfall, or rain. Before the tourists scattered for the evening. He hurried back along the main thoroughfare to *Piazza del Duomo*, envisioning what he must do.

From atop the cathedral's steps, he studied the crowd of tourists, hawkers, and locals coming and going. Amongst the chaos, patterns emerged. The tourists meandered, their heads craned to take in the cathedral—or tilted downward, focused on the rectangular devices in their hands. Some clustered near the baptistry, foreigners packed shoulder to shoulder, gawking at the intricately carved eastern doors. It was a perfect trap, and Alessio soon had his mark.

A lone man, probably British, pushed his way through the crowd, his knapsack partially unzipped and dangling from one shoulder as his wallet bulged in his rear pocket.

Alessio knew from the delinquencies of his youth that the rear pocket pinned a wallet close to the body and was ill-suited for lifting. But not this time. The man's pants drooped at the waist and the pocket sagged open, torn at the corner.

"Forgive me, Father," he whispered as he waded into the crowd. Alessio approached the baptistry doors, feigning awe, as if he too had never seen the site before.

The onlookers crushed against one another, man and woman alike, each pushing forward for a closer look, their photographic devices raised overhead. Alessio neared the man with the opened backpack and stumbled forward, intentionally. As he bumped the target's shoulder, his hand darted out, plucking the wallet from the slack pocket. The man turned around, alarmed. Alessio apologized, and having surmised that English had become the de facto language of the tourist circuit, added, "Your bag is unzipped, you should close it before something goes missing."

Alessio glanced at the bronze doors, and his eyes, as if pulled by a higher power, settled on the panel depicting the story of Moses receiving the Ten Commandments. He squeezed his eyes shut, defiant. *What choice did you leave me?* He slipped between the onlookers behind him and hurried toward the north side of the cathedral, the wallet clutched tight within his jacket sleeve.

His heart raced as he skirted a leather shop and several cafés, bypassing the line of visitors waiting to climb to the dome. He pulled open the door to a hotel and, trying his best to fit in, slowed his pace and followed a red carpet down a lengthy hallway to the lobby.

"*Buon Giorno,*" he said with a terse nod to the clerk before taking a seat on a leather couch behind a partition. Alessio knew the key to being discreet lay not in trying to be invisible, but in perfecting an air of the ordinary.

His palms were sweating. He hadn't picked a man's pocket in years. *How many? Forty? Ten? Two hundred?*

Was it always this easy? Would it be worth it? He dropped his hands between his knees and carefully unfolded the wallet, his legs shielding his gains from view. Alessio extracted the slippery currency from the billfold as a man settled onto the chair across from him.

Alessio did his best to affect an air of nonchalance. He slid the wallet into his pocket while stealthily stuffing the cash into his jacket. He offered a polite smile, as if the two were waiting for a train, the only passengers on an otherwise empty platform.

The man appeared Oriental, probably no older than Alessio but it was hard to tell due to his closely shorn hair. He was dressed in blue denim, a heavy wool sweater rolled at the neck, and thick-soled boots. The man stared with his head canted to the side, a bemused look on his face, and his hands folded loosely in his lap.

Alessio stood to leave, only to see the man rise in unison, his gaze fixed on Alessio. Wondering if he had been caught, his string of petty thefts ran through his mind, lashing him with guilt: the cleaning fee, the boots, and now a wallet. *You call yourself a Catholic?*

Like a cornered dog, Alessio stared back with menacing eyes. On the verge of demanding to know what the man wanted, he thought better of it. He softened his expression, nodded politely, and turned to retreat to the crowded streets beside the Duomo. That's when a hand grabbed him by the wrist.

"I believe I can help you," the Oriental said in whispered Italian.

"Who are you?" Alessio demanded, wrenching his arm free of the Oriental's grasp. He puffed out his chest and glared at the shorter man.

"My name is Hiromasa. Please sit so that we may speak." His voice was sweet yet firm, like chilled honey, and he smiled with a disarming innocence as he motioned to the couch.

Alessio wanted to berate him for his insolence, but was trapped, stunned by a shimmering light radiating off the man, fringing him in blue, like a holy aura. He wondered how he hadn't seen it earlier. Alessio's eyes watered as he stared at the angelic glow, entranced. Fearing he might be experiencing a migraine, he sat—and immediately cursed himself for having done as told.

Hiromasa sat alongside him with a pitying look often reserved for idiots. "I'm sure you had a noble reason for stealing that man's wallet." Alessio felt himself stuttering as his heart raced. He'd been caught. But he was at a loss for words, spellbound by the light.

"Never mind the wallet," Hiromasa said, exposing a mouth of crooked, yellowing teeth, "Though I suppose if you'd like to confess your sins, I may be able to accommodate you."

Alessio replayed the scene outside the cathedral, scanning his memory for the man now sitting next to him. He hadn't seen him in the crowd. "How did you see me?"

"Let's say that you had a way of catching my eye."

The comment seemed to allude to something Alessio didn't understand, a riddle of sorts. "Don't toy with me," Alessio said, rising again to leave.

Hiromasa laughed and placed his hand on Alessio's arm, halting his departure. At once the shimmering fringe of light sparked and leapt, like the flames of St. Elmo's fire on a ship's mast. But the glow, this aura of Hiromasa's, seemed to be trying to connect with Alessio, building near Hiromasa's fingers and leaping toward the bare skin of Alessio's wrist.

"You see it too, don't you?"

Alessio blinked and rubbed his eyes, willing the light away. Hiromasa removed his hand and continued talking, but he spoke with such swift delicacy, Alessio couldn't make out the words. He scrutinized him, struck by the incongruity of this foreigner speaking such fluent Italian. Alessio glanced toward the reception desk, then whispered, "*Conosci l'italiano?*"

"Yes. Italian and English. And *Nihongo*, of course."

Alessio made a puzzled face.

"Westerners call it Japanese."

Alessio hadn't met a Japanese before, and never knew any to speak Italian. The barrage of surprises was exhausting and he wanted to be free of this man. "Explain yourself or let me be. I tire of this," Alessio said in English.

"As I said, I can help you."

Alessio raised his eyes in doubt. "With confession?"

"Well, I was connected with the church."

"You're a Christian?" Alessio leaned back and surveyed the man from head to toe. "A Japanese Christian," he said, scoffing at the idea.

"My name is Hiromasa Uchida, but if you prefer, my Catholic name is Oliverio Pedroza."

"It sounds Spanish."

"It's a long story," Hiromasa said, his toothy smile returning.

"Well, I'm sure it's very interesting, but I must be going. Unless the confessional booth has a bed and a toilet, it won't be much help."

"What is your name?"

"Alessio. Alessio Argento."

"Come with me, Alessio." Hiromasa rose as a family of tourists entered the lobby. They stood blocking the hallway, studying a paper map.

Alessio noticed that the glimmer trimming Hiromasa was absent on the family. He eyed Hiromasa, unsure if he should trust him.

"You have questions, I'm sure," Hiromasa said, no doubt sensing his reluctance.

"None you can answer. I too am sure."

Hiromasa clapped his hands. "I believe, in time, you may be proven wrong. Nevertheless, I have a place for you to stay and work. At the campground across the river. The cabin is cold, but there's plenty of work. The pay is not great, but it's honest." His eyes shifted to the jacket pocket where Alessio had stashed the money.

"Why help me?"

Hiromasa didn't answer, and instead brushed past the family. If Alessio was honest with himself, a little company would serve him well. And he could certainly use a job. Not to mention a place to stay.

Yes, there were the practicalities of Alessio's situation to consider, but the soft-spoken man seemed to know things. Alessio suspected he could not only trust him, but that Hiromasa may even be the key to understanding his situation, to helping him return home. There was only one way to find out.

Chapter 13

TUESDAY, MAY 5 — NIPIGON, ONTARIO, CANADA

Kara eased her wracked body onto the curb and slumped forward, aching from her toenails to eyelids. She tried massaging her thighs through the spandex tights, but the effort was pitiful. She was spent.

And it was becoming a daily occurrence.

They passed a perfectly good campsite fifteen miles back, but Edward wanted to keep moving to "take advantage of the long days" and "stay on schedule."

What schedule?

Kara had been asking herself that question for over an hour, chewing on it as her depleted legs spun the cranks in ever-slowing circles. They had food in their bags, plenty of water, and had spent most of the day in the saddle. There was no need to keep moving. But Edward insisted— and she relented. And now they were here, at a grocery store they didn't need, in a town with no obvious place to camp.

They had only crossed into Canada yesterday afternoon but were already at the northwest corner of Lake Superior, in the fishing town of Nipigon. Eighty miles today, seventy-eight yesterday. Kara yawned and stretched, reaching for the stars from the seat of her pants, welcoming the popping she felt as she rolled her head in circles.

At least we got to camp at Fort William last night, she told herself. As a child, the fur trade era fascinated her, due in no small part to it being the only time her American History classes discussed her region of the country. These days, the fort was more theme park than outpost, but Kara didn't mind. She took her time in the visitor's center, reading each placard and studying every artifact. And when Edward went outside to wait, saying the dioramas reminded him of the body he saw in Montana, she let him go without comment.

"Must be tough pedaling all that gear over the hills, eh?"

Kara looked up as a lanky man in a plaid hunting jacket crossed the street toward her, a case of beer tucked under his arm. His beard was gray and patchy like stubborn drifts of snow refusing to melt.

"I'm feeling it today."

"Not surprised," the man said. He kept a respectful distance, which Kara appreciated. "Where you coming from?"

"Fort William."

He eyed the bikes and smirked. "No, I meant, *where did you start your trip?* But all the way from Fort William today?"

Kara nodded as she stood, her legs rebelling under the strain. She felt twice her age.

"I don't even like driving that far," he said with a snort. Kara chuckled to be polite. Rarely did a day go by without someone making the same lame joke.

"Well, I hope the truckers were being nice. Ain't much room for bikes on 17."

Kara admitted as much. Highway 17 through Ontario was by far the most dangerous road they'd ridden since leaving Seattle. With a shoulder barely wider than a bicycle tire, she spent the bulk of the day staring at her mirror.

"Yeah, a real shame. Seems every year a cyclist gets killed out there." The man shifted the case of beer to his other arm and shook out his hand. "Well, I better be goin'. You be safe."

"Before you go, any chance you know a place we could pitch our tent for the night?" *Maybe your backyard,* she added to herself, fearing the only option might be back the way they came.

"There's a campground by the beach. Down that road there," the man said, pointing beyond a small barbershop.

"Oh, that's great."

"Kayakers use it in the summer, but you should have it to yourself this time of year."

The man wished her well and walked off, taking the stress of the day with him. Between navigation, traffic, food, and finding a place to camp, there was no shortage of details to fret over while touring. In hindsight, a few extra miles were no big deal. When Edward finally exited the store, Kara was so eager to get to camp, she forgot being miffed about the long day. She led the way down the hill as a plastic grocery bag swung from Edward's handlebars like a pendulum.

A half-dozen primitive campsites dotted a forested cove at the base of the bluff, steps from the water. Traces of snow served as mortar on the cobble beach, an iceberg floated offshore. They chose a sheltered site, hoping the pines would block the wind, and set about clearing the winter detritus. Judging by the amount of pine cones and fallen branches covering the pitch, nobody had used the campsite since fall.

"Too bad the wood is so wet. Would have been nice to make a fire," Kara said while feeding a pole through the tent to Edward.

"The market had firewood. I'll go buy some. About time we had a campfire, eh?"

"Eh?" Kara imitated. "Two days north of the border and you're speaking Canadian?"

"I've no idea where that came from. I didn't even realize I said it."

"God help us when we get to Scotland. I'm not going to understand a word you say." Kara laughed and lobbed a soggy pine cone at him.

He bent to collect some ammunition of his own, then rose, pointing. "Wonder what that canoe is doing over there."

Kara followed his gaze to a red fiberglass canoe at the campsite nearest the lake. "Think it's abandoned?"

"Looks pretty new to me." Edward gave her a quick kiss and grabbed his wallet. "Check it out while I get the firewood."

She watched him go, then looked to the canoe. There wasn't anyone nearby, or even a tent for that matter. But the canoe looked too shiny to have been there long.

Kara stepped lightly through the forest, the moss-covered ground softening her footfalls, the damp aroma of the pine drawing her forward, perfuming the air.

From the edge of an adjacent campsite Kara saw that the canoe, lipstick red and showroom clean, propped against a paddle lodged handle-first into the ground, was actually a makeshift shelter. And there, beneath the upturned boat, shivering violently in a yellow rain suit, sat a man shoveling canned meat into his mouth with bare fingers.

Intrigued, but cautious, Kara crouched behind a tree and watched as he continued eating, unaware of her presence, his bushy mustache smeared with SPAM. His bulbous nose glowed as red as the canoe, and his hair was a frenzy of black waves. Yet despite his disheveled appearance and obvious lack of warmth, the man seemed oddly relaxed.

He tossed the tin toward a pile of other empty cans and moved to lie down. Kara clamped a hand over her mouth to muffle a nervous giggle. *He's sure got a taste for SPAM.*

Stretched out on the ground, it was clear the slicker and pants were too large for him, as the material was bunched at the elbows and knees. He was short, probably no taller than Kara, but solid. His chest and arms bulged comically against the rain suit as he crossed his arms, hugging himself for warmth.

Then he began to sing. With his eyes closed and fingers tapping in rhythm against his arm, he serenaded the forest. His voice was soft and barely audible over the wind rustling the trees, but the words were certainly French.

But what is he saying?

Kara needed to get closer. She glanced over her shoulder, then advanced. Inching stealthily from tree to tree, ignoring the beads of sap on her fingers, she crept within ten yards, near enough to hear the peculiar dialect, to feel the energy of his tenor.

A lump caught in her throat. She'd seen this before. Not him exactly, but his appearance, the canoe, and the song and everything else she had observed. Everything about the man resembled the French-Canadian voyageurs, the canoemen who plied this region in the early 18th century. This stranger resting beneath his canoe was just like the wax figures in the museum, the spitting image of the drawings in her history book.

She couldn't steal her eyes from him. And it wasn't just curiosity that had her risking detection. The man wasn't attractive in the least, yet the butterflies in Kara's stomach fluttered all the same. She flushed as she gazed upon this barrel-chested man lying upon the bare ground. And the longer she watched, a voyeur hiding amongst the trees, the more she was drawn to him. There was a quality to him she'd never seen in a man before, not even Edward. Something primal.

A whiff of smoke caught Kara's attention and she realized that she had been holding her breath. Her eyes stung from not blinking. She looked once more at the man then retreated to camp, where Edward had already lit a campfire.

"So, what's up with the canoe?"

Kara could barely speak, as if she had been shaken from a dream, stunned and disoriented. She filled in Edward the best she could, being careful not to paint the man as too shabby, and conveniently omitting the more private reflections. There was no way to explain them to her husband when she didn't even understand them herself.

"Do you remember your French?" Edward asked.

"*Oui, oui, monsieur.*"

"Why don't you get changed and invite him for dinner." Edward placed several pieces of kindling on the fire and blew at the embers.

"Are you sure?" Kara cursed herself for having even mentioned the man. "What happened to not trusting strangers?"

"Nobody should have to live off SPAM. Besides, it's about time we paid some of our good fortune forward."

Kara crawled into the tent, unsure what to think. On one hand she was happy to see Edward in a generous mood, but dinner with the two men could prove awkward. After all, she could control her desire to stare, but a racing heart skipped to its own rhythm.

Twenty minutes later, after freshening up and laying out the sleeping bags, Kara emerged from the tent having decided she and Edward would eat alone.

Edward was hunched over their stove, pushing bratwursts around a frying pan with a plastic spatula. Behind him, approaching from the trees, all dimples and teeth, was the man from the canoe.

"*Bonsoir,*" the man called out, stepping from the trees. His gaze locked on Kara, who felt herself flush. He smoothed his mustache then ran a hand though his tangle of hair.

Kara hadn't accounted for the possibility that he would invite himself and now had to make the best of it. "Good evening," she replied in French, while wondering if he had seen her watching him.

"Looks like someone smelled the dinner bell." Edward intercepted the man's approach with his hand extended, only to be enveloped in a bear hug. The man's hand clapped Edward on the back with a thud. He was even shorter than Kara thought, barely rising to Edward's shoulder despite the thick soles of his galoshes, which looked to be several sizes too big.

"*Parlez-vous anglais?*" Kara asked, hoping an air of polite formality would mask the unwelcome warmth rising in her.

No, he didn't. Only French. Left, right, left, she turned her head. Air kisses. The man smelled of processed meat, yet she relished the brush of stubble against her cheeks, thrilling at the intimacy of such contact with a mere acquaintance. It was one of the European traditions she enjoyed most during her semester in France.

Edward cleared his throat, snapping her back. She initiated introductions, but Edward seemed distracted by the man's appearance. His name was Jean-Benac. He said it proudly, thumping himself on the chest twice as he spoke. He repeated Kara's name softly, as if his voice was pronouncing each syllable for the very first time. She expected Edward to interject again, but he was too busy staring, head cocked to the side, squinting as if trying to read a faraway sign.

"Ed," she hissed, "You're being rude."

"But he's glowing." His voice was laced with confusion and awe.

"What?"

"Little blue flickers ..." he said, his voice trailing off.

Kara glanced at Jean-Benac, then, shaking her head, said to Edward, "You must have been staring at the fire too long. You're seeing things."

Kara motioned to a log across the fire. Jean-Benac tugged at his rain pants as he sat, lest he trip over the dragging cuffs. He licked his lips as Edward forked a bratwurst onto a bun, but Kara could feel his eyes on her, not the food, as she topped it with mustard and relish.

Jean-Benac was hesitant, sniffing the food before taking a bite. He chewed slowly, as if unsure it was edible, then his face lit up as he took another bite. Then another.

"It's like he's never seen food before," Edward said, smirking. "Ask him where he's from."

Kara did, her French returning to her slowly. But between his peculiar patois and mouth filled of food, she struggled to translate. Nevertheless, she discovered he was from Trois-Rivières, in Quebec, and headed to Grand Portage, Minnesota. Whether to find work at the casino or as a canoe guide at Fort William, she couldn't be sure.

Edward appeared dumbfounded, as Grand Portage was ninety miles away. He wanted to know why the man was in Nipigon.

Jean-Benac made a paddling motion with his arms as he explained that he came ashore because of the storm, that the bay was sheltered by large islands that provided protection from the waves. He said he was used to much larger canoes, and paddling with a crew, and that he didn't trust the boat, but was hoping to leave tomorrow.

"Ask him how many miles—" Edward was cut off as Jean resumed speaking.

Jean stared at Kara as he spoke, his voice rising and falling with a flustered intensity that mimicked the brewing storm in his eyes. The sedate man she watched sing beneath a canoe an hour ago was now loosely corked, shaken, and ready to burst. Kara tried to keep up as Jean described coming ashore here before. A horrible storm—the worst he'd ever seen—forced his canoe into the bay. One of his friends went overboard. He never saw him again. The town was much smaller, he said. Then, shaking his head, "*Tout le monde parlait Francaise.*"

"I think he's describing a dream," Kara said to Edward. "He says everyone here used to speak French."

Edward made a face that mimicked Kara's own confusion. He bent to add another piece of firewood to the campfire. Meanwhile, Jean-Benac kept talking, staring at Kara, who listened the best she could.

"What's he saying?"

"It's hard to tell. He said he remembers growing older. That the paddling eventually became too difficult. He took a job as a steerman—"

"In a canoe?" Edward asked.

"Yeah, I guess," she said, thinking back to the thirty-foot canoe on display at the fort's museum. "He seems confused, though. Says he was older the last time he was here."

Edward made a doubtful look then shook it away sarcastically, turning his attention to the frying pan.

Kara felt something troubling the stranger and asked if he was perhaps experiencing déjà vu or if he had been dreaming. He didn't think so, he said, not looking away.

"I remember waking up a several days' paddle from here, in a village to the east. It looked different though. The buildings were larger and the canoes shone like colored glass. I don't know how boats made of glass can last in these waters. So many rocks. And icebergs. A log will shatter them, no?" he said.

"Go on," Kara said, trying to focus him.

Jean leaned forward, resting his elbows on his knees, and stared into the fire, his eyes watering, reflecting the crackling flames, as the sloshing of the lake against the beach filled the temporary silence. "She wasn't there."

He answered Kara's unspoken question in a whisper: "Claudette."

The butterflies Kara felt earlier, alone behind a tree, returned, sent into a frenzy by the bolt of jealousy crackling through her. She couldn't explain it, this man, a stranger, was nobody to her, yet she felt dominion over him. Kara wondered who Claudette was, how long they'd been together, and what Claudette looked like. If she was prettier. Kara gave a self-conscious glance at her chest and tugged the hem of her jacket as she pulled her shoulders back. She looked across to Jean-Benac and wondered if he saw the effect he was having on her. As if reading her mind, his lips split into a grin.

"Who's Claudette?" Edward asked, brusquely, shimmying his seat closer to Kara's as he spoke.

Kara cleared her throat and translated the question, hoping Edward wasn't getting jealous.

Jean-Benac blushed as he looked from Edward to Kara, then took a deep, pitying breath. Claudette was his lover, one of the many girlfriends he had around the lake, but the only woman he hoped to marry. Until one day she made him choose between the canoe and her love. "How could I stay ashore? A voyageur's heart belongs to the water."

Kara gasped. Had he just referred to himself as a voyageur? There were plenty of similarities, she reminded herself, but the profession hadn't existed for centuries. Kara considered the possibility of him being one of those history buffs who took their reenactments too far, but disregarded it. *He looks lovesick.*

"I went to her, to beg forgiveness, but her cabin was no longer there. Perhaps …" Jean-Benac devoured Kara with his eyes, taking in the whole of her with a slow, rising study. "She is here. Perhaps my Claudette has returned."

"What is it? What did he say?" Edward demanded, an edge to his voice.

Kara ignored him, unwilling to lose the moment, refusing even to blink.

A hand clasped on Kara's knee. It was Edward's. He'd pulled his chair closer still—their knees were touching. "What did he say?"

"He had a girlfriend near here."

"And—"

Jean-Benac reached to touch her hair, but Kara pulled her head back, suddenly feeling uncomfortable, sensing Edward's dwindling patience. Jean-Benac offered Edward an apologetic look. He then spoke slowly, enunciating every syllable, as if willing Kara to understand him clearly. "Your hair is different. Your clothes are very strange. And you're older, but I feel it. Here," he said, placing his hands atop his heart. "I feel as I always did around you."

A wave of warmth surged within her as she struggled to form a response.

But Jean gave her no time to speak. He turned abruptly to face Edward and spoke to him directly. "How did you know Kara was the one for you?"

Edward made a face, waiting for the translation.

"He wants to know how you knew I was the right one for you," Kara said.

"I just knew. I guess you'd say it was love at first sight." Edward spoke without hesitation, his tone devoid of passion, unlike the man across from her.

"Ah," Jean-Benac said, smiling wide. "But sometimes we don't only see our love with the eyes. Sometimes we see with our soul. It was the same for me. Then ... *and now.*" He faced Edward as he spoke, but Kara knew those last two words were only for her. And she wasn't about to offer a direct translation.

His words echoed in her mind as she admired the simple beauty of his comment, a theory that made her own feelings easier to comprehend. This man wasn't much to look at, but there was something there, a connection that spawned a nervousness bubbling within her, an inability to look away, to breathe, or blink for fear the moment would end. She had experienced this sensation only once before, when she was first dating Edward. She remembered the anticipation before class, thrilling at the sight of him, every bit as sure he'd be there as she was terrified he wouldn't. In truth, he was always the first to arrive, his jacket draped across the adjacent desk, reserving it for her. Yes, that was exactly how she felt now; the completeness she felt slipping into the chair beside Edward.

Kara was lost in her thoughts, theories rising to a point and disappearing, like the flames of the campfire. But one idea stuck with her: Maybe what people called love at first sight had nothing to do with the eyes, but an explosion of joy caused by their soul finding its mate.

Kara stared through the campfire haze at Jean-Benac as her mind dove back in time to her crush on Edward. The hand on her knee clamped down, pinching her. Yanked from her daydream, she turned. Her husband glared at her, his chest puffed out, nostrils flared. Edward rarely showed a trace of jealousy, but she liked it. She patted his hand and nodded.

"*Tu dois partir,*" Kara said, telling Jean he should go.

Edward and Kara put down their plates and rose with their guest. To Kara's surprise, Jean wrapped an arm around Edward and leaned in to talk to him. "It's okay, *monsieur*. I am happy for you. Take good care of my Claudette. Perhaps I will find myself another woman in Grand Portage. A younger one," he shouted, clapping Edward on the back.

Kara fictionalized his words for Edward's benefit, amused by Jean-Benac's verve. He stepped to her, jolting the hairs of her neck. She needed him gone, now, knowing her feelings were so inexplicably wrong, but wishing them to continue forever.

"Your soul is as beautiful as ever." He whispered in her ear ever-so-faintly as he kissed her cheek. Kara blinked the mist from her eyes and watched him leave, recognizing the couplet he sang on his walk back to the canoe.

"Now I wish those red roses were on their vine today, while I and my beloved still went our old sweet way."

Chapter 14

WEDNESDAY, MAY 6 — ROSSPORT, ONTARIO, CANADA

The canoe was gone come morning. Edward noticed its absence upon rising, happy to enjoy his breakfast of instant oatmeal and black coffee without interruption.

The sky reflected in the still waters of the lake, where small icebergs rafted about like coasters adrift on a glass coffee table. The conditions were perfect for paddling, he thought, recalling Jean-Benac's journey to Grand Portage. But he didn't like the looks of the clouds to the west. They had better get going.

Edward watched his mirror closely throughout the morning, on guard for trucks overtaking them on the too-narrow roadway. The Trans-Canada Highway was no place to ride a bicycle, at least not in Ontario. But they had no choice. With a near-impenetrable wall of pine flanking them, the route proved simultaneously stressful and monotonous. Worse still, the puffs of gray he watched grow large in his mirror soon darkened and opened.

Seeking a break from the rain, Edward and Kara stopped at a tiny resort community to warm up over a hot lunch. There, the waitress served up news that snow was burying the uplands to the east. And more was due overnight.

Outside the café, Edward spotted a phalanx of small cabins aligned near the beach. A sign said the property was closed for the season, but the lights in the main house were on. Edward and Kara crossed their fingers and rang the bell. Lucky for them, a retired widower had purchased the property last fall and, in his younger days, had cycled across Canada—and still remembered the generosity of the strangers he met along the way.

"I can open up one of the cabins for you. There's no heat, but the water's on. You'll have to use your own bedding, though. I'm not quite ready for vacationers yet."

"Thank you so much," Kara said. "We really appreciate it."

"Happy to help. Come up to the house once you're cleaned up. You can probably use a drink."

By the time Kara and Edward unloaded their bikes and changed, the storm had intensified. Rain pelted the cabin's tin roof while the lake seethed with whitecaps. Thirsty and wanting company, they sprinted for the main house as the wind swirled around them, whipping their rain pants and inflating their jackets like balloons.

Inside, decades-old travel brochures sat piled atop dusty furniture. The home more closely resembled an antique thrift shop than a rural lakefront home. Nevertheless, it was dry, and their host, Robert, was happy to dig up some cold beers for them. Edward joined Kara at the window, where she stood staring at the churning lake.

"Don't be mad, but I can't help worrying about Jean." Kara said. "You think he's okay?"

Edward bit the insides of his cheeks and took a deep breath. "He's fine."

"But look at it out there."

"He probably made camp as soon as the storm came up. He might have taken some chances if he was in a kayak, with a spray skirt, but alone in a canoe—"

"You two know someone canoeing today?" Robert asked, handing them each a bottle of Molson.

"Thanks. Yeah, we ran into a guy last night in Nipigon. Said he was canoeing to Grand Portage."

Robert scrunched up his face, as if he was trying to remember some forgotten detail. "Nipigon, you say?"

"Yep. Said his name was Jean-Benac," Edward said it with the air of an aristocrat, "He only spoke French—"

"I translated for us," Kara interrupted. "He joined us for dinner."

"A red canoe, by chance?" Robert asked, his demeanor stiffening. Edward and Kara nodded.

"And about this tall?" he said, holding his hand up.

"That's the guy. Sounds like you know him."

"Know him? That bastard stole my canoe! He showed up here back in February, naked and hollering, trying to break into one of the cabins. I was gonna call the police, but then I saw how cold and scared he was. February's no time to be running around in your birthday suit. Got him a blanket and brought him inside. First time I tried using the translation app on my phone, but Google could barely make sense of his accent."

Edward was about to speak, but forgot what he was going to say, knocked into silence upon hearing that Jean-Benac arrived naked, in February, just like the Blackfoot.

"They used to speak French here," Kara said, flatly, turning back to the roiling lake.

Robert gave Kara a puzzled look, then said to Edward. "So he's headed to Grand Portage? Guess I'll have to drive down there and get my boat back. Ordered ten of them last month. Brand new. Kevlar. You should have seen him. I swear he acted like they descended from outer space."

Edward could tell Kara was chewing on a question, and he had a hunch what it was.

"Anyway, I let him help out through the winter. He earned his keep splitting firewood and shoveling snow and the like. Strange guy. Acted like everything was new to him. I mean, forget the smart phone, plenty of people up here hadn't seen one of those before, but the television, the lights, the refrigerator. At first I thought he was just pulling my leg, but nobody could keep up that kind of charade for a full month. Nah, I think it was genuine. Like he was frozen in time and just woke up," he said, laughing.

The remark about him being frozen made Edward recall the blue glow he was so sure he had seen, but Kara cut off his line of thinking.

"Did he mention a woman named Claudette?" she asked, turning abruptly from the window.

Robert tilted his head and tapped his fingers against the beer bottle while he thought. "Come to think of it, he did. I didn't understand much of what he said, but I do recall him yelling for someone named Claudette the night I found him. He sounded apologetic. Desperate, even."

"He told us he woke up in a small town to the east where there used to be a few cabins."

"I don't know what to say. All the houses here are at least sixty years old, some more than a hundred."

Edward listened attentively, storing away the information, not quite sure what to believe. Or how far to let his imagination run. But he was curious. "Any chance there are some older structures nearby. Maybe in the woods?"

"I hadn't walked every inch of the property yet—the snow came pretty early this year—but I did spot what might be an old foundation in the woods out past the cabins. Used it for my leaf pile last fall."

"Come on," Kara said, zipping her rain jacket and flipping up the hood.

"Now? Kara, it's pouring out."

"Just come with me. I need to see it."

Edward rolled his eyes and handed Robert his drink.

"You two go ahead. I'll light a fire in the stove. I reckon you'll need the warmth when you get back," Robert said.

Outside, Edward jogged to keep pace with Kara as she strode across the grass behind the row of cabins lining the beach. He glanced at the barn as he passed and counted nine canoes identical to the one Jean-Benac had stolen.

Kara hesitated at the edge of the trees, leaning forward to keep the rain off her face.

"What are you looking for?"

She didn't answer. Not at first. He watched her advance into the woods, stepping over fallen branches, brushing past the sopping wet undergrowth without notice. "There," she pointed.

Dozens of rocks, chunks of granite the size of cinder blocks, were scattered about. Moss-covered and weathered, they had no doubt shifted with time, but their rectangular arrangement was clear. "Must be a hundred years old," Edward said.

"At least." Kara stepped around the ruins of the foundation, moving slowly, as if the ground was sacred.

He watched her go, following the orange of her jacket through the fog of his breath. She moved with a purpose, sweeping the ground back and forth, like a beachcomber with a metal detector. The scent of fire caught his attention. Behind him, a wisp of smoke spiraled out of the chimney.

Kara let out a startled scream, her voice wavering in the dampness of the forest.

"Kara?" Edward sprinted toward her, snatching a tree branch from the ground as he ran, fearing she'd startled a bobcat or, worse, a bear. He scanned the woods for obstacles and threats, seeing nothing. Nor did he hear a single noise beside the rapid footfalls of his shoes on the sodden ground and the panting of Kara's breathing.

"What is it? What's wrong?" he asked as he closed on her.

She was trembling in place, her gaze locked on the ground, her hands tented over her mouth and nose.

Edward followed her stare to a lichen-stained tombstone leaning upon a boulder. The inscription, softened with age, but still legible read:

Voice le Corpse de
CLAUDETTE
Fille de Pierre Leblanc
Noyé le 1er octobre 1739
28 Ans

Chapter 15

SUNDAY, MAY 24 — MONTREAL, QUEBEC, CANADA

For two weeks, their journey was marked with Inuksuit, rock cairns shaped like prehistoric men, guiding them across the vastness of Ontario, threading a path between the wilds of the lake's northern shore and the cities to the south. To Edward, the days blurred together in a dripping mass of cold and rain, the monotony of the rolling hills broken only by the sight of a moose, the stench of roadkill.

Edward passed the time reflecting on his weekly phone calls to Tom. They were brief, as the older man maintained an air of the permanently distracted. Nevertheless, the Thursday check-ins gave Edward a purpose, a small taste of the accountability he thrived on—and craved. He didn't know if it was even possible to cycle around the world in six months, but he was determined to try. And so he continued to dig deeper each day, pedaling further than before, hoping Kara wouldn't object. Or think it suspicious.

Peak-a-boo views of Lake Superior provided daily reminders of Jean-Benac. For the second time in as many months they encountered someone who seemed of a different era, naked anachronisms along their path. Coincidence? Edward hoped so. *But what about the tombstone?*

Edward wasn't sure what Jean-Benac told Kara about Claudette—he suspected there was much she failed to translate that night around the campfire—but whatever it was, the sight of the grave seemed to strike her to the marrow, chilling her spirit. Edward shivered at the memory.

Days later, at an overlook above a cobbled beach fringed with lingering snow, she asked him how easily a canoe could be capsized.

"Thinking about Jean?" Edward said, careful of his tone.

She took a deep breath. "I keep imagining him tossing about in that storm, struggling to stay afloat."

The comment reminded him of a dream he had at the cabin, steps from the grave marker. He was alone in heavy seas, aboard a canoe, as helpless as an untethered buoy. The wind and rain lashed his face as he clutched the gunwales with both hands, bracing himself, fighting to stay alive. Then everything went dark. He awoke from the dream with a jolt, shivering uncontrollably, gasping for air.

"I'm sure he's okay," he said, repeating the words he used that night by the window, believing them even less.

Spring greeted them a thousand miles east of their brush with Claudette's grave, on a trail halfway between Ottawa and Montreal. Seemingly overnight, everything changed. The musty smell of forever-damp wool gave way to the floral essence of lilac-covered riverbanks and fences draped in honeysuckle. Narrow highway shoulders were replaced by the crushed gravel of Quebec's network of bicycle trails. Even the insects were a welcome change after so many days spent trying to outpace the last vestiges of winter.

They stopped to camp at a trailside picnic area, on the eve of their arrival in Montreal. Edward sipped a beer while looking over a map when Kara stepped from the tent, barefoot in a flowing, ankle-length skirt and sports bra, her hair falling loose along her shoulders. She spread her arms to the evening sun and sighed with delight, as if every molecule of stress she'd ever known was confined to the winter clothing they'd no longer need.

He stared, transfixed by this beautiful being standing before him, glowing with the radiance of an eclipse, blinding to behold, but impossible to ignore.

"Finally," Kara said, smiling at the sun, her eyelids squinting against the light. "Just you and me and a sunny campsite."

Edward could only smile back at her, unwilling to interrupt the moment with his voice.

She twirled in place, her arms stretched wide, then dropped onto the freshly mowed grass with the carefree grace of a schoolgirl. "I can't believe we're almost to the Atlantic."

He smiled, his eyes fixed on her stomach, perspiration glistening.

"You're going to love Cape Cod. And Fourth of July in New York! It's going to be amazing." She shielded her eyes from the sun, beaming. "I love you."

"I love you, too," he said. And for the first time he allowed himself to think ahead to the day he could tell her about the contest, his new job, and the income that would allow him to give her anything she desired. She'd be ecstatic. He was sure of it.

The ride into Montreal proved far longer and more complicated than Edward anticipated. With no directions to go by and only a small-scale map of the city to reference, Edward struggled to navigate. Congested roadways, multiple river islands, and surprisingly steep hills conspired against them, making the going as stressful as it was confusing. He knew their hostel was in the historic quarter, not far from the Basilica de Notre-Dame, but he wasn't sure how to get there. And it didn't help that the signs were in French.

He knew Kara could read the street signs but, for whatever reason, she was in no mood to offer assistance. She only spoke to voice her frustration with Edward's inevitable mistakes. With every additional hill and wrong turn, Kara soured further, muttering complaints about their lack of a GPS, the long miles, and the weeks of enduring a too-fast pace. Edward did his best to ignore it, knowing she would perk up once they got to the hostel. *We all have our days*, he figured.

He slowed to a stop at a red light, finally inside the city limits, thanks to the compass on his handlebars. He was straining to read the street signs when he heard a commotion, followed by the blare of a car's horn.

He turned in time to see Kara struggling to stay upright, as much atop her bike as she was inside the passenger window of a car. But it didn't register. Four thousand miles of uneventful cycling dulled him to the dangers of their endeavor. Then it hit him.

Edward leaped from his bike, heaving it onto the sidewalk, and ran to her, his heart racing.

"It's okay. I got it," he said, grabbing the bike, hoping not to scratch the car.

"I couldn't unclip. My foot's stuck in the pedal," she said, grimacing as she pushed herself out of the open window of a red Honda Civic stopped alongside her. "God damn these shoes!"

The driver shouted at them in French. Noise.

Edward grabbed her shoe and twisted it free, mindful of the ankle it was connected to. "Okay, it's free."

Kara stood, her face as red as Edward's panniers, tears welling in her eyes. "I lost my balance. The shoe got stuck."

The cars behind them honked while the driver of the Civic continued to berate them. At least he waited until Kara and her bike were clear of his car before speeding off. As Edward walked Kara's bike to a nearby bench, her bicycle helmet flew past his head. Was it meant to hit him? He wasn't sure.

"I can't do this anymore. I can't." Kara stomped past and slumped onto the bench, sobbing into her hands.

Edward watched her, unsure what to say. They'd been arguing throughout the day and he didn't want to make it any worse. He picked up the helmet and sat, leaving room between them. He spun the helmet in his hands, waiting for the dam to break, for whatever was really bothering her to come spilling out.

"We're never *there*. We're always going. Every day, another destination. I just want to get there." Her voice cracked as she spoke. "*I'm soooo tired.*"

Edward didn't know what to say. One moment she's twirling like Julie Andrews in the Austrian countryside, and now she's crying her eyes out five miles from their hostel.

"*This is sooo hard.*" Kara wiped the tears and faced him, looking desperate. "I want to get to the beach and sleep for days."

He took her hand in his. He hated seeing her like this and a part of him knew he was to blame. The long miles, the minimal days off the bikes. That was his doing. His guilt beat down upon him, crushing his words into silence.

"And you're in such great shape. It makes me so mad because I ride all the time, and you just get on your bike and a few weeks later are faster than I'll ever be. I can't keep up with you."

So that's what's bothering her? Edward looked at his legs, carved lean, a braided river of blood pumping through the swollen veins. His racer's legs were back.

"Baby, you're not slowing me down. I'd have to wait twice as long for the guys I rode with back home. You know that."

Kara sniffled and turned away, never one to be patronized.

Edward wrapped his arm around her, pulling her to him. "Nobody likes being waited on. That's natural. But I'd wait all day for you if I had to. Hell, I'd carry you if I could."

Kara wiped the snot above her lip, then sighed. "It's not just that. I feel useless. This trip was my idea and you do all the navigation and you're the one keeping the bikes running—"

"With your help," he interrupted.

Kara rolled her eyes. "I feel like all I do is wash our dirty shorts and lay out the sleeping bags." She blinked away another tear. "You even do the cooking."

"Kara, there's not been a single moment when I felt you were useless. I'm so damn impressed with you each and every day. How many other people could do what we're doing?"

A trace of a smile creased her lips. Then, after a moment she said, "I'm sorry. Maybe I'm just feeling sorry for myself today."

"Remember. The highs are higher—"

"And the hormones are stronger too," she said with a chuckle.

Edward handed back her helmet and looked to his bike, still lying on its side by the street corner.

"Can we take a few extra days off in Montreal?"

He flinched. He couldn't help it. *A few?*

"Absolutely," he said, staring straight ahead, knowing how precious every day's progress was, updating the math in his head, wondering where he could shave some miles.

Chapter 16

SATURDAY, MAY 30 — HIGHGATE, VERMONT, USA

Kara watched as Edward rifled through the pages of his passport, searching like a child who couldn't find his homework.

"He didn't stamp it."

She shrugged as she tucked in the ends of a tortilla and rolled her second burrito. Jelly squirted onto her fingers as she took a bite.

"A whole month in a foreign country and I don't even get a stamp? That sucks."

"Canada doesn't count."

"Of course it counts," Edward said, his voice cracking into a falsetto, reminding her of Jerry Seinfeld. "They use a different currency, the road signs are metric, and Quebec—"

"I'm kidding," she said, tonguing the peanut butter stuck to her teeth. She found his disappointment cute, the man who never wanted to travel anywhere suddenly upset because he didn't get a passport stamp. "Don't forget to eat."

A plain tortilla sat on his plate, turning doughy in the sun. Edward fanned the pages of the passport a final time and tucked it beneath his thigh. They sat atop a low wall at a sleepy border crossing in northern

Vermont, enjoying an early lunch on their way south after four days at a hostel in Montreal, and two more in Quebec City. A mild breeze blew, rustling the emerald leaves of the trees, fanning the scent of freshly mowed grass.

"At least the border agent was friendly. The 'Welcome home' was a nice touch."

"And he didn't find anything to confiscate," Kara said.

"That reminds me. Should we replace the pepper spray they took on our way into Ontario?"

Kara didn't care. "If we see some." They would be at the beach soon. Definitely wouldn't need it on the Cape. In New York? Maybe.

"As long as it's not law-enforcement grade," Edward added, imitating the stern wording of the customs official who had taken their original canisters. Anything not intended for use against animals was banned in Canada—and using theirs against a human could have been considered a pre-meditated attack. Kara didn't think they really needed it in the first place, but knew Edward appreciated the security it provided. He'd always pretend it was for wild dogs, but she knew the truth.

She thought back to their day riding through the Blackfoot reservation, the guys at the taco joint, and then later, Edward's hesitation outside the American Legion. Always protective, forever cautious. She figured he was like a lot of guys that way: smart enough to know the odds of needing a weapon were low, but wary enough of the greater world to want one anyway.

The terrain in New England proved unlike anything they had ridden thus far. The mountains didn't reach as high as those out west, but the roads were steeper—and the hills came in bunches, unlike in

Washington. Here, they were grinding their way through multiple ascents a day. The downhills were over in a blink, barely long enough to dry the sweat from their arms before their wheels tilted into the next climb.

Kara attacked the corduroy landscape with newfound energy. Crossing the border had her feeling like a thoroughbred at the quarter pole of the Kentucky Derby—knowing a white sand finish line lay less than a week away.

Nearly three months in the saddle had whipped her into shape, but their ride across Ontario left her exhausted. The quickened pace and excessive mileage was grueling, the time off in Montreal proving only a tease. Now, she couldn't wait to park the bikes, to spend enough time in the same place so she wouldn't have to wonder where the bathroom was if she got up to pee in the middle of the night.

She had read the warnings of other globe-trotting cyclists before they left—burnout was inevitable. It was important to take time off every few months. And that was her plan for Cape Cod. It wasn't just a chance to return to where she summered with cousins as a child. It was an opportunity to have a proper vacation. As much as she enjoyed the awe with which strangers now viewed her, bicycle touring was a really tough way to see the world.

Kara tingled with excitement, thinking ahead to her two weeks on the Massachusetts coast with Edward, and rode each day harder than the last, chasing the respite over the horizon.

"Boston? I thought you'd be in Europe by now. What's with all this north-south crap, Ed? You're supposed to be heading east."

Edward cupped a hand over the earpiece and twisted in the armchair, trying to shield Tom's booming voice from the hotel receptionist, but the lobby was small and the telephone's coiled cord short. He cursed himself for leaving his cell phone on after last week's call, allowing the battery to die.

"We ran into snow in Ontario. And the cycling wore Kara down in Montreal so we took some days off."

"I'm not going to pay you to make excuses. And neither will our clients. Here's a tip. The number one rule for working for me is be a man. Own your mistakes. You want to spend a few nights eating *foie gras* in Montreal with your pretty little wife, that's fine. But own it! I've got no respect for men who hide behind their wives. Did she *make* you spend a few days in Montreal?"

"No," Edward muttered, wondering why Tom was so worked up. *So long as I'm ready to start in October, what difference does it make?*

"Good. I expect to hear some French waiters in the background the next time you call."

Down the hall, an elevator dinged and Edward froze, fearing Kara had come looking for him. A couple stepped out, arm in arm, dressed for a night on the town. Edward exhaled, but his relief was quickly replaced with embarrassment as he became acutely aware of his disheveled hiking pants and wrinkled tee shirt. Meanwhile, condescension oozed from the phone as Tom lectured him with the tone of a drill sergeant.

Edward massaged his forehead and sighed.

It'll be easier back in Seattle. Once the office is set up, I probably won't even have to deal with Tom that much.

"Uh, huh." Edward struggled to focus.

"So I got myself a map and started plotting your position and ..." Tom's voice trailed off. Edward could hear him rustling papers. When he resumed, his voice took rose in octave and tempo, as if he was explaining a revolutionary discovery. "I've run the numbers and, depending how far north you go, you need to average 97 miles per day, due east, to win the job. Unless of course you want to head to the Arctic."

Edward imagined a basketball spinning atop his finger, the seams converging toward the top, spreading at the logo. He began to sweat, thinking how many unnecessary miles they packed on by heading south.

"Now, I don't care if you bike the whole way or take a train. Hell, take a goddamn hot air balloon for all I care. But I want to see progress. If you'd rather spend the summer zigzagging all over the place or riding in circles, that's fine. Tell me now and I'll call it off."

"No need for that, but I'm curious. Why does it matter where we go so long as I'm ready to start on time?"

Tom snorted. "Ron said you were good at finding loopholes."

"Ron ... *Madsen?*" Edward ground his heel into the red and gold carpet at the thought of his former boss.

"Yep. He offered me a side bet after I told him about our little arrangement."

Edward groaned.

"Ron doesn't think you've got what it takes to get around the globe in six months. Thinks you're too soft—especially when it comes to your wife. We'll see ..."

Edward had been twirling the phone's cord around his arm and now tugged it tight enough to restrict circulation, make his fingers numb. He wanted the job. More than ever. And most of all, he wanted to be there when Ron paid up, to watch him squirm. Edward couldn't believe he had the nerve to mention Kara, as if he'd ever begged off overtime because of her.

"So, what are the stakes?" Edward asked, his voice laced with the detachment of an assassin inquiring about his next hit.

"Don't worry about that. You just get to Europe and cover those miles." Tom kept talking with barely a pause to breathe.

The bet with Ron changed everything. For both of them.

"When can you get to Europe?"

Edward sighed, realizing the bind he was in. "Kara, er ... We were going to spend a few weeks at the beach, and then head to New York in July."

"Last I checked New York wasn't on the way from Boston to Rome."

"I'll think of something." Edward rubbed his forehead, grinding the skin across his skull as if he could erase the details of the past few months.

"Well, you'd better decide now. Otherwise, just return the signing bonus and I'll tell Ron he was right."

Edward's shame hardened like a diamond. Sharp. He wanted to explain Kara's desire to go to New York City, but knew Tom wouldn't care. "You're asking an awful lot, Tom. How do I know you won't go back on your word?" He pictured the moment the autographed baseball shattered the window. And the security escort out of the building. "It wouldn't be the first time I've had that happen."

"Are you questioning my integrity?"

"No, it's just—"

"Listen here, you ungrateful son of a bitch. I'm the only one willing to take a chance on you. Don't question my word again. Is that clear?"

Edward agreed through clenched teeth, flashing his middle finger at the phone. Across the room, the receptionist watched him, giggling conspiratorially.

"I'll hold up my end of the deal. All you need to worry about— listen closely—*all* you need to worry about is holding up yours. I'm just here to keep you on track, like a coach. Now get to Europe."

Edward's heart pounded in his chest. The elevator chimed again. At once, he was certain Kara would pass through and see him on the phone—see him ready to blow. And once the questions began, they'd never stop. He had to hang up immediately. "We will. Thanks again. Hope you and Brenda have a nice night. I'll call next week."

Edward cradled his sweating head in his hands. Why did he mention Brenda? He was only trying to be polite, but now he couldn't stop hearing Kara's description of the woman echoing in his mind. She was lonely. She lived like a widow. Kara called her the *Ghost of*

Housewife Yet to Come. But what did she mean by that? Did Kara feel that way too? Was she afraid he'd become like Tom?

He smothered the doubts and questions beneath a blanket of determination, knowing what he had to do. Just this once, he figured. She'd understand.

It never occurred to Edward that Kara might be in the hotel's business center. But there she was, occupying one of two adjacent computer terminals. The cramped, undecorated room smelled as if it had been recycling the same stale air for months.

She saw him before he had a chance to turn around.

"How'd you know I'd be in here?" she asked, spinning atop the office chair, her feet tucked beneath her. "I was just about to go looking for you."

Edward watched her, round and round, a silly smile on her face. Behind her, an oscillating fan glared at him like a cyclops with a lazy eye, its stationary blades coated in dust.

"I didn't," Edward said. "I thought I'd take a look at airfare." The words dribbled from his mouth, soaking his shirt in shame, spilling his honest intent.

"Great. We can look together." She patted the burgundy chair next to her, sending a poof of dust into the air. She spun the long way around to face the computer she was using. "First, you gotta see this great place I found. We can rent it for two weeks and still have enough time to get to New York City for Independence Day."

Edward sank into the chair and looked at the screen, speechless. His tongue felt as scratchy as the driftwood decor in the photo on Kara's monitor.

"It's only a cottage, but it's right near the beach. A perfect way to celebrate our cross-country ride." She clicked through the photos to the bedroom and leaned her head on his shoulder. "We'll be able to see the dunes from bed."

Edward kissed her forehead. He wanted to tell her it looked wonderful, but what was the point?

"And we can go skinny dipping," she said, giving his earlobe a lick.

He shivered as a bead of nervous sweat ran the length of his back. He pulled the mouse and keyboard closer and searched for airfare from Boston to London, leaving the next day.

"Oops, I think you meant to search flights leaving New York."

This wasn't how Edward had envisioned this playing out. He didn't expect to be working out the details *and* breaking the news— *her heart?*—simultaneously. He considered telling her about the contest, but couldn't. She'd never understand. Not yet. He braced for her reaction.

"Actually, I was wondering what you'd say about heading to London from here."

"Why would we do that?" She shot him a puzzled look.

Because your husband … Nothing. He felt his mouth go dry as he opened it to speak. But it didn't matter; he was tongue-tied even in thought.

"So, we'd ride back to Boston after New York?" she asked, confused.

He took a deep breath and worked the computer, clicking the mouse, trying to ignore her questions. Delaying, stalling, searching for a flight. His animal instincts were kicking in. *Fight or flight,* that's what they call it. He was in line for both and knew it.

"Tomorrow?" she asked, pointing at the screen. "No way. I've been looking forward to Cape Cod for months."

Edward stared in silence. They had to get moving. Tom was right. He sorted the fares by price and scanned the results. Kara swung her feet to the floor and leaned forward, her eyes burning into him.

"Are you even listening? What's going on? Answer me."

"Just let me look—"

"This is bullshit. You know how much I want to take time off," she said, her voice climbing an octave.

"We'll take it in London. Let's get someplace new." He couldn't spend two weeks idle, but he knew he'd feel a hell of a lot better once they got across the ocean. And maybe once they were in London, Kara would be excited enough to keep moving. Preferably east, he thought.

"We didn't even get to the coast yet. Boston Harbor is hardly the Atlantic Ocean."

"Well, we didn't exactly dip our wheels in the Pacific either," he countered.

"Puget Sound was close enough. Plus, it was March. And we live there."

"Seattle to Boston has a nice ring to it," he said, as much for his own benefit as hers. Riding across the country was something he knew he'd look back upon with pride; he regretted not having left from the coast. He sorted by departure times and waited for the results. "This one works. It leaves tomorrow night, which gives us enough time to get the bikes boxed up."

"Edward," Kara said, her voice cracking as she turned his chair to face her. She gripped his knees and stared at him. "London will still be there next month—"

"And so will New York. If we go now, we'll beat the crowds. Then we can get through France before the country shuts down in August." He watched himself saying these words as if he was floating above, clinging to the fluorescent lights. He saw his mouth moving, the blank look on his face, and the shock and heartache in Kara's response. "And the weather is supposed to be nicest in July," he continued, knowing he could talk her into almost anything. It was an advantage he held over her. She trusted him. "You said it yourself, it will be perfect."

"This is anything but perfect," she shouted.

He hated doing this to her, but he had no choice. After all, what would he say? *Hey babe, I know this is your dream, but I've got this job offer. How about we skip all the best parts and hurry home?*

Edward clicked on the tickets and left the mouse hovering over the purchase button as he dug out his wallet. Kara's eyes followed his hand.

"I can't believe you're going to do this."

Edward stayed quiet.

"You're not even listening to me."

He wanted to console her, to tell her he heard every word, and that he was in agony, but he couldn't. Wouldn't. He propped the credit card on the keyboard.

"I couldn't wait to show you that cottage and now we're not even going. No matter what I want to do, it's never good enough for you."

He shook his head, willing Kara to disavow her own feelings.

"You don't care at all about me or what I want. What did I do to make you stop caring?" Her tone had turned desperate, her words tapped out in code as her fists beat atop her thighs.

"Of course I care. It's why we're here. This whole trip was your idea, wasn't it? New York City is only a five-hour flight from Seattle. We can visit anytime. But London? How often will we get to London?"

Kara shot him a disgusted look, then looked away.

"I've seen enough of North America. I want you to show me around London and Paris." He put his arm around her, pulling her closer. "Show me where you went on your semester abroad."

She bit her lower lip, but didn't face him.

"Let's get some fish and chips. Wuddya say, guvnor?" It was his first attempt at a Cockney accent and it sounded awful. *What a dork,* he thought.

Kara shot him a look he deserved. One that said he was an incorrigible asshole, but she was relenting. When she spoke, it was only to express a whirlwind of concerns about packing the bikes, navigating in London, and finding accommodations.

"I'll take care of it," he assured her.

"We can't even go for one week?" she asked, motioning at the beachfront cottage on her screen. Edward could practically hear the seagulls in the photo.

He shook his head and squeezed her knees softly between his own, his hands on her hips. "I love you so much, Kara. I'm sorry I make you mad sometimes." He fixed his eyes on hers, ignoring the deception tearing his insides to shreds. *I'll make this up to her.*

Kara's lips drew tight and pinched upwards ever so slightly. If it was a forced smile for his benefit, he'd take it. He knew he didn't even deserve that much. But her hands remained balled into fists, the tendons contracting on her forearms. This wasn't a disappointment he could hug away. She wouldn't give in quickly.

Now or never.

Edward typed the credit card number into the form. He felt the heft of Kara's stare with each press of the keyboard. It was done. They were booked on the red-eye tomorrow night.

"Aisle or window?" he asked, smiling.

Kara stood, gently slid her chair under the desk, and left the room without saying another word.

Chapter 17

FRIDAY, APRIL 3 — FLORENCE, ITALY

Alessio emerged from the dimly lit shed, anxious to escape the festering scent of fertilizer and rotten lawn clippings. He raised a gloved hand to his brow and squinted, scanning the campground for Hiromasa as a cobweb dangled from his thumb, tickling his nose. Pruning shears hung holstered to his belt, a bucket of gardening tools and chemical miscellany knocked against his leg.

Six weeks had passed since he accepted Hiromasa's offer of work at the campground. Six wintry weeks spent painting bathrooms, stitching tears in canvas tent-cabins, and cleaning more windows than he cared to remember.

He once looked forward to spring, especially the fanciful floats of Carnival that ushered in the season of Lent on Malta, but here at the campground, trapped in his current situation, the drudgery persisted. Today's chore: pruning rose bushes.

Alessio shuffled along the path leading to the main gate, his shoulders slumped, feeling like a prisoner forced to toil for his room and board. The seasons changed, yet he idled no closer to understanding how he'd come to live in modern Florence—or why. He only knew he wasn't cut out for this world, this life. An artist—a gallery owner at that—had no business laboring away at mundane maintenance tasks. Even the prospect of trimming flowers held little appeal. But what choice did he have? Not an hour passed without some new discovery startling him; not a conversation shared without words and meanings soaring over his head, like the mechanical birds he'd seen birthing trails of clouds in the sky.

Hiromasa called them airplanes.

Hiromasa always seemed to know what things were called. How customs changed.

Alessio set the bucket down at the far end of the shrubbery and withdrew the snips. He started high, removing the winter damage, pruning the interior, ensuring the rose buds had plenty of light. He went about his task in a daze, his ability to focus lost in the fog of his thoughts. He sought refuge in the memories of his life in Malta, the *when* he knew.

"Be sure not to snip the buds." It was Hiromasa's unmistakable accent, approaching from behind.

Alessio looked at the clipping he felled, a thin branch with a bud on the end. He shrugged, turning to see Hiromasa.

"Here, I'll show you." Hiromasa reached for the clippers.

"I know how," Alessio said, dropping the tool into the bucket. "But I'm glad you're here. You once said you might have answers, but have been stalling for weeks, avoiding me except when others are around. It's time you explain."

Hiromasa cocked his head. "What would you like to know?"

"Don't be coy. You're hiding something, aren't you? I watch you. You're quite skilled at pretending, but I see the surprise in your face, the curiosity. You act like this is your world, that you're like these other people, but you're not. You have this." Alessio grabbed Hiromasa's gloved hand and, with his other hand, pushed Hiromasa's shirtsleeve upward, exposing a fringe of shimmering blue light, an essence that arced like miniature flames that nipped at Alessio's skin.

Hiromasa sighed. "I have no explanation."

"I've waited long enough," he said, his voice rising. "Tell me where you came from. Tell me what you know."

"Why ask questions whose answers only necessitate dozens more questions?"

Alessio's nostrils flared as he looked away in anger. Though he had yearned to share his secret, to admit aloud that he somehow traveled through time from the nineteenth century and woke up naked in a strange bed, he had to be careful. He suspected Hiromasa had a similar story, but what if he didn't? *If I'm wrong about him, he'll claim me a lunatic.* Alessio's mind flashed to the asylums of his era, the unspeakable horrors he heard described in whispers, stories too coarse to be repeated in the company of women. He shook his head, refusing to risk it.

When he turned back, he saw that Hiromasa's face had relaxed, as if he was relieved to be changing the subject. But then, with a wink, he said, "Florence has changed considerably, has she not?"

Alessio knocked the bucket aside stepping to Hiromasa and grabbed him by the arms. "What do you know? Tell me."

The smaller man's ease vanished as his eyes went wide. "I don't know what you're talking about." Alessio glared at him, then released his grip, suspecting he wouldn't get anywhere through intimidation. Hiromasa smoothed his shirtsleeves and took a deep breath.

"You do know." Alessio said. "When are you from?"

A spark of understanding flickered in Hiromasa's face. *When.* The magic word.

"I knew it. You're from the past too."

He nodded. "Like you, I also woke up one day in this strange new world."

"In February?"

"Yes."

Alessio stared at him as he digested their similarities, wondering how deep their connection went. "Where?"

Hiromasa blushed as his lips parted in a smile, revealing his crooked teeth. "One moment I was an old man in Rome. Next, I was young, completely naked in the street, freezing on the ground. Not far from here ..." His voice trailed off as he spoke, as if the thought was too painful to fully recall.

A feeling of weightlessness permeated Alessio's being, the burden of his predicament lessened through sharing. He wasn't alone.

"I woke in a similar predicament." Alessio recalled the room's barrel-shaped ceiling, the brick floor, the hint of linseed oil used to polish it. He thought of the nights spent in that room—with Sylvia. "In a guesthouse that I used to stay during my travels. I would visit several times a year to collect work from my gallery in Malta."

"Interesting," Hiromasa said, his face scrunched in thought.

"Why do you say?"

Hiromasa turned to the rose bush and pinched a branch between his finger nails, snapping it from the cane. "Tell me, what were you feeling when you woke up?"

"I was scared. And confused. Weren't you?"

"Of course. But that came after I realized I was in a strange place and time. How did you feel when you first woke?"

Alessio thought back to the moment when he first stirred. When his hand padded the empty space beside him on the mattress, before he realized Sylvia wasn't there. That moment when the pang of his broken heart and the anger of being made a fool rushed in, mixing, swirling and coating him in humiliation. The shame.

Alessio shut his eyes to the memory as his hands went clammy inside the rubber gardening gloves.

Hiromasa nodded and said, softly, as if the recollection still caused him distress, "My heart, too, was quite heavy when I woke."

The comment landed like a thunderclap, sending Alessio's hair on end. For nearly two months he'd puzzled his fate, doubted his faith, and admonished his Lord over the absence of a sign. And yet the answer may have been working and living alongside him all this time, bottled up within the shoulder-high enigma named Hiromasa.

"What do you know? Please tell me now," Alessio urged, grabbing Hiromasa's arm.

Hiromasa took a step back, his palms out. His smile didn't waver, his deep brown eyes didn't flinch. His was the practiced calm of a man used to easing runaway emotions. "I have only a theory. I cannot be certain, but let me ask you—"

"No. No more questions, I want answers."

"What was her name?"

Alessio recoiled as if slapped.

"You cannot expect answers if you're unwilling to assist in the solution."

Alessio tucked his hair behind his ears and crossed his arms in front of his puffed-out chest, the veins of his arms pulsed with the resolve of a man willing to kill to protect his claim. He glared at Hiromasa, challenging him, refusing to say a word about Sylvia until Hiromasa came clean, and shared all he knew.

Hiromasa stared back for seconds that stretched like hours, then, at once, his shoulders went slack. His eyelids fell shut like feathers falling from the sky. He took a deep breath and when he began to speak, he looked at Alessio with the sorrow of a man forced to relive the worst day of his life.

"I knew her as Isabelle …"

Chapter 18

Edward slumped against the wall near the doors of the oversized baggage area, his handlebar bag between his feet. Their panniers and duffel bags stacked alongside him, creating a yellow and red vinyl wall he now hid behind. Their plane landed over an hour ago. Across the room, three suitcases lapped a squeaky carousel in perpetuity, forgotten.

He wouldn't normally trust an airline with his bicycle, given the paltry sum for which they insure them, but he had little choice. There was no time to have the bikes shipped ahead, not if they were going to make the flight.

Now, as he sat waiting at Heathrow, a slice of him secretly hoped the bicycles had gone missing, jettisoned somewhere over the Atlantic. It'd be so easy then. Of course, he'd have to feign outrage and hurt in equal portion to Kara's, but she'd get over it. A quick trip to the tropics would soothe her pain. Then, back home to start his new job. After all, despite her fib back in Montana, the bikes held no sentimental charm. Least of all to him.

He didn't even like them.

They were reliable, his and hers steel beasts of burden that didn't begrudge any load or road surface. But, in Edward's eyes, they were donkeys. Ugly ones. Quality components were important, he'd say to friends looking to get into cycling, but never underestimate the value of aesthetics. The key to getting into better cycling shape was to ride every day. And the only way to do that was by buying a bike you yearned to ride every time you caught sight of it.

Their touring bikes didn't pass that test. With their indecorous frames, overbuilt wheels, and middling components, the bikes were utilitarian. Strip away the panniers, fuel bottle, and various adventure-themed accessories and the bicycles were as unremarkable as the family minivan.

Edward watched as two golf bags emerged from behind the doors. He sighed. As much as he wished for a shortcut home, he didn't really want the bikes to go missing. Though it might get him back to work sooner, he knew stolen bikes were a commute paved in too many of Kara's tears. Feeling guilty for having thought it, he counted down from twenty-nine, his age, a childhood trick to make the wait tolerable.

Kara approached carrying a single cup of coffee as Edward resorted to counting down fractions, stalling for time. "Still no bikes?"

"Nope." His eyes shifted to her cup. "Didn't get me one?" Edward asked, feeling a pang of guilt as he surveyed the distance she kept between them.

"Didn't know you wanted any."

Edward forced a disarming laugh. "When have *I* ever not wanted coffee?"

"We don't always get what we want. Do we?" Kara arched her eyebrows, then turned away.

Two gray doors swung open in time to save him from putting his foot in his mouth. Their boxes slid out, the large THIS SIDE UP arrows pointing at the floor as an attendant called their name. Edward could see one of the corrugated bicycle boxes had a gaping hole in the side. The corner of the other, personally sealed by Kara with at least five layers of packing tape, had also been torn.

Edward huffed his indignation as he stared at the attendant while pointing at the arrows. Kara's anger was less passive, but the man merely shrugged off their complaints and retreated to the safety of the Employees Only area.

Kara sipped her coffee with narrowed eyes while Edward righted the boxes, cringing at the rattling he heard from within. He slid the first box toward the stack of panniers. He was returning for the second as Kara struggled to push it with a single hand. The box toppled sideways and fell flat across the floor, a whooshing slap that echoed through the concourse.

"Just …," Edward started, as he yanked the box upright. "I've got it," he said through gritted teeth.

Kara's bike went together without a hitch and it wasn't long before Edward had straightened the handlebars to his own, bolted on the pedals, and raised the seatpost back to riding height, thankful for having marked the position with nail polish. But as soon as he went to put the front wheel on, he noticed the skewer that held the front wheel to the fork was missing.

"Goddamn it, it's always something with airlines."

Kara, who had already reattached her drive-side panniers and was spinning the bike around to lean against the wall, asked what was wrong.

"The damn skewer's gone."

"Didn't you leave it on the wheel when you boxed up the bikes?"

"I couldn't, it wouldn't fit. I taped it to the down tube, right here," he said flicking a piece of packing tape hanging from the frame like a taupe-colored flag of surrender. "Shit! It must have gotten loose in the box and fell out that damn hole. Watch our stuff."

Edward stormed across the tile floor to the baggage office but paused before ringing the bell. He took a deep breath, held it, and opened and closed his fists five times, pumping them quickly. He exhaled in a long, calming whistle.

The blonde-haired, round-faced woman who greeted him spoke with such a British accent, he could barely understand her. Amidst the drama surrounding the change of plans and packing the bikes, he had forgotten that he was halfway around the world from home.

"Hi, my name's Edward Vaughan," he said, smiling. "I was a passenger on the flight from Boston, and one of the items in my bicycle box is missing. Would it be possible for someone to check the area to see if it fell out?"

"Does the missing item have a luggage tag or any other identification?"

"No," he said, taken aback. *Why the hell would it?* "Like I said, it's a small bicycle part that was inside a box. The box got torn and the part fell out."

"Well, sir, the airline cannot be responsible for inadequately sealed luggage."

Is this woman listening to anything I say? "Sure. I understand, but the item *was* properly sealed inside a perfectly *sound* shipping box and one of your employees, whether here or in Boston, managed to rip a hole in it. And now a critical piece of our equipment is missing."

"Well, sir, I do apologize. If you can just fill out this Missing Items Form—"

"Never mind," Edward said, turning his back to her.

Kara was near the bikes, her arms wrapped around six dripping water bottles. "Any luck?"

"She told me to fill out a form for lost and found."

"So ... no?"

"What do you think?"

"Don't get mad at me," she said, sliding the bottles into their cages on the two bikes.

Edward heard her add a couple of barbs under her breath, and figured they were directed at him. He squeezed his fists once, slowly.

"I'm not angry with you. But I'll be lucky if I can roll it through the terminal without the wheel falling off."

Edward dragged the empty cardboard boxes toward the recycling bins, strapped the last of his bags to his bike, and followed Kara through the customs checkpoint and into the hustle of Heathrow's Terminal 3.

"Wait here." Kara leaned her bike alongside a water fountain and withdrew her wallet.

"More coffee?"

She shot him a look that reminded him he was still very much in the dog house. "Your turn to babysit the bikes." Kara thrust her helmet at Edward and walked off.

He watched as she threaded her way through the crowd, holding her line as the sea of skittering suitcases and aimless travelers parted around her. She planted herself at the information desk across the concourse. A young brunette smiled a greeting, her polished hospitality visible at twenty paces. The girl nodded with too much enthusiasm then turned her attention to a computer terminal. There was a flash of a pen. Some scribbling, and then she pointed. Edward couldn't tell at what; he saw only escalators.

Kara returned, a tourist map trailing from her right hand.

"I'm gonna take the train into the city and buy us a new skewer."

"You sure you don't want me to go?"

"I'll be fine. There's a bike shop near a station I'm familiar with."

"Maybe you should stay here. Get some rest. It was a long flight."

She rolled her eyes. "Has it occurred to you that I might want some time alone?"

It had. That's what made him nervous.

Edward watched her walk off as he stood alone, rocking in place. No kiss goodbye. No goodbye at all. She simply left. He stared after her, willing her to come back, to not split up so hastily, the gulf between them left stretched and jagged.

At home, neither left the other to go anywhere without a hug, a kiss, or without the one staying behind offering an *I love you, be careful.* It was as automatic as checking one's pockets for their keys and phone.

Kara must have heard his thoughts, for she was suddenly on her way back. He couldn't wait to hug her. Only now did he realize how tortuous the past two days had been.

"Forgot my passport," she said, unzipping a pouch on her bag without looking at him.

He couldn't be certain, but her pace seemed faster the second time she left.

Kara's frustration faded in size-seven increments with each step toward the escalator. For two days she ground her teeth and kept her venomous tongue bottled up while silently simmering over Edward's abrupt change of plans. No more. By the time she reached the bright tile floor, deep beneath the airport terminal, she'd left both her husband and her anger behind her. She had London to look forward to.

She bought her ticket, fed it into the turnstile, and retrieved it on the other side with the efficiency of a daily commuter. It was good to be back. As much as she had enjoyed her semester abroad in France, it was the twice-monthly trips into London that she remembered most fondly. Similar, yet foreign; crowded, yet cheerful; and old, but clean—unlike Seattle in every way.

She took a seat on the train, practically vibrating with nervous excitement. The feeling reminded her of those initial moments spent pedaling away from home, beginning the journey she hoped would give her marriage a fresh restart.

Kara caught herself wondering how many do-overs they'd get.

All around her travelers crammed aboard the train, their suitcases and backpacks making egregious advances into personal space. Phones in hand, the unshaven, jet-lagged passengers seemed not to notice, too fixated on their first hit of information after so many hours in airplane mode. *Thank God we didn't bring a phone*, she thought.

As the sprawling hive of suburbs in west London lurched by one station at a time, well-dressed commuters took their place alongside the tourists. Kara relished not fitting in, a member of neither team. Hers was the uniform of the adventure cyclist and she wouldn't be headed back to work for years. Dressed in road-worn cycling shoes and a wrinkled nylon blouse she reserved for low-mileage days around town, Kara straightened with pride. The chartreuse top didn't breathe well and clung to her shoulders and stomach when she sweat, but it could pass for casual wear, provided nobody noticed the salt streaks decorating the seams.

A nearby woman, old enough to be Kara's mother, stared at her, unable to conceal her curiosity. "Bicycle tour," Kara said, as if the two words were a hall pass that would excuse any and all foreseeable dress code violations —and create envy in everyone along the way. The woman frowned disapprovingly and shuffled to the door, leaving Kara to giggle.

Eight stops later, Kara emerged onto a crowded street a block from the bicycle shop. The store wouldn't open for thirty minutes according to the sign, so she took a seat on a bench and watched the people march by, entertaining herself by the ease at which she could sort locals from tourists. Guidebooks, cameras, and the ubiquitous folded, partially torn tourist maps (Kara kept hers hidden in a zippered pocket) were dead giveaways. She sought tougher clues: bulging security belts, men with their wallet stuffed in their front pocket, khaki vests and reversible skirts. The hallmarks of the camouflaged traveler.

A double-decker sightseeing bus rumbled by. A picket of selfie sticks jutted from its open-air roof, GoPros and iPhones raised like spears. She wondered how many home videos she'd appear in and settled further into the bench. *Her bench*, she thought, feeling a triumph over those without the luxury of loitering.

A man with cropped brown hair, capri-length pants, and a wool jersey dismounted a fluorescent green bike. A fixed-gear with handlebars narrower than his waist. "Ya waiting for the shop?" he asked, as he leaned the fixie against the glass. Kara pegged him for twenty-three. Cute, too.

"Yeah. How'd you know?" she said, straightening in her seat.

"The socks gave it away."

Kara looked down and realized if the shoes weren't obvious enough, the "Save the Tatas" breast cancer awareness cycling socks certainly were.

"Where's your bike?"

"Back at Heathrow. We just flew in and ..." she hesitated. She was going to say husband. She always said husband. "We somehow lost a skewer."

"Ouch," he said, then looked at his watch. "I'm not due to open for another fifteen minutes, but you're welcome to have a look around the shop while I get the lights on." He took a massive key ring from his pocket and unlocked the door.

The store resembled the showroom where she and Edward bought their Audi, only much smaller. Six high-end racing bikes hung from mannequin arms bolted to gray walls. Spotlights shone upon the bikes, each a brand she'd never heard of, but the store was otherwise dimly lit. A display case of boutique sunglasses took center stage. Hangers hung from a support column, each displaying a jersey from a different pro cycling team. It was nothing like the shops she frequented back home, where dozens of mountain bikes crowded the floor, hemmed into homemade wooden racks, locked together with a heavy steel cable threaded between their frames. Worse still, she saw no accessories, workbench, or spare parts of any kind.

"Uh, do you carry components here?" she asked, approaching the iPad serving as a register.

"Absolutely. I'm Mark by the way." he said, wheeling a metal stool out from behind the counter.

"Kara."

He eased himself onto the seat, his blue eyes fixed on hers, watching her over the rim of a travel mug. "So, you just got to London," he said between sips. "From the States?"

One question led to another as Kara told him about their plans for Europe. She didn't correct him when he referred to Edward as her "cycling friend," as she was relishing the attention, but her heart winced all the same.

It was refreshing to meet a guy who didn't ask questions as a way to redirect the conversation to himself. He seemed genuinely interested, asking about her work as a graphic designer, the trip, her life in Seattle, and before she knew it, an hour had passed—and Mark had inched close enough that she could smell the tea on his breath.

"Wow, they're going to wonder what happened to me," Kara said motioning to a clock on the wall. "I better get that part."

"Oh, right. Did your friend write down what he needed?"

He? Why'd he assume she was with a man?

"No, but we just need a skewer—"

"Right," he said, interrupting. "But I need to know what kind of bike he's riding. Not all wheels are alike. Care to call his mobile?" He opened the door to what Kara thought may had been a closet, revealing a concealed workshop. Multiple work stands held bikes in various states of assembly, ringed by shelves stacked with hundreds of parts.

"We're not carrying a phone. But I know the part."

Mark made a look that told Kara that, despite the niceties, he was just another bike shop bro who had yet to discover that women might know a thing or two about cycling.

She cut him off before he could say anything stupid. "We're riding steel mountain bikes, set up for touring. Hundred millimeter XT front hub, thirty-eight spokes. Six-bolt disc brakes, nine millimeter axle. Quick-release, preferably." Data overload, but she felt like showing off.

He cocked his head, impressed. "What size tires you running?" he asked, opening a drawer.

"Seven hundred by thirty-eight Schwalbe Marathon Pros."

Surprise whistled forth. "Why so much rubber?"

"We're expecting rough roads in Morocco and Central Asia. And they helped with the snow."

"You were touring in snow? You Yanks really are crazy."

He pulled a skewer from the drawer and took two boxes from a shelf. "Here's a used skewer. No charge. And you can probably use some spare tubes with the miles you're putting in."

Kara declined politely. They didn't have room for extra tubes. But he insisted and she relented and withdrew her wallet.

"Free. Consider it a welcome gift." He pulled the stool a bit closer, stepped in front of it, and leaned back, shortening himself to match her eye level. His knee made the slightest contact with hers.

"Well, thank you," she said, tucking her bangs behind her ears. The fabric of his pants brushed back and forth against her legs as he slowly oscillated against the stool. Kara caught herself admiring his dimples and took a small step back.

"My flatmates are having a party tomorrow night. You should come," he said, reaching for a pen. "And bring your friend too."

It was precisely the type of opportunity Kara hoped for. Chance encounters leading to invitations to meals, parties, and weddings were the Holy Grail of independent travel. She couldn't say no.

He thinks he's going to get some. Yes, there was that. He'd been flirting the whole time. *Why didn't I stop him from referring to Edward as a friend? Why didn't he notice my wedding ring?*

"Sounds like fun. We'll be there."

Mark clapped his hands and smiled a cocksure grin, likely imagining her naked. "Party starts at nine, but come anytime."

She thanked him again and grabbed the tubes and skewer, noting the color. "Oh this is great, it's the same color as the one we lost."

"The least of my talents," he said, stepping closer.

"I bet it is. My husband's gonna be thrilled. Thanks again, Mark." she said, turning for the door, smiling proudly.

Edward gazed toward the escalators, watching travelers disappear into the depths of the airport for what felt like hours. He wanted to chase after Kara, to deliver the goodbye kiss she denied him. To tell her he loved her.

She hates me.

Does she? He wanted to believe it wasn't true, that she was merely angry and yes, disappointed, but she'd forgive him. They'd embrace, he'd apologize for rushing them off to London. All would be fine. Water under bridges.

It's not only about skipping Cape Cod.

Of course not. That's why he couldn't shake the idea of her never coming back. Edward returned to the bikes, anxiety working him over like a boxer on a heavy bag, the memories of his lies landing like punches to the gut.

He rested his hand on the saddle of her bike and stared until his eyes blurred. What would he do if this was all he had left of her? If she abandoned him? He wasn't stupid. Edward had long suspected that Kara wanted more from him than he gave, that she didn't place as much stock in the money and security he aimed to provide. He always chalked it up to her youthful impracticality, figuring she'd see it differently when they got older, had kids. Now, he wasn't so sure.

It'd be so much easier if Tom had given him a full year—or if he thought Kara would believe he'd have more time for her with the new job.

The airport intercom crackled to life, all static and outdoor voice, announcing the baggage carousel for passengers arriving from Toronto. A family shuffled past, "Welcome Home" balloons bouncing along behind them. A young boy clutching his mother's dress smiled and said, "I like your bikes."

That makes one of us, kid. Edward returned a fake smile.

Being idle was no good. He needed to make himself useful before his imagination left him in pieces. He eyed the panniers and shrugged, knowing how disorganized they'd become.

One by one he unpacked each of his bags into a tidy pile. Edward rerolled every article of clothing, consolidated the contents of each pocket, and shook three months of North American leaves and grit onto the floor. He sorted their tools and cookware, then took stock of their purification tablets, waterproof matches, and repair patches.

He repeated the task for Kara's panniers, taking satisfaction as the mound of pine needles and dirt grew. Progress.

The last bag contained her clothing. Edward turned the stuff sack over in his hands, as hesitant to open it as a widower standing before his beloved's armoire. Then, with a deep breath, he tugged the drawstring and spilled her clothes into his lap, releasing a cascade of blouses, skirts, socks, and underwear. Two of each. He so rarely came into contact with her unworn clothing that he never before realized how petite it was, how delicate the items felt. Working from the larger items to the small, he repacked her clothing with a care he'd never shown his own.

The pile shrank to a single pair of silk briefs, and a pang of uncertainty bore into him. He held them, caressing the sleek material, wondering when she last wore them—and if he noticed.

I'm gonna lose her, he thought, his earlier fears rushing back, kicking down the flimsy blockade built upon distraction. Edward's eyelids fell shut, the silk bunched in twin fists against his forehead as he struggled to recall the last time they were intimate.

Had sex or made love?

He ached as months of bedroom memories swirled in his mind. Fragile recollections of Kara lying beside him, spooning, Edward pumping away for a minute or two before falling asleep. Their passion no hotter than a November drizzle. More partners in life than lovers on a journey.

It wasn't always like that. The sex used to be great. Then came the promotions. And the late nights, and the weekends spent with clients instead of Kara.

"I'm such an ass," Edward said, his voice muffled by the crumpled underwear he held to his face. He breathed deeply, siphoning off the detergent scent, hoping to detect a trace of her essence, a single molecule to remember her by.

Awareness rushed in, reminding him where he was—and how pathetic he was acting. He laughed at himself, hoping nobody was watching, then took a deep breath and blinked away the last of his emotions, gaining the clarity he sought. They had a fight. That was all. And Kara would forgive him.

This time.

He couldn't worry about that now; he could only make it up to her and hope he didn't have to hijack the route again for several months. By then, he suspected, even Kara might want to fast-forward to home.

Edward returned her stuff sack to the pannier then scooped the pile of dirt with his hands, relieved to be as free of the grime as he was the burden of his misgivings.

"It's bad luck to wear that indoors, ya know?"

Edward spun, tearing the helmet from his head as his pulse quickened. He'd just finished mounting the mirrors to the other side of the helmets in preparation for British roads. "You came back."

"Yeah, sorry it took so long—" Kara began, pausing as a curtain of concern descended on her face. "Are you okay?"

Not really, he thought. He looked away as he spun the helmet in his hands, not wanting to sound pitiful.

"Of course I'd come back." Kara moved quickly, wrapping her arms around him. A small shopping bag slapped against his back. He felt himself melt into her as she whispered words of compassion into his ear with the tone of a woman honored to see a man's weakness on display.

"I'm so sorry, Kara."

She nodded slowly. "I know."

"I was so selfish. It wasn't fair," he said, feeling his resolve crumbling. He hated the lies, the secrets, the guilt. "There's something I need to—"

She silenced him with a kiss—a lifeline—and for the briefest moment he was convinced she knew about the contest. The impossible thought flashed like lightning, replaced instantly by the pressure of her lips against his, and the crackling realization that he'd nearly said too much, given up the dream he had for them. But no. He had her forgiveness, her blind permission to keep his secret. To go for it.

Edward returned the kiss with the fervor of a man brought back to life.

Edward woke before dawn the next morning, still in the clothes he wore to dinner, with a wrinkled sightseeing map unfolded across him. Confusion set in as he forgot where he was, a side effect of life on the road. A dog-eared travel guide thudded to the floor as he stretched, jogging his memory. He'd borrowed the book from the lobby of the inn, a cramped guesthouse in west London's Hammersmith area.

Nowhere near the tourist attractions, but easy to reach by bicycle from Heathrow. And with a proper English breakfast included.

Kara lay beside him, an angel in repose, every muscle at peace save for her lips, which seemed to curl at the corners, pursed in secret delight. Edward kissed her forehead, hoping he'd remember to ask about her dream, but knew she seldom remembered them. Whatever it was, he was happy she had it.

He gathered the map and guidebook, switched the bedroom's electric kettle on for tea, and freshened up as quietly as he could. Not wanting to wake Kara, he settled onto the floor nearest the bathroom light and set about planning the day's itinerary. He knew he had to make it good.

Two hours later, down three flights of narrow, twisting stairs, Edward sat pushing sautéed mushrooms around his plate, wondering why anyone would want beans and mushrooms for breakfast.

"You eating these?" Kara asked, stabbing a tomato with a fork.

He crinkled his nose in disgust, wishing for a plate of pancakes and bacon. *Real* bacon, he thought.

"So, what's the plan for today?"

Edward warmed at the question. "It's a secret," hoping he sounded as confident as he wished. It was risky, but he was determined to treat her to a special day. After Cape Cod, he needed to nail this.

First came the macarons. A pastel spectrum of airy decadence at the Chelsea Farmer's Market where he and Kara sipped cappuccino beneath an oversized umbrella. Edward couldn't take his eyes from her as she sat cross-legged opposite him, swinging her foot hypnotically. A simple walking shoe dangled from her toes with the style of a stiletto, the curve of her foot distracting him from her stories about London. Just as it used to distract him from the professor's lecture. *When did I stop noticing this?*

From the market, they strolled to Rainbow Row in Notting Hill, where a collection of brilliantly colored townhomes stood brick to brick as if the street were a box of crayons. Kara flitted about with her camera, moving from house to house like a butterfly in a garden. Edward watched on, proud of the day he'd arranged, but still mindful of the eggshells he walked upon. After a few selfies, he led her to Hyde Park for a lazy picnic lunch. On the way, he took her hand, tentatively, as if for the first time.

Though Kara spoke little as the day unfolded, Edward wasn't about to risk ruining the moment by saying something he'd come to regret. He could tell she'd forgiven him. It was in her smile during coffee, in the kiss she gave him while snapping photos, by the way she rested her head against his shoulder as they walked. In the park, Edward leaned against a tree while Kara napped in his lap. The rough bark ground against his shoulder blade, but he bore the discomfort without disturbing her.

Hours later, they were seated high above London's south bank, at an Americana-inspired lounge in the Shard, a futuristic skyscraper befitting its name. The view from their table offered a sweeping panorama of the city's landmarks.

Kara cozied up against Edward's chest on the sofa-style seating, heating the air between them, and pointed her wine glass as she identified the major sights, from St. Paul's Cathedral to London Tower.

"You can't really see it, but Shakespeare's Globe is right below us," she said, "near the Wobbly Bridge."

"The what?"

Kara laughed and pointed at a pedestrian bridge. "It's technically the Millennium Bridge, but it swayed so much when it opened, the city had to close it for two years to fix it. Locals have called it the Wobbly Bridge ever since."

"That's hilarious."

"They have nicknames for everything. That's the Walkie Talkie," she said, pointing at a concave tower across the river, "and the one behind it is the Cheesegrater."

Edward shook his head, amused.

"And that egg-shaped one over there—"

"With the diamond windows?"

"That's the Gherkin. Like the pickle."

"So *that's* the Gherkin," Edward said, putting place to name.

"You've heard of it?" Kara sounded surprised.

Edward felt the heat rise in his face as the name carried him back to the office, to the boisterous tales of thousand-dollar meals and private clubs. "Madsen used to brag about going there. 'Members only,' he'd say."

"Probably snobs."

Edward cringed. He'd been promised a chance to tag along on Ron's trips to Europe once he got his promotion. It was one of the perks he was most looking forward to.

Does she think I'm a snob?

He tipped his glass and poured the thoughts of Ron Madsen into the oblivion of his gullet. A server materialized as Edward sat his glass on the coaster a little too forcefully.

"Another Merlot, sir?"

"Maybe something a little stronger." Edward flipped open the cocktail menu and snorted when he saw a drink called the American Dream. He ordered it without as much as a glance at the ingredient list.

Minutes passed in awkward silence as Edward waited for the mention of Ron to pass, as if waiting out a raincloud beneath a bridge. The air had changed around them and he feared Kara may have sensed it too.

"I ... well, *we,* got invited to a party," Kara said, her voice hesitant, laced with suggestion.

"You did, did you?" Edward said with a smirk, trying to conceal a pinprick of jealousy. "By whom?" he asked, his voice rising in a faux-accusatory tone.

Kara blushed. "The guy at the bike shop."

Edward's drink arrived not a moment too soon, and he hastily took a sip as his jealousy deepened. It tasted sweet but contained a smoky finish that reminded him of the Scotch he had with Tom.

"And what'd you tell this guy at the bike shop?"

"What do you think? I said my husband and I would try to make it." Kara placed a hand on his knee. "But we don't have to go."

The storm had passed and Edward felt himself expand with relief. "The only party I want tonight is with you." His cocktail-moistened lips alighted on the lengthy expanse of her neck. He dragged his tongue ever so slightly to the wisps of hair beneath her ear. "No falling asleep in our clothes tonight."

Back at the inn, they unbuttoned, unbelted, tugged, and loosened each other blindly, their mouths biting and searching. They tumbled as one onto the bed with its cheap, fraying quilt, knocking the pillows to the floor.

Kara's sleeveless blouse was unbuttoned to her navel, her bra unfastened and pushed aside; skirt flipped upwards, panties dangling from a solitary foot—the silk ones he'd been fondling in the airport. Edward, shirtless, knelt between her toned legs in admiration of her bewitching blend of sexuality and strength. His pause was brief, a fleeting genuflection at the altar of his love.

Outside, the seesawing siren of a British copper Dopplered past as Edward bent to explore and taste and wrap himself around and within Kara's warmth.

Chapter 19

MONDAY, JUNE 8 — LONDON, UNITED KINGDOM

Edward crawled out from under the sheets and flopped alongside Kara, flushed. He arched his back and stretched as a nearby fan blew a revitalizing breeze. Across the room, window blinds cut stripes across the purple-blue glow of daybreak.

He scooted his pillow closer to Kara and rolled to his side. She smiled, glistening. And Edward was in love. He studied her blissful smirk, the rising and falling of her chest as she breathed, the gentle flaring of her nostrils. She licked her curling lips and he could tell she sensed him watching her.

Kara took a deep breath and blinked away the last vestiges of sleep. When she turned to face him, a loving twinkle danced in her eyes. Right then, a thought rocketed through him, exploding with such force he felt his chest recoil: *I can't ever risk not seeing her look at me this way.*

"Morning," she said, her voice brimming with a delicious heaping dose of naughtiness.

"Sleep well?"

"I don't remember you letting me," Kara said with a yawn.

They stared at one another beneath twisted sheets with twin grins. The room was still, save for the oscillating fan and the lazy march of sunlight across the walls. Thoughts drifted by like plankton through a fishing net as Edward sank deeper into her gaze.

Kara broke the silence with a beleaguered sigh. "It's probably time we start packing for Scotland."

"We don't have to." He placed his hand on her hip, hoping to punctuate his sincerity.

"You want to stay another day?"

He shrugged, not knowing what he wanted other than to stay in this moment.

Kara tilted her head, as if he was a sculpture needing to be studied from another angle. "I thought you couldn't wait to get to Scotland. What about the Whiskey Trail? And Edinburgh?"

He repeated the questions in his mind. It was complicated. His comment was such a simple remark, an echo of the romantic mood he was in, meant to be ignored or agreed to without deliberation.

But the moment was lost. Awareness flooded his mind. It was Monday, another week begun. Only four days until he had to call Tom. The Atlantic suddenly felt much smaller from Europe.

Edward rolled onto his back and balled his fists behind his head, knocking a pillow to the floor with one elbow, almost bumping Kara with the other. *Can't I have one fucking day without worrying about Tom?*

"What's wrong?"

Edward laced his fingers and squeezed the back of his head in frustration. Pain surged behind his ears, his skull being crushed in a vise of his own making. The ache was intense, but gratifying. A release. Like when he threw the baseball at Madsen.

He snorted at the memory and relaxed his grip, taking a calming breath as relief filled the void left by his waning adrenaline. He knew it wasn't a good look—God knows his mother hated seeing his father pound and slam his way through life—but it felt good. To blow the valve off every now and then and vent. But he had to be careful. After all, it was his temper that landed him in this mess to begin with.

Since when is spending every day traveling the world with your wife a mess?

He could feel Kara staring at him as she repeated her question. He ignored her, searching his imagination, hoping for an idea. To his right, he felt the mattress sink and rebound as she got out of bed.

"It just occurred to me," he began, an entirely true statement, "that it would take two months to cycle around Great Britain—"

"Yeah," she interrupted. "That's why I thought we could take a train to Inverness and cycle south."

"They have direct trains from London to northern Scotland?"

"I don't know. Maybe."

Edward hadn't ever ridden a train in the States, least of all with a bicycle—his experience with public transit began and ended with the Puget Sound ferries. He envisioned rushing on and off trains, fetching their bicycles from luggage cars, and changing platforms with two bikes and ten bags. "That could be a nightmare with all our gear."

"What do you suggest?"

"I'm not sure. I really wanted to see Scotland. Probably more than any other country, but ..." His voice faded into a sigh as Tom's bellowing voice echoed in his memory: *East!* Edward gritted his teeth at the unwelcome intrusion, deciding right then that one romantic day in London wasn't enough. And neither Tom nor anyone else was going to make him leave.

"Let's stay here," he said. "Just another day or two."

"Really?" she asked, wrapping a discarded quilt around herself.

"I'm serious. Let's spend another day in London then look into taking a ferry to Denmark."

Kara put her hand to his forehead, as if checking for a fever. "Are you sure you're feeling okay? Scotland was your pick."

A good question. The man who built a career on smart investments and due diligence felt ideas being turned to words faster than his brain could process. But he knew skipping Scotland would pay dividends in the long run.

"Yep. I feel awful about you missing Cape Cod. It's only fair if I miss something too, right? Then we'll be even."

Kara bobbed her head side to side while mulling over his words.

Edward wasn't sure where the idea came from, but he loved what he was hearing. He sat up in the bed, excited, his hands drumming on his knees.

"There's gotta be a boat to Denmark," he continued, his tempo soaring as guilt and trepidation danced a quickstep across his mind. "And I know you wanted to visit as many countries as possible. We can ride back along the North Sea through Germany to the Netherlands. That gets us an extra country and still gets us to the mainland sooner than if we pedaled from Scotland. It'll be perfect."

Kara appeared tempted by the offer, but remained silent as she paced. The past twenty-four hours had been some of their best in recent memory. And he knew she felt the same way. "Well?" he finally asked, encouraging her with big-eyed excitement.

"The continent," she said after some time.

"Huh?"

"The continent. You said the mainland. That's not what Europeans call it."

"Good to know." After a moment's silence, he raised his eyebrows, begging for an answer.

"If it's what you want—"

"Is it what *you* want?"

"I guess. I mean, I'm not sure. It sounds okay. It's really different than I envisioned."

"A little spontaneity is good for us, right? Isn't that what you always said?"

Kara nodded politely. "It is. I just never thought you'd be *this* spontaneous. Promise me something."

"Anything."

She walked to his side of the bed, the quilt trailing like a wedding train. "Promise me this is it with the sudden detours. Don't get me wrong, I'm glad you're being more impulsive, but I feel like the trip is slipping away from us, like we're fast-forwarding through a dream."

He swallowed hard. *Whose dream?*

"Say you promise." Her voice hitched with nervousness.

He took her hands in his, hoping she wouldn't notice their shaking. "Of course," he said, feeling the sting of guilt as he spoke. "Now, come back to bed," he said, pulling her on top of him, rolling with her across the bed. He tickled her as he landed kisses all over her neck and collar bone, relishing in the sensation of her hair brushing against his face. He rose into a plank above her, hovering, his eyes locked on hers.

"I promise," he said, knowing it was a promise he couldn't keep.

Kara balanced atop the nose of her saddle, stomping the pedals with all the power she could muster. Sunscreen-scented beads of perspiration pimpled her skin. A drop of sweat hung from the tip of her nose, tickling, swaying in rhythm with her pedaling. She snapped her head to the side, flinging it to the gravel, only to feel another drop form.

Her heart pounded in her chest, but she refused to ask him to slow down. Not again, not so soon.

They were in Denmark, the Jutland Peninsula to be exact. A two-day ride out of London brought them to the seaside town of Harwich, where they boarded an overnight ferry to Esbjerg. Now they were headed north, not deeper into Scandinavia, but retracing earlier miles thanks to Edward's stubbornness, in search of a detour.

To her left, an earthen levee restrained the North Sea. To the right, cattails jutted from a narrow marsh, beyond which stretched an emerald field, wavering in the wind like velour brushed by an invisible hand. Towering windmills ticked by like mileposts, breaking up the landscape, the monotony, and distracting her from the brackish stink. At least the wind was with her.

She knew the tailwind would become an obstacle soon enough, but for now it helped speed her along the trail back the way they came, in a country she hadn't intended to visit.

Kara was surprised by Edward's decision to skip Scotland. His suggestion to take a ferry to Denmark shocked her even more, given the nightmares he'd suffered while cycling around Lake Superior. She thought he'd developed a phobia of the water at the time. But unlike herself, Edward slept fine aboard the ferry.

The cawing of the Danish shorebirds carried Kara's thoughts across the North Sea and the Atlantic, all the way to Canada—and Jean-Benac. It wasn't the first time. Two nights earlier, Kara took a midnight stroll around the ferry's deck. She'd leaned over the railing, staring at the inky darkness splashing below, wondering if Jean-Benac was safe—if he somehow survived the treacherous seas that plagued Edward in his sleep. She also wondered about Claudette. The grave. It had to have been a coincidence, she reasoned. After all, how could Kara remind someone of a woman who died in 1739? Nevertheless, thoughts of the grave marker led her to recall the innkeeper's story about finding Jean-Benac, naked in the snow and wild with terror, calling out for Claudette.

Back on the bicycle, in Denmark, she looked up in time to see Edward lower his hand, his palm facing Kara at a shallow angle. He was slowing. *Finally.*

They stopped in front of the fence they passed earlier. Kara waited as Edward backed through the spring-loaded gate and yanked on the handlebars, tugging his bike like an obstinate bull. Once through, he held the gate for Kara. She pushed past without looking at him, then leaned her bike against a signpost.

"Well, that was a fun extra six miles. You know how much I *love* backtracking," she said, stretching her legs.

"Sorry. I didn't know there'd be a river," he said with a smirk that begged to be slapped.

She stared at him in disbelief, her gaze narrow, and pointed at the sign where NO PASSAGE TO GERMANY was written in three languages, English included.

"I thought the warning was only for cars, that we'd find a way through."

"We're on a bike path, Ed," she said, her arms raised and hands flailing, as if trying to ward off the stupidity she was hearing. "There aren't any cars!"

Kara knew he was practically incapable of admitting a mistake. Where most people would shrug their shoulders and accept that they screwed up, Edward would double down, determined to make any miscalculation seem more the casualty of his genius than the result of his blunder. It was the thing that irked Kara most about him, but what really pissed her off was that she went along with it. She let out a sigh that could have turned a windmill. "Why didn't you listen to me?"

"I thought it'd be a shortcut," he said.

Kara chortled. She couldn't help herself. He was in such a hurry, he wasn't even making sense. "This isn't a race. Nobody's waiting to give us a trophy if we get across Europe a few days faster."

Edward looked away, but not as a concession. He was avoiding her, concealing something. Kara stared at him, waiting. Something felt off, but she didn't know what.

"At least we got a bit of tailwind out of it," he said, offering a conciliatory smile.

Kara shook her head, ignoring his blatant attempt to change the subject as she mounted her bike. She led the way to a road angled inland, to the south.

Progress was a poultice and Kara quickly forgot her frustration over the errant detour as she pedaled into northern Germany. But she couldn't shake the feeling that Edward was hiding something from her, especially when he accelerated past, his derailleur shifting into a taller gear.

Kara spent the week trailing Edward as they crossed the Elbe River west from northern Germany to the Netherlands. Their destination: Amsterdam. The winds were favorable, the weather sunny, and Kara had a list of hosts lined up for them to stay with, arranging them an easy day's ride apart before leaving London. She expected some of the most pleasant, relaxing days of the entire trip.

But Edward had other plans.

She held her tongue as they raced across the apple and onion country of the German-Dutch borderlands, averaging eighty miles per day. The roads were flat and the daylight long. Edward thought it best to take advantage of it. "There's not much to see," he reasoned. "The faster we get through the countryside, the more time we'll have in the cities."

Kara believed the wonder of bicycle touring resided in the spaces in between but swallowed her objections. She was in shape and could handle the miles, she told herself—all in effort to keep the peace.

Towns passed like billboards on the side of a highway. Saint Peter-Ording, Bremerhaven, Grosse-Meer, Leek, and Lelystad, all places they could have spent a day or more exploring, all towns Kara would retain no memory of.

Instead, they rode until dusk. They camped on the side of fields, under bridges, and tucked in the woods, out of sight, hoping to avoid detection, like teenagers secreting away to drink shoplifted bottles of liquor. And while Edward hunched over their camp stove cooking the nightly batch of pasta, Kara stewed.

One night, at a campground a day's ride from Amsterdam, suspicion birthed an idea: Maybe he had some sort of trophy waiting for him. She replayed the past two months in her mind, cataloging the times he pushed for longer days, overruled her suggestion, or downright ignored her and skipped ahead. The flight out of Boston still hurt every bit as much as his decision to skip Scotland surprised her. There had to be a reason.

He's up to something.

She snatched her toiletry bag and change of clothes, turning the idea over in her mind as she marched to the shower. There, under the tepid trickle of water, she once again felt the excitement of the tour slipping through her fingers. But it wasn't just the trip. It was their marriage. She'd been lonely before, but never angry. Never wanting to slap him. Or curse him out at the top of her lungs.

Maybe it was the twenty-four seven contact, she thought, wondering when she last had a day to herself. Or having to wash their clothes in a bucket, only to pull on underwear that was still damp come morning. Or the endless string of cold, dirty, campground showers. Kara rinsed the shampoo from her hair and bent to shave. She didn't get halfway up her calf before the razor nicked her, as if right on cue.

Kara bit her lip, grimacing from the sting, as blood trickled down her gooseflesh leg. She hurled the razor at the floor. Her chest convulsed, ringing months' worth of emotions from her heart, but no tears came. She was too tired to weep.

"We were supposed to be in Cape Cod," she croaked.

She leaned into the stream of water and rested her forehead against the cold tile, beating her palm against the bathroom wall, drumming up the courage to confront Edward. It was like February all over again, she realized, thinking back to the day she dialed up the nerve to ask for a divorce. And with that memory, the tears finally came in waves.

Things had to change. She couldn't do this anymore.

They reached Amsterdam the following afternoon. Kara, exhausted and emotional, stayed on guard, ready to blow the whistle at the first sign of Edward trying to speed them out of town. To her surprise, he said nothing when she checked them into the hotel for three nights. Nor did he demur when she told the receptionist they might extend their stay. And later that evening, while she watched with side-eyed suspicion, he didn't flinch when she suggested taking a full week off the bikes when they reached Paris. For every trap she set, hoping to snare his intent, Edward skirted it with ease, calming her bated breath, disarming her doubts.

She wondered if he was simply tired, or if he truly preferred the cities to the farmscape. *Maybe he's just humoring me.* Her lingering angst refused to dissipate. Instead, it bubbled amid her confusion like vinegar in oil.

That night, she slipped into bed with a heavy sigh, too exhausted to confront him and unwilling to risk an argument. Edward climbed into bed minutes later and reached for her thigh. She rolled away, pulling the covers tighter around her.

The following morning, Kara stood beneath the hot shower, testing ways to approach Edward about spending the day apart. She didn't want to hurt his feelings, but knew a day alone would do her well. Him too.

She pulled the shower curtain back and startled, nearly slipping on the wet porcelain, as Edward's reflection stared back at her in the cramped bathroom's mirror. *Can't I even use the bathroom by myself?*

Kara toweled herself off and waded gingerly into the conversation, probing for the proper it's-not-you-it's-me balance before diving in. "What would you say to sightseeing separately today?" Then, before he could react, she added, "It's nothing personal, just that we haven't had much time to ourselves since we left home."

She watched him brushing his teeth in the mirror as she spoke. To her surprise, the spark in his eyes went dim as his face appeared to melt. The toothbrush dangled from his mouth, limp in his grasp. "We don't have to. I just thought it might do us some good," Kara said, backpedaling.

Edward appeared to weigh her words carefully, then bent and spit into the sink. When he straightened, she could see the wheels turning in his mind as he began to nod. "That sounds fine," he said, smiling. "So long as you're not trying to get rid of me."

She grabbed him by the chin and squeezed. "Not unless you have another week of eighty-mile days planned."

Kara bounded from the hotel thirty minutes later, tourist map in hand, and hurried off to the Anne Frank House. It was the first attraction she thought to visit, the place she most associated with Amsterdam, and she didn't want to waste a minute mulling over the decision. The queue already stretched down a neighboring street, and she was in no mood to wait. She looked up at the house, imagining the interior of the famous attic, recalling the face of the girl whose diary became obligatory reading half a world away. The slightest bit of shame rose within her, but she extinguished it quickly. This was her day, and she'd spend it doing the thing Anne couldn't: enjoying the city at her leisure.

Kara stuffed the map into her pocket and walked off, not caring where she went. She wanted only to float along, like a leaf adrift on the city's canals.

She meandered slowly, aimlessly, crossing dozens of bridges as she wended her way through the medieval city center. Kara bought herself a multicolored bouquet of tulips at the flower market and carried it past dozens of museums, cafés, and boutiques, occasionally lifting it to her nose. She wandered for miles, from the gauntlet of bicycle racks outside *Amsterdam Centraal* station to the dirt trails of *Vondelpark*, to the Van Gogh Museum. There, while standing in front of the ticket booth, she caught herself thinking about Edward: *What was he up to?*

She wanted the day to herself, but only needed a few hours. For as much as she wanted time alone, she hated the thought of creating memories without him. The museum would wait until tomorrow. They'd visit it together.

Kara retrieved the map from her pocket, noted the circle the receptionist had drawn, and hurried back to the hotel, hoping he'd be there.

Edward nearly jumped from his seat at the touch on his shoulder. Guilt and panic surged within him as he heard Kara's unmistakable giggle over his shoulder. His hands darted out, grabbing mouse and keyboard, closing the browser window with the speed of a mongoose striking a cobra.

"It's just me, silly." Kara laughed. "When did you get back?"

Back? He looked around the room for a clock. "I … I didn't leave," he stammered.

"Seriously? It's almost four o'clock. It couldn't have taken *that* long to route us to Paris." She swatted him playfully across the back with a bouquet.

He shrugged, hoping she didn't notice his concern. "Guess I lost track of time." *Paris?* She saw the screen, one of a hundred routes he'd spent the day drawing on Google Maps. But which one? And how much of it? He'd been plotting far beyond Paris. He glanced at the screen again, checking to see if he left any other windows open.

Kara gave his shoulder a friendly squeeze. "Let's get a drink. I want to tell you about my day."

A week later, in the Belgium town of Dinant, Kara caught her reflection in a bakery window. Turning to admire the definition of her bronzed legs, she couldn't get over the bump of her calf, the ridge along her thigh. She twisted and gazed over her shoulder, barely recognizing the transparent lookalike standing before an audience of éclairs and profiteroles.

Her back and shoulders rippled beneath her sleeveless jersey with the muscles of a rock climber. Kara smiled as she spun around, relishing in her newfound physique, strong but feminine. Wrestling an eighty-pound bicycle around the world wasn't easy, but it certainly had its benefits.

The smell of fresh-baked baguettes sent her mind wandering ahead to Paris. She twirled in place, daydreaming ahead to a stroll along the Seine with Edward, her lithe body glowing in the sun. Kara lifted the hem of her shorts, exposing a swath of skin as white as meringue. She recoiled in disgust and cursed her ridiculous tan lines. "So much for a minidress."

After a picnic lunch in Dinant, under the shadow of the town's clifftop citadel, they continued thirty-six miles to the famed brewery town of Chimay. It was their last night in Belgium—a detour of Edward's choosing—and their second brewery in as many days. But Kara happily obliged, in too good of a mood not to. The past week rolled by in soft-focus tranquility. Ever since Amsterdam, he'd slowed his pace, agreed to shorten their daily mileage, and embraced the trip as vacation, as if he had read her mind.

They crossed into France the following day, bumping along a web of dirt roads through the rural Champagne-Ardenne region, seeking passage south. Tilled fields rolled like waves to the horizon, masonry farmhouses floated like buoys, and Kara and Edward pedaled along the array of roads, adrift on shifting winds. They rode for hours, their view often blocked by walls of corn, hoping to reach the city of Reims by sunset.

Stopped for a check of the map, Kara leaned over Edward's shoulder, chatting, when a voice called out behind them.

"Hello. Are you lost?"

She and Edward exchanged a puzzled look and turned as an aging man, as thin as a rake, approached the stone wall bordering the dirt road. He wore a floppy brown hat and a wrinkled dress shirt stained in the sweat and dirt of a man who didn't dress down to work hard.

"You speak English?" Edward asked.

The man nodded. "I was in the French Air Force and worked with many American pilots. They taught me English."

His mention of the military reminded Kara of where they stood: the Ardennes, the Western Front of World War I. Kara scanned the fields, trying to visualize the trenches, the constant bombing, the millions of soldiers who died. But the bucolic modern landscape refused to be overlain with such horrors. Her brain wouldn't allow it.

"Now I farm. And this is my orchard," he said, motioning to the twenty-odd trees behind him, planted in rows. "I'd offer you some apples if they were ripe, but harvest isn't for months."

Kara and Edward broke into simultaneous laughter.

"What is it? Did I speak incorrectly?"

"Not at all," Edward said. "We've been hearing we were two months early since March."

"You began your trip in March?"

"Yep. We started in Seattle," Kara said.

"That's incredible. And where is your destination today?"

"We were going to Reims, but we had to take a detour due to bad directions—"

Edward interrupted with a snort. "Thanks, Google."

"Reims is still fifty kilometers away," the man said, pronouncing it *Rance,* rolling the R. Kara made a note to stop saying *Reems.*

"What do you think?" Edward asked, looking at Kara with his eyebrows raised.

"I don't have another thirty miles in me today." She turned toward the Frenchman. "Do you know of a campground nearby?"

The man stroked his chin briefly. "I'll be going out for the night, but you are welcome to tent in my orchard."

Kara took a sudden interest in a pebble near her foot, expecting Edward to decline the offer, saying it was too early to stop for the day.

"That's very generous. We'd love to," Edward said, much to her surprise.

The man who never offered his name, nor asked theirs, opened a gate in the stone wall and showed them where they could set up their tent. He pointed out a spigot on the side of a barn and bid them *adieu,* turning back to his house.

"Excuse me," Edward said, catching the man's attention. "Would you mind if we used your bathroom before you left?"

"Yes, yes, of course. I will show you," he said, smiling.

Kara and Edward followed and, an hour later, they were not only changed into their camping clothes, but clean from a shower too. Kara need only get caught glancing at the shower to coax an offer to use it. She felt a little guilty over social engineering additional hospitality from the man, but he seemed happy to offer.

Outside by the tent, Kara paged through a French phrasebook, refreshing her memory, as Edward approached with a bottle of wine. Their titanium coffee mugs dangled from his finger.

"I couldn't let us spend our first meal in France without some *vino.*"

Kara smiled, opting not to remind him they weren't in Italy. "Were you carrying that all day?"

Edward laughed. "I'm flattered, but you think too highly of me. I asked Louis if I could buy a bottle from him while you were showering."

"Louis?"

"The guy who owns this place. Anyway, he refused my money. Says it's local." Edward removed the cork with his teeth and sloshed two generous portions into the mugs, which he set on the grass. "He also gave us this." Edward unveiled a block of cheese from his pocket. Kara warmed with delight. This was the France she knew most Americans never got to see. The generosity, the desire to share. And she was so happy Edward could experience it. "See what happens when we slow down?"

Edward nodded thoughtfully, then took a sip of the wine. He smacked his lips. "That's really good."

Kara took the flimsy plastic cutting board and knife from the bag of kitchen supplies and sliced the cheese as Edward scooted next to her. He took another gulp of the wine and turned to face her square on, anxiousness written all over his face.

"So, I was thinking—"

"I can tell."

He laughed. "That obvious, huh?"

She nodded.

"I was wondering if you'd want to head through the Alps after Paris, instead of going through the Pyrenees."

"The Alps?"

"Yeah, it'll give us more time in France," he said, plucking a piece of cheese from the board. "And we can try some of those big climbs in the Tour de France. Maybe Alpe d'Huez. Doing it fully loaded would be tough, but we can handle it," he said, giving her leg a squeeze.

"What about Spain? You know how much I want to see Madrid and Barcelona."

Edward paused. It was brief, but Kara noticed it, like a derailleur slow to shift gears. "Oh, yeah, that's right. Of course," he said apologetically. "I'm sorry. I wasn't thinking. Forget I said anything."

Kara watched as Edward forced a smile onto his face. Was it an honest mistake? Had he just been buttering her up this past week, hoping she'd agree to forfeit the one destination she wanted most to visit?

She rolled the mug of wine between her palms as she questioned her own intuition, wondering why his request so unsettled her.

Chapter 20

FRIDAY, MAY 15 — FLORENCE, ITALY

Alessio rushed through his evening duties, restocking toilet paper and wiping sinks and mirrors with the haste of a schoolboy scribbling his homework so he could play. Now he stood behind an empty table, his grip tight on a plastic tray as he watched the cafeteria door. Why did Hiromasa insist on inviting him to dinner if he wasn't going to be punctual?

Worse, it was too early to eat. The tourists haven't even wandered in yet, but Hiromasa had taken to suppering as soon as he finished his work. His landscaping efforts left him ravenous and he liked to turn in early, he often said. Their disparate schedules were exacerbated by the start of the campground's high season, and they seldom saw one another for more than a few minutes each day.

Alessio scowled at the mound of pappardelle with Bolognese sauce heaped before him, sprinkles of pancetta clinging to the ribbons of pasta. He twirled his fork in the noodles with disinterest, having grown as bored with food as he had with what he'd come to consider his twenty-first century imprisonment. His freedom to venture beyond

Florence (*and go where?*) offered no comfort. He was as much inmate as jailer, tarrying for God's pardon.

Hiromasa entered five minutes later, appearing freshly showered, his black hair damp against his head, a clean uniform shirt tucked into pants free of grass stains. Alessio shifted uncomfortably in his seat, the residue of the day's toil clinging to him.

"Not eating?" Alessio asked, as Hiromasa approached empty-handed.

"The pizza oven isn't ready. But don't wait for me. Eat."

"Only the elderly eat at this hour."

Hiromasa waved Alessio's comment away with a flick of his wrist and laughed. "Oh, Alessio, you're always so grumpy." He shook his head in a tsk-tsk motion. "You should enjoy life."

The door swung open before Alessio could respond, and Hiromasa turned anxiously to look. A young couple entered and waved. "Pardon me," he said to Alessio. Then, motioning to the pasta, "Go on, before it's cold."

Hiromasa approached the couple as if they were long-lost friends. He shook the man's hand and hugged the woman, smiling his toothy grin as they kissed cheeks. The couple nodded along as Hiromasa gestured helpfully in various directions.

Alessio didn't know which bothered him more: that Hiromasa seemed to make friends so easily, or that he acted as if he'd been here his whole life.

Alessio forked a crisped chit of pancetta and recalled their talk amongst the rose bushes. Hiromasa had sailed to Italy in 1615 from Nagasaki, a translator with the Keicho Embassy. He and the other Japanese Catholics aboard the ship were baptized in Mexico, then continued on, over land and sea, to the Vatican. Hiromasa remained in Italy to further his language studies, eventually learning English in a pontifical college in Rome.

Hiromasa described falling in love with a Florentine woman named Isabelle, his perfect companion. "I felt our souls melding as one, like the Chinese yin and yang of harmony," he said when telling the story. Alessio remembered himself nodding, innately knowing what was meant even if he himself didn't understand the exotic phrasing.

Now he stared as Hiromasa joked with the cook rolling the pizza dough. The Chinese reference was still lost on Alessio, but the sentiment had been echoing in his mind for weeks. As were the specifics concerning Hiromasa's appearance in modern Florence.

After much prodding, Hiromasa had also divulged how his relationship with Isabelle unraveled. Though he had considered the clergy's suppression of life's greatest joy to be unhealthy (a comment that made Alessio blush, recalling his own celibacy), he respected their rules prohibiting marriage despite having never been ordained. And when Isabelle forced him to choose between her and his future in the church—

"Well, here I am," Hiromasa had said, snapping a rose stem.

"Here you are," Alessio repeated, lost in the memory.

"Yes. Sorry to keep you waiting. Wine?" Hiromasa placed a carafe between them and slid a glass over.

Alessio looked from the wine to Hiromasa, not noticing his return. "You perplex me."

"Really? How so?"

Alessio leaned over his plate and whispered. "You've overcome an additional two hundred years of change and are more at home here than I will ever be."

"Must we really discuss this again?"

"How can you not be curious about our situation?"

"You're mistaken. I'm very curious. I spend my entire day asking questions, learning, studying." He scanned the room in a quick motion and lowered his voice. "Sometimes I sneak into the office to use the computer. There's a machine called the Internet—"

"That's not what I'm referring to," Alessio interrupted.

Hiromasa sighed. "Yes. I know." He took a sip of wine and licked his lips. "Perhaps it's my Buddhist upbringing that separates us. But, I have chosen to accept that which I cannot control."

Alessio shook his head and retreated to the state of palpable ennui he'd been cultivating for weeks.

"You must learn to accept this new reality for what it is," Hiromasa said.

Alessio rolled his eyes, thankful he hadn't burdened his earlier life with such well-intentioned friends. "What reality?" he challenged.

Hiromasa spread his arms across the table and smiled.

"This isn't real," Alessio countered, locking eyes with Hiromasa, finally deciding to see what Hiromasa thought of his theory. "We didn't one day wake up in the future. This is purgatory. We're dead— being here is our soul's punishment."

Hiromasa's eyes narrowed. "Is that what you believe?"

"Nothing here is real. This food," he said, inverting a forkful of pasta, "We eat out of habit, not because our bodies need nourishing. We work to earn shelter from cold, but not because we will freeze to death. We're already dead. We just don't remember dying."

"Then why do we not see the glow on others?" Hiromasa reached his hand across the table toward Alessio. His blue energy arced toward Alessio, as if his aura was trying to bond.

Alessio pulled his arm away.

"What is this sin you feel you're being punished for? I ask not out of curiosity, but because I am here with you. And for all that is holy, I cannot see a reason why God would penalize me."

Alessio ran a hand across his face. "It wasn't my fault," he said through clenched teeth. Alessio balled his fists and glared at Hiromasa, his eyes stinging with fury while his nails dug into the meat of his palms.

Hiromasa tipped his head and affected a look of kindness. "Perhaps confession could ease your burden?"

"You're no priest."

"No, but certain allowances can be made for our situation."

Alessio looked around the restaurant. The young couple had left and the cooks were either in the kitchen or outside smoking. They had the room to themselves. But why confess? He was being punished for another's sin—he had neither knowledge nor consent.

Hiromasa prodded gently, as if trying to coax a skittish squirrel out of doors. "Tell me."

Alessio took a deep breath as his reluctance crumbled. "She made a fool of me."

"Sylvia?"

He winced at the sound of her name. "Yes."

"Were you together long?"

"We met the prior year, in 1844. I traveled to Florence twice annually, to gather art and supplies for my gallery in Valetta. We endured the time apart knowing it made the reunion that much sweeter, but ..."

"Pre-marital relations are not uncommon, my friend."

Alessio shook his head. "That wasn't it. She wanted me to stay. Before I left in the spring."

"I'm sure she knew she would miss you."

"Perhaps, but I couldn't ignore my gallery. I had nine trunks filled with paintings. Early summer was my busiest season. I had to be there before the British boarded the steamers heading north."

"So you returned to Malta. And Sylvia?"

"She stayed in Florence. I promised I'd only be gone a few months, like usual. And I stayed true to my word. I returned in August and called for her." Alessio reached for the wine and drank deeply as he replayed the memory of their rendezvous, the emerald gown she wore, the scent of her violet perfume. "She accompanied me straight to the guest house—"

"The one where you awoke in February?"

Alessio stared into his lap as he searched for the words. "The time away made me realize how much I needed her in my life. I decided to propose to her, hoping she'd overcome her reluctance to move to Malta if she were my wife—"

"Did she say yes?"

Alessio looked up after several seconds, dizzy with anger. He could feel his chest growing hot, his nape on end. "We made love. Afterward, I was helping her fasten the hooks on her dress, when, with my hands on her hips, she reached into a pocket and slipped a ring onto her finger. 'I married,' was all she said."

Hiromasa exhaled a long, pitying breath.

"She pulled on her hat, collected her purse, and left me standing there. I could barely breathe, let alone speak. From the doorway, she hesitated and, without turning to face me, said, 'I still love you, Alessio Argento, but I will not come second to your gallery.'"

Tears blurred Alessio's vision, but he refused to acknowledge them. "Sylvia walked out of my life forever that afternoon, with no idea that in my attaché was a most splendid engagement ring."

Hiromasa slumped in his chair, solemnly shaking his head. "Your Sylvia and my Isabelle made the same choice."

"She made me an adulterer!" Alessio roared, slamming the table, causing the plates to jump and the carafe to wobble. "I would have never bedded a married woman."

Hiromasa recoiled, but kept quiet.

"And now I'm stuck here. Was it not enough to wake that morning having to experience the heartache anew? After decades alone, replaying every moment and decision that led to her rejection, now I'm stuck in this future world—a Florence of foreigners!"

"You must remember to trust in the Lord with all your heart—"

"God's will be damned," Alessio hissed. Guilt forced him to reflexively seek forgiveness for his shocking words, but he stopped halfway through making the sign of the cross. Piety was getting him nowhere.

"Perhaps there's a way back to our own times, although I must admit that I find the notion of voluntary time travel absurd." Hiromasa tented his hands and tapped his fingertips as he thought. "But it is curious that we are here together, in unison. There must be a reason for our shared reincarnation."

"Reincarnation? Time travel?" Alessio was disgusted. "As a Catholic, you ought to know better."

Hiromasa shrugged. "Do you?"

Alessio took a deep breath. *No.*

All he knew was that their lives had been upended. Through divine intervention or otherwise, they had been returned to the place where their respective loves had abandoned them. *But why together? And why now?* Alessio reached his arm across the table and watched the bluish glow concentrate near Hiromasa's fingertips. "What do you see?"

"I see the blue energy on your fingers trying to connect with me," Hiromasa said.

"As do I, but what is it?"

"The light behaves like quicksilver," Hiromasa said, squinting. When Alessio began to speak, Hiromasa raised his finger, silencing him. "Though I cannot see my own skin glowing, I envision the particles dividing and joining seamlessly like liquid mercury." Hiromasa dragged his spoon through a puddle of sauce on Alessio's plate for effect. "Do you know what I think?"

"I have not a guess."

"I can't help but wonder if we are seeing a split soul trying to reunite."

Alessio cocked his head and gave a puzzled look, believing he mustn't have heard him correctly.

"Think of the similarities between us. Our only difference is the time we lived. Perhaps we are connected not only through circumstance, but because our bodies served as vessels for the same soul."

"Are you suggesting you were reincarnated into … *me?*"

Hiromasa let loose with a raucous laugh. "I suppose I am. Though probably not directly. There may have been others between us. After all, you were born nearly two centuries later."

As interested as Alessio was in hearing Hiromasa's theories, the idea of his soul being shared with another man disgusted him. "Your blasphemous remarks aside, how could a soul inhabit two people simultaneously?"

"I don't know," Hiromasa said shrugging. "But perhaps that's why we've been brought back to Florence. Look at us. We're not old men. We were, once, but we've returned as young as we were when our beloveds abandoned us."

"You sound like a poet. Any more wine and you'll start quoting Plato."

Alessio delivered the quip by instinct, his quick tongue always ready with a sarcastic jab or obscure reference. But the allusion to *The Symposium* wasn't in vain. As soon as he said it, he realized the Greek philosopher's concept of soul mates may have been exactly what Hiromasa was hinting at.

Hiromasa stared from across the table, his face as wide and bright as the morning sun. "I hadn't considered it before, but our reunion, at the time and place where they—our soul mates—deserted us, cannot be coincidence."

Alessio mouthed the words, *soul mates*, feeling the pang of his broken heart return. "Do you believe Isabelle and Sylvia shared the same soul as well?"

"I do. Isabelle and I. You and Sylvia. I see no reason why their soul and ours couldn't have found one another countless times over the centuries."

"The world is a big place," Alessio said, unconvinced.

"But a magical one, would you agree? There could be millions— *billions!*—of souls in the air, passing time, waiting to join and split." Hiromasa again placed his hand near Alessio's "Look. Just like the sky above."

Alessio tipped his chin in the direction of a cook approaching with Hiromasa's pizza. He refilled their glasses with the house red as he waited for the man to leave. "But I still don't understand why we returned."

"If there are others sharing our soul, then perhaps something happened with those properly alive in this time, a trigger that brought us here."

The notion that Sylvia may have also returned invigorated Alessio. And even if she hadn't, Hiromasa's suggestion made some sense to him. Their souls might be present in this era, inhabiting a couple alive today. It was unlikely, a guess at the unexplainable, he knew, but comforting nonetheless. What if his return to Florence wasn't punishment, but a trial? What if this was a reward for his devotion. He had to find her: Sylvia or her modern vessel.

Would he recognize her?

He looked across to Hiromasa and watched the Japanese man eat his pizza. *Sylvia could be anywhere in the world*, he thought. *Anyone.*

But they were soul mates, as Hiromasa said. Their paths would have to cross.

With that thought came the kernel of a plan, one that would absolve the wrongs of the past—and in the process return him to his proper time.

"I'm going to find her."

"Who?"

"Sylvia, of course," Spittle flew from his lips as he spoke. "She's the key to my going home. We'll adjourn to the Florence of my memory. As one." Alessio vibrated with a purpose he hadn't felt since waking in February. He stood abruptly, knocking over his chair, and looked into Hiromasa's stunned face. "Thank you."

Chapter 21

THURSDAY, JUNE 18 — PARIS, FRANCE

They arrived in Paris sweaty and flustered. Edward came to understand that the pedals in and out of major cities were the most stressful, but Paris tested his nerves more than any other so far. He expected to get lost, or be squeezed for space alongside inattentive drivers, but not to have to detour around a sea of angry faces holding signs, shouting in protest of who knew what.

"Typical Paris," Kara said, once outside the hotel. "At least we didn't get caught up in one of the roller-blading mobs."

Edward gave her a puzzled look.

"It's a weekly thing. Thousands of Parisians roller skate through the city every Sunday. I borrowed skates from my host family last time, but I'm sure we can rent some."

"We should," Edward said, already anticipating the wackiness of it. Especially if it meant fewer hours spent in a museum.

He handed Kara his passport and detached the panniers while she ventured up the stairs of the skinny, nondescript hotel with the weather-beaten sign. It wasn't long before the bikes were locked to a pipe on a second floor terrace, safely confined within the center of the ring-shaped hotel. Together, he and Kara shuttled their bags up four flights of stairs, to a tiny box of a room with peeling paint and the aroma of disinfectant. A framed pastel of fruit, its coating of dust visible from the doorway, hung crookedly over the bed.

Hours later, Edward stared at the lone piece of thrift-store art, unable to sleep in the sticky stillness of the room. He kicked the sheets off in frustration long before midnight, cursing the hotel for its lack of air conditioning. At twenty past one, he yanked the curtains aside in hope of coaxing a nonexistent breeze. By two thirty-five, he was convinced the street lamp outside was pointed directly at his pillow. And by four o'clock, he resigned himself to staying awake.

The red digits of the alarm clock read 4:44. Edward turned the alarm off before it buzzed, thankful he wouldn't have to explain to Kara why it was set.

Kara's hand slid across his chest as he made to leave and Edward felt her inch closer, whispering in her sleep.

"I'm gonna get some fresh air," he said, and kissed her forehead, just above her eye mask. "Keep sleeping." Her lips curled into a peaceful smile as he slid out from under her arm.

He moved carefully, stepping over their panniers, trying not to bump anything as he groped for the phone hidden in the shadows. Edward padded down the stairs to the terrace, barefoot and shirtless, clad only in shorts, the Blackberry in hand. There, he stared at the phone, practicing his pronunciation of *bonsoir* as he waited anxiously to hit the call button. He hadn't spoken to Tom since Boston—his call last week went to voicemail—and Edward couldn't wait to hear Tom's reaction to them being in Paris.

"Thursday already, Edward?" Tom asked, picking up on the second ring without so much as a hello.

"*Bonsoir*, Tom."

"Huh?"

"Good evening," Edward said, rolling his eyes. "Though, it's already morning here in Paris."

For a moment, Edward was afraid the call dropped, but he soon heard Tom muttering and the rustling of paper. Tom mentioned a map on an earlier call and Edward now pictured him leaning over his desk, pen in hand, perhaps drawing a line, or stringing colored yarn between push pins.

He knew it was silly, but he wanted Tom's approval, or at least acknowledgment of how far he'd gone in two weeks. Edward risked a lot to get to France so quickly—they were nearly three months ahead of schedule by his estimate—and he deserved some recognition.

Instead, he heard only silence.

"Hello. You still there?"

"Yeah, yeah, hold on a second," Tom barked back, before continuing to talk under his breath. It sounded like he was calculating something.

Edward paced the terrace, enjoying the swishy sensation of the artificial grass carpeting on his feet. Above, the blackness of night absorbed a purplish hue.

"I figured you'd have taken my advice to heart and picked up the pace. Weren't you taking a ferry to Denmark last week? Why are you headed southwest?"

Edward's head lolled back on his neck as he searched the heavens for patience. *Because we can't just pedal across Russia, you horse's ass.* He took a deep, calming, breath. "Because we had to get south, for logistics."

Tom sighed. "You better not cost me my bet with Ron. How many miles are you averaging per day?"

Edward balled his fist and fake-jabbed at the brick wall "Sixty-three, sometimes seventy."

"And you're riding every day, right?" In the background, Edward heard what sounded like Tom tapping on a calculator.

Edward bit down on his lip. Of course they weren't. The pros don't even ride every day in the Tour de France. *What the hell is wrong with this guy?* "Mostly. We take a day off every week or so," Edward said, not about to tell him he intended to spend the better part of a week in Paris.

"I suppose your wife wants some time in Paris."

Edward dragged his finger along the frame of Kara's bike, absently wiping away a smear of dirt as he said yes.

"Well, while she's out sightseeing, I've got something you can work on."

"Okay," Edward said, unsure he wanted to hear what it was, wondering if he wanted any part of Tom at all.

As if I have a choice. Edward felt a pit forming in his stomach.

"You need to find office space for your team. Seattle's a hot market. Goddamn tech companies buying up every inch of real estate out there. You need to lock something in soon. October's just four months away."

He shrank to the ground, balancing atop the balls of his feet in a squat, with a hand on the outdoor carpet for balance. The strength to stand abandoned him. *Four months? Impossible.*

Tom continued talking, his words forming a disorienting fog Edward couldn't see through. "It'll take a few weeks to furnish and get the branding in place. So you got to decide soon. You also need to start interviewing candidates for your support staff."

Was he hearing this right? How was he supposed to find office space and conduct a candidate search from halfway around the world—while still trying to bicycle seventy miles a day? The absurdity of Tom's request snapped Edward out of his stupor, jolting him like a speed bump struck during a mountain descent.

"That's impossible. I'm hardly ever near an internet connection, not to mention the time zones—"

"You'll figure it out."

"I don't see how. Can't someone in your office help with the hiring?"

"Why? They'll be *your* employees, not mine."

Edward's eyes went wide. *My employees?* Did Tom expect their pay to come out of Edward's salary too? It sounded like it. How could he have been so stupid not to get the details in writing? He pumped his fist in a calming motion. *Deal with it later. I don't even have an office yet.*

"Fine, then what about the office space? Can't your assistant help with that?"

"I've got more than enough to keep my team busy. You've yet to bring in one dollar for this company. Don't shunt your responsibilities off to my staff."

"No, it's just—"

"I've warned you about excuses, Ed. I'm starting to think you're more trouble than you're worth."

The feeling's mutual.

"I'll have my gal here in Minneapolis text you a link to our hiring protocols. She'll coordinate getting the lease signed. Just send her the details once you pick a site."

"Uh-huh." Edward's head swam as one obstacle after another crashed atop him, waves of responsibility dragging him under, choking his breath. He'd never felt more overwhelmed in his life.

"Another thing. These calls are too late for me. Call me at nine o'clock from now on. That'll be better for the both of us."

"Well, actually, that would mean—"

"And every other week is fine, okay? Great. Two Thursdays from now at nine. *Au revoir,*" he said, chuckling. In that moment, Edward envisioned Ron Madsen laughing alongside Tom, clinking glasses, celebrating Edward's struggle.

The phone fell silent as Edward grasped his stomach, feeling for the knife he'd surely been stabbed with. Instead, he felt only nausea, and the suffocating onset of panic-laced discomfort. He'd dreamed of one day setting up his own office, hiring his own staff. But here? Now?

He bound up the stairs three at a time, racing to reach the bathroom before he vomited, dashing to hide the phone before Kara woke, clinging to an unraveling strand of hope.

Edward rinsed his mouth in the sink and stared at the mirror. He'd never been one of those people who paid attention to the subtle changes in another's complexion, but he knew his own face well. Despite his cyclist's tan, it looked several shades paler than healthy.

He replayed the phone call in his mind, the knot in his stomach cinching tighter with every word, eventually wringing himself empty once again. He flushed the toilet and turned the faucet to full blast, but no amount of cold splashes could allay his dread.

There was a light tap on the door. "Is everything okay?"

Edward jumped at the sound. "Just a second," he called back, his eyes darting to the phone atop the sink. He searched the indecorous bathroom, feeling like a prisoner in possession of contraband, but it was no use. He stashed the phone in his shorts pocket, dried his hands, and opened the door.

Kara greeted him with a pitying look. "Aww, you look awful."

He clutched his stomach and winced as he stepped past her, mindful of the phone in his pocket and moving swiftly to avoid a conciliatory hug.

"Maybe something you ate?" she asked.

He shrugged, unsure how much to reveal. Or how much to lie. "We both had the shawarma last night. You're okay, right?"

Kara nodded and looked at him, her face a wealth of concern. She stepped into the bathroom and shut the door. Edward quick-stepped to his pannier and buried the phone in the stuff sack containing his winter gloves and hat.

He made sure to be in bed, the sheet pulled to his neck, when Kara returned. She felt his head. "You're not warm."

"It's my stomach. Couldn't sleep at all last night."

Kara sat down next to Edward on the bed. "Is there anything I can do to help?"

He doubted it. "It's probably stress. I'm sure I'll feel better this afternoon."

She scooted closer and looked surprised. "What's got you worried?"

Edward hesitated as his heart raced. Everything he told her was true. He was stressed. And he'd been sick and felt he might vomit again any moment.

What can I say? She's too good to me. I can't lie.

But he had to. And she was in the nurturing mood. "My knee," he said.

"Really? You should have told me. Since when?"

He rolled on his side to face her and grimaced, for her benefit. "We're cycling around the world. I'm not going to make a big deal out of every little ache and pain." If she noticed him avoiding her question, she didn't say anything.

"No, but if it's causing you stress—"

"I can ride, but the mountains have me worried."

Kara angled her head, whether with sympathy or suspicion, he couldn't tell.

Edward took a deep breath, finding the nerve to plant the seed. "I don't know how I'm going to get through the Pyrenees if it doesn't get better soon."

She stroked his head, running her fingers through his hair gently. "Don't worry about that now. Just get some rest."

He nodded.

"We'll think of something," she added, undoubtedly aware he couldn't do anything *but* worry about it.

Kara shifted to lie next to him. Outside, the purple pre-dawn light gave way to a frail blue. Songbirds were in full throat, but no match for the sound of the water gurgling through the pipes behind their head. Paris was starting to wake.

"I don't think I'm up for sightseeing today," Edward said.

"That's fine. Maybe you'll feel better tonight."

He doubted it. "What about you?"

"Well … Since I'm awake, I'll probably head up the hill to Sacre-Coeur and grab breakfast," she said, shrugging. "Probably just wander the city."

"Save the Eiffel Tower for me, okay?"

"Of course," she said, patting his hand. Kara looked around the room, disapprovingly. "It's too bad we don't have a phone or a laptop you can occupy yourself with. That TV looks older than us." Near the door, a tube television, yellowed with age, sat askew atop a mini fridge.

"I'm sure I'll find something to do," he said, noticing for the first time, the green lights of a Wi-Fi router on the ceiling above the door.

Edward's mind raced at full gallop by the time Kara left. For as much as he tried to calm his nerves—and his stomach—he couldn't swim free of the day's current, its undertow dragging him to oblivion. An hour earlier, he couldn't wait to update Tom, so certain he was of finally receiving his due praise. Now he was in bed, sick with anxiety, and pretending to be injured.

Being idle only made his problems worse. Tom's latest demands were a call to action, to advance or surrender. And with a full day at his disposal (Kara said she'd be back by dinner), he had a perfect opportunity to get online and see what he was up against.

He pulled on a pair of pants and a short-sleeved shirt and went in search of food and the hotel's internet password. He descended two flights of stairs before realizing he was limping. Whether a trick of the mind or a sign that he'd become too adept at lying, he didn't know, but he hated himself for it. He gripped the iron banister, wanting to drive his knee into it, to give himself something worth limping about, he thought, recalling his father's echo. But he paused, letting the adrenaline of his shame dissipate.

The receptionist directed Edward across the street to a corner café, where he ordered a *petit déjeuner* consisting of a croissant and espresso. He slid another euro coin on the counter and ordered a second breakfast, knowing Kara would never have allowed such a gluttonous faux pas.

The caffeine and carbs wouldn't help settle his stomach, but he felt his mental fog lifting, allowing him to focus. Back in the hotel room, with the door locked and the chain drawn, he retrieved the mobile phone and a notepad and flopped onto the bed.

A certain element of him was excited to have a task, a sense of purpose for the day, but he didn't know where to begin. He'd never hired anyone before, let alone staffed a department. He decided it best to start with the office space. After all, prospective employees would want to know where they'd be working.

His search turned up a number of options, but mostly for shared desks, business incubators, and the types of coworking places geared more toward creatives like Kara. He wanted a proper office, with a locking door, and bookcases, and a wall where he could hang his diploma.

An office like he had, one that looked the part.

Edward continued his search, wading through an endless stream of listings. The options overwhelmed him, the descriptions containing more questions than details. How many desks would he need? Open floorplan or private offices? What were his conference room demands? "How the hell should I know?"

Every link bragged about the views, each outdoing the next with photos showing off the Space Needle, the house boats on Lake Union, and Mt. Rainier.

He scrolled through the assorted hometown scenery, his mind wandering from the search for office space to the more pleasant quest for a place to live once he won the job.

A shadow flew across the wall, distracting him from the Blackberry's screen. Even in the dim light, the room was a dump. A rat trap he endured to maintain the illusion of them still being on a budget. Kara never complained, but he suspected she hated it. How could she not?

"She won't have to put up with it much longer," he mumbled to himself, knowing they'd soon be home.

October was only four months away.

I can't win.

Edward felt his pulse accelerate as visions of a calendar flashed in his mind's eye. He closed the browser and opened Google Maps. He stumbled as he typed, his fingers feeling as if they'd been slept on. Finally, a line stretched over eight-hundred miles from Paris to Madrid. He zoomed out as his breathing intensified. Another four-hundred miles to Barcelona. Three weeks at a minimum with no days off.

"That'd leave us three months," he whispered. Three months to get from Spain, across Asia, to Seattle?

Kara wants to bike through Morocco next.

Edward flicked the trackball and sent Europe zipping across the screen. He flicked it again to Italy. Another flick landed in Turkey. Again. Uzbekistan. Again. China. And China once more on the next flick.

He panted, as if his breathing sought to match his ever-quickening pulse. His numb fingers had gone slippery with sweat by the time he scrolled to the blue of the Pacific. Flick. Blue. More blue. Blue again. His body shook erratically, his heart and lungs racing side by side down the backstretch to …

Where the fuck is America?

Edward threw the phone aside and leaped from the bed. Bad idea. The dingy linoleum floor seemed to wobble beneath him. Bird shadows swooped across the room, circling him, closing in, landing atop his chest, squeezing out his breath, boiling his blood.

Four months?

He crawled back onto the bed, clawing for the phone. He pulled the sheet over his body as he curled himself in a ball, shivering, hyperventilating, and drenched in sweat. Clutching the phone between his hands, Edward squeezed his eyes shut with all his strength, and having never experienced anything like this before, he began counting. "One Mississippi, two Mississippi, three Mississippi …"

By the time he reached fifteen, his breathing had grown from sips to gulps. By twenty, he felt well enough to sit up.

Edward went to the bathroom, filled the sink with cold water, and plunged his face into it. The stinging chill delivered the smack he needed—dread lingered, but he no longer felt certain to implode. When he returned to the bedroom, he noticed the phone's screen was centered on Paris. The combination of buttons he'd mashed in his fit of terror somehow landed a pin on the Gare de Lyon train station.

The name sounded familiar. He zoomed out and, sure enough, the city of Lyon laid to the southeast, not far from Switzerland, the Alps, and the Italian border. He tapped a few keys and stared as a map of the Eurail train network filled the screen with colored lines radiating like spokes on a bicycle wheel. One led south through Geneva to Milan, and down the length of Italy.

The door bumped against the chain with a thud around noon. "Ed, you awake? Open up, it's me."

Shit, she's early.

Edward cinched the straps on his duffel bag and added it to the pile. He limped to the door, his phantom injury returning.

It will be okay. She'll understand.

Kara leaned forward to give him a kiss, then hesitated, holding him by the shoulders as her eyes grew with concern. A shopping bag hit the floor, but it sounded miles away.

"You're as pale as a ghost. Are you still sick?"

He didn't know. His skin itched with nervous pinpricks, anticipating the conversation to come.

"And you're soaked. Look at your hair. You look like you've run a marathon," Kara said, stroking his head.

He shied from her touch and ran his hand across his face. It glistened, slicked with sweat. Trembling.

"You're panting. Let's get you in bed."

His breathing was the only sound in the room. Fast, nervous breaths, his nostrils flaring wide while his chest heaved like a bellows. "I was packing," he confessed, unblocking her view.

Kara's eyes flashed to the bed, where their panniers and duffel bags sat, freshly cleaned, packed, and arranged in identical piles. "What's going on? Do we have to change rooms?"

"Sort of." Then, in a whisper, he said, "To Madrid."

"What?" she demanded, grabbing him, turning him to face her.

"An overnight train to Madrid."

"We just got to Paris last night!"

Edward shuffled his feet as the floor seemed to undulate beneath him. He placed his hand against the wall for balance. "We need to keep moving," he said between breaths. He clamped his eyes shut, wishing the panic away. "To see the art," he added, struggling to explain his reasoning, his thoughts swirling like finger paint.

"You're not making any sense."

Through the din of the attack, he imagined telling Tom to go to hell. Telling him that no job was worth the strain he was putting on his marriage—or his health—but he couldn't. The Edward Vaughan standing in the decrepit Parisian hotel wasn't that brave.

He almost called it off a few hours earlier, before he bought the train tickets. Before he realized he could hire an assistant to set up the office and perform the candidate search. All he had to do was make one more leap ahead. Just a train ride. He had four months. It was still possible.

He hated how each successive lie came easier. Even to himself.

"You promised no more sudden changes."

He looked away.

"Dammit, Ed, I'm sick of this," she shouted, shoving the pile of panniers onto the floor. She stared at the tangle of bed sheets, her breathing as intense as when pedaling a mountain pass. "What about the Eiffel Tower?"

"The train leaves at seven."

Kara felt the train slowing, the subtle rhythm of the steel wheels clicking and clacking along the rails had changed from a tango to a waltz. She stretched her neck and looked at her watch. It was nearly five in the morning. *Ten hours to get to Barcelona?* It seemed preposterously slow. *No wonder we had the berth to ourselves.*

Edward sat across from her, the upper bunk on his side of the *couchette* flipped out of the way. He bit his fingernails as his bloodshot eyes studied the tickets. Presumably, to see what time they transferred for Madrid.

Aboard the train, Kara read while Edward played Solitaire. Their picnic dinner of baguette, ham, and Brie was consumed in awkward silence, the macarons and wine untouched. And now the silence continued as Kara wondered why he avoided her, pretending to be distracted by the tickets, when she felt him staring at her moments ago.

Kara reached to open the curtains when the gargled static of the intercom broke the tension. The voice, speaking in French, instructed the passengers to prepare to disembark. They'd be arriving in *Milano* shortly.

Milan?

Before she could question her own ears, the speaker crackled to life again. A different voice now spoke—in unmistakable Italian. And the gist was clear. They were on the wrong train.

Kara jumped from the bunk, catapulted into action. "Did you hear that? We ended up in Italy."

Whatever response she was hoping for failed to arise. Edward's gaze didn't shift, he didn't blink. He only stared at the papers in his hand, saying nothing as his legs bounced nervously on his toes.

With every bump of the train, Kara's suspicion hardened, arming her tone with an edge. "I'm talking to you, Ed. How the hell did we end up in Milan?"

He glanced briefly at her then looked away, as if searching for an excuse in the folds of the curtains.

"Let me see those." Kara snatched the tickets from his hand. Milan to Florence, leaving in twenty minutes. "Florence! Why Florence?"

"It was an accident," he said, his voice soft. "I don't know what happened. I must have bought tickets for Milan by mistake."

"That doesn't even make sense. The tickets are for Florence. See," she said, thrusting them at him. "It says, *Firenze!*"

"I bought them last night from an attendant. Once I realized we were headed to Italy."

Kara spun her back to him and grabbed the stuffed Sasquatch she used as a pillow. She twisted it, winding its fluffy spine, wanting to rip it in two.

"I thought you'd be excited. Isn't Florence the cradle of the Renaissance? There's probably dozens of Picassos there."

She buried her mouth in the plush animal to muffle her scream. *The cradle of the Renaissance? Picasso?* She could almost forgive him for thinking they had anything to do with one another—though it would certainly be nice for him to have some elementary knowledge about her interests—but it was as if he'd never listened to a thing she said. Kara hated the Renaissance period. Ever since her high school art history class. "Nothing but Bible paintings and portraits of rich dead guys," she'd said at least a thousand times.

Kara felt his hand on her shoulder. "Babe, I'm sorry. I should have woken you. Heck, I should have had you buy the tickets in the first place. The damn website was in French—"

"I'm sure there was an English version," she seethed, bristling under his touch.

"I know. I panicked." He sighed. "There's no excuse, but when I saw we were headed to Italy, I bought us tickets for the first place that came to mind."

She wheeled on him, kicking aside his red duffel bag. Could he really be that stupid? That clueless? "Why not just ask for tickets to Spain, or back to Paris? Or, I don't know," she said in her most sarcastic tone, her head shaking in faux astonishment, "maybe ask where *I* want to go. Has it ever occurred to you that I might like a say?"

The train lurched to a stop as the conductor's voice intervened. "*Benvenuti a Milano Centrale,*" he said, like a referee separating fighters at the bell.

"We've got to hurry to get the bikes," Edward said. "The train leaves in twenty minutes."

"How convenient," she said through gritted teeth. She then realized she could refuse to go, that she could buy a one-way ticket to Madrid for herself. A tempting thought, but a trigger she wasn't ready to pull. Kara shot Edward her most incensed look, a promise that this discussion was far from over, then turned and thrust the Sasquatch and her copy of *The Sun Also Rises* into her duffel. "So much for the bullfights."

An hour later, Kara stood alone at the end of the passenger car, staring out the vestibule window, watching the northern Italian countryside slip past at high speed. In the light of day, with the stress of changing trains behind her—not to mention her first espresso kicking in—the pieces of the puzzle started to fit together.

The hypnotic motion of the train awarded Kara the clarity and time to reflect back to Paris. They were in front of the train to Barcelona, she was sure of it. Then, suddenly, Edward came running and asked if she heard the announcement. "They changed the platform," he said. Kara hadn't heard anything, but didn't give it a second thought. There was no time. Only now, in hindsight, did she realize that they were the only passengers rushing to a different platform.

And once aboard, Edward effectively quarantined her throughout the night, gently discouraging any wandering, diverting her from the dining car, and even shadowing her to the restroom. She thought it odd, a little protective, perhaps. Or just funny timing between the two of them. But now she wondered if it was his way of preventing her from discovering the truth.

Would he really do that?

She didn't want to believe it. Kara picked absently at a sticker on the vestibule's bare metal wall, wondering if she ever had a reason to suspect Edward of lying.

But if Milan was a mistake, he would have woken her. And he would have laughed, or been angry. He wouldn't have hidden it. That wasn't like him at all. And he certainly wouldn't have gone in search of an attendant to buy tickets from.

So what happened?

The door opened, releasing a cacophony of wind and rumble as someone passed between the cars. Stepping out of the way, Kara noticed the rail operator's logo on the door and stiffened with fury as the truth hit her at once. They changed train companies in Milan. *There's no way the attendant could have sold him those tickets!*

"My husband lied to me." Kara's eyes watered as a pit formed inside her, like a black hole, expanding, swallowing everything she thought she knew about her marriage.

Her mind jumped to the previous morning, when she woke to the sound of Edward vomiting. He was worried, he said—about his knee. But just the prior night, while out getting dinner, she saw him running up and down the stairs and leaping to grab tree branches. She thought of the rush at the Paris train station, after the so-called announcement. Edward ran, lugging the two bagged-up bicycles without any trace of a limp.

"He was faking it," she said, whispering his lie to herself. He faked being hurt to leave Paris. But why?

Kara braced herself against the cold, metallic wall as she stared out the window, her vision blurred. She hadn't just been lied to; she'd been played a fool. He'd been hijacking the trip for months, ever since Canada. Maybe earlier.

They should have still been at Cape Cod. Instead, they were almost clear across Europe, with little hope of going back.

Outside the window, the Tuscan countryside rolled by, all hills and valleys she wouldn't pedal, rivers she'd never dip her toes in. In the silhouettes of hilltop towns she saw the centuries-old alleys she wouldn't stroll, the photos she'd never take. For months Kara had dreamed of the magic of the road, the countless postcard moments she'd share with Edward. And now it was over. Without ever happening. Almost from the start, the trip had been nothing like she imagined. Every day a test of endurance, a measure of their ability to cover miles and find water, food, and a safe place to spend the night. Ride, sleep, repeat.

Kara sobbed, feeling more isolated than ever before. Halfway around the world, on a runaway journey, with a man who thinks her a fool. Worse, he didn't care about her dreams.

I should leave him, she thought, recalling the legal papers she had drawn up. Only a plane ride away. But this was her trip. She wasn't about to end it early.

The train slowed as a sign marking the border of *Firenze* passed. In the distance, the rust-colored tile of the cathedral's cupola came into view.

Behind her, the door slid open once more. This time, a familiar voice spoke to her. "There you are. I was wondering if you got locked in the toilet." She felt Edward's arm slither around her waist, as if everything was fine between them.

Kara spun from his grasp and made herself small against the wall. "Don't touch me."

"Whoa, what's going on?" He looked genuinely surprised.

"You've been lying to me for months. Admit it."

"What? No, that's not—"

"Say it!" She glared at him, challenging him to test her fury, to utter a single syllable that didn't explain his actions. Her mouth opened in silent rage, ready to bite.

Edward's lips quivered, but he held quiet.

"I can barely stand to look at you," she spat, shoving past him as the train nosed into the shadows of the Florence station.

Alessio stood and stretched his back, wiping the sweat from his brow as he did. He took a swig from the water bottle he carried ever since the heat of summer descended upon the Arno Valley. The scorching temperatures were unlike anything he had endured back home, where the sea breeze would funnel up the stairs and alleys of Valetta, providing relief from the heat radiating off the city walls.

He bent to scoop a pile of weeds for the bin and noticed two bicycles leaning against the campground office. These were unlike any bicycles he'd yet seen, loaded as they were with clever luggage. Red and yellow pouches hung alongside the wheels like saddlebags. Alessio pulled his hair back, tying it with a blue rubber loop that had come wrapped around a bundle of asparagus, as he pondered the bikes, sensing something special about them, the way someone can sense an approaching storm.

"I'd forgotten how hot summers could be in Florence," Hiromasa said, a smile in his voice.

Alessio grunted, not having seen him approach. Every day Hiromasa came calling for him, armed with another mundane pleasantry. Alessio rolled his eyes and bore the routine, grateful for the distraction nonetheless.

"Have you seen those?" Alessio asked, pointing.

Hiromasa followed his gaze and whistled, clearly impressed.

"Are they Gypsies?"

Hiromasa laughed. "Perhaps, in their own way. They're bicycle tourists. The campground has special rates for them. They're probably German or Dutch."

"What would make them travel that way, instead of by motor?"

Hiromasa began to answer, but when his mouth opened, the only sound was a gasp.

Alessio turned from Hiromasa in time to see a man exiting the office. Even from this distance, he could see the man's legs and arms glowed blue. Just like he and Hiromasa had seen on each other. "Do you—"

"Yes. Absolutely," Hiromasa confirmed, stepping to Alessio's side. From atop a small rise in the path they watched as the man leaned on the bike, his back to them.

A woman exited moments later and walked briskly toward the yellow bags. Alessio watched as the man reached for her hand, only to see her pull it free and continue on. She yanked her bicycle away from the wall and started up the path, pushing it straight toward them while the man lagged behind, his head hanging.

She didn't look in their direction. But Alessio could tell by their posture—both hers and the man's—that something had soured between them. And just as Alessio began to wonder what it could be, she raised her head and looked his way.

Alessio's heart leapt into his throat as the tremor in his right hand returned, this time matched by a nervous shaking in his legs. All over his body, he felt his nerves firing, as if the fibers of the aura he wore— the one only Hiromasa could see—were now alive and dancing, celebrating to a song only she could sing.

Sylvia?

Beside him, he heard Hiromasa gasp again.

He senses it too. For as much as Alessio wanted to sneak a glance at Hiromasa, to see if his glow had intensified, he couldn't bear to take his eyes from her.

The man pushed his bike after her, yelling. "Kara! Wait up!"

Kara.

She didn't slow. She, this *Kara*, pushed her bike with all her might, grumbling as she did. She approached, near enough to see her scowl.

Kara looked right at Alessio, locking eyes with him for the briefest moment, but it was all he needed. His search was over. It wasn't the body of the woman who spurned him for another man and tricked him into adultery. No, that woman was not here. But his heart—his soul—could see what his eyes could not.

He found his pathway home.

PART THREE

Chapter 22

FRIDAY, JUNE 19 — FLORENCE, ITALY

Edward fed the poles through the tent's nylon sleeves, a sliding swish of aluminum the only noise. A wall of hedges hemmed in the campsite and green netting hung overhead, casting the site in midday shade. Kara paced beyond the collapsed tent, gnawing on her anger, spitting silent invectives. His wish for quick forgiveness evaporated, leaving him as brittle and mute as the wilted azalea blossoms littering the ground.

He dreaded having to set up the tent alone. While technically possible, it was infinitely easier when they did it together. So he waited, crouched in the corner, hoping she'd slot the poles into their pockets on the other side. An awkward minute passed before Kara eventually helped, their well-rehearsed routine allowing her to continue ignoring him. She then gathered the bedding from her duffel bag, tossed Edward's items at the bushes, and set to laying out her own.

Weren't they still a team? Edward tried to imagine being so mad that he'd refuse to cook her dinner or fix her bike, but the betrayal that would require was too painful to consider.

He picked up the bag containing his air mattress and knelt beside her in the sleeping area. Kara yanked the bag from his hand as he tugged on the drawcord. "I'll do it," she snapped.

"I don't mind."

"I said I'll do it." She stared at him without blinking, the same way she dared him on the train.

He yielded—again—and backed away, reluctantly.

Kara exited the tent several minutes later carrying a pannier. Edward looked up from wiping down his bike, an unnecessary task he busied himself with, waiting for her to speak to him. She scanned the area with disgust then slammed the bag in the dirt. "And not even any Goddamn picnic tables."

Edward bit his lip and buried his face in the rag, concealing a titter. He'd been complaining about the conspicuous lack of picnic tables since they arrived in Europe. And every time he did, Kara would tell him to get over it, adapt, and think like a European. Whatever that meant.

If she noticed his reaction, she didn't acknowledge it. Instead, Kara tucked a toiletry bag under her arm, rolled a change of clothes within her towel, and left for the showers, tension trailing in her wake.

He wanted to rush after her, but what could he say? Whenever he imagined trying to apologize, he only heard her words piercing him anew, buckling his knees. *Don't touch me.* He knew what he should do. What he should have done back at Heathrow. Or earlier.

Kara's words played on a loop in his mind as he retrieved his toolkit and flipped her bike upside down. She wasn't only mad about Madrid, he knew, removing the rear wheel. He'd been lying for months.

"It's over," he said, talking to her bike. "I blew it." Edward wondered how he could begin to repair the damage, without pushing her further away. To tell her about the contest meant admitting a litany of lies and deception. But to not tell her … "She's too smart for that."

Edward's mind drifted ahead, to a future home, as he removed her worn brake pads from the caliper. What would he do for money?

"Dammit," he said, pinching his finger in the needle-nose pliers. On the third try, he got the new pads in place, and he soon had the wheel spinning freely and the brake rotor perfectly centered. He ran the chain through a rag, wiping away a week of grit. Edward continued tinkering on her bike, soothing his nerves with each turn of a hex wrench, fine-tuning his explanation to Kara.

He hoped the hot shower had managed to be as therapeutic for Kara as the bicycle maintenance was for him. But if not, at least her bike would be in great shape for ... wherever she wanted to go, he thought, daring to hope it'd be with him.

Kara returned as Edward locked her bike to a lamppost. She looked gorgeous in a dress he hadn't seen before, white with red and yellow flowers falling into a pile at the hem. Her hair was combed back and he needn't get close to smell her perfume. A summer-sweet scent he wasn't familiar with. Her eyes darted toward him (or was it her bike?) but she didn't break stride. She disappeared into the tent momentarily, then emerged with her camera and purse.

"You look really nice," he said, but she didn't acknowledge him.

Edward watched her nervously. He couldn't take it any longer, his earlier calm straining under the heft of her silence. He swallowed the lump in his throat. "I was thinking of getting some lunch."

"Not hungry."

"I don't mind waiting."

Kara stopped in her tracks, her back to Edward, her hands on her hips. "If you're hungry eat, if not, don't. Just leave me alone."

"Kara." He spoke her name as if it was the last word he'd ever say.

She spun to face him. "You want to have lunch and go sightseeing, Ed? Is that it? You want to act like everything's fine? We're in Florence!" Kara was practically vibrating with anger, her fists clenched at her side. "Did you forget you lied to me?"

Edward inched toward her, yearning to be closer. "It was an accident," he said, shaking his head, so used to lying that he couldn't stop himself, even now. *What difference does it make, she already knows.*

Kara stomped her foot and took a deep breath. "How dumb do you think I am? You expect me to believe the attendant sold you tickets in the middle of the night for seats on another company's train?" The pain of his deception wept from her every pore.

"Kara, I'm ..."

"You tricked me," she shouted, pushing him with both hands in the chest. "I can't believe you would do this to me."

Edward bothered the rag in his hands, searching for the words like an actor trying to remember lines from an unwritten script. His chest tightened, choking him from the insides, suffocating his thoughts, his voice, his breath.

"So, that's it? You've got nothing to say?"

The words were there, but refused to be spoken. He wanted to come clean about everything, to swear his love, and tell her they'd head to Madrid in the morning, but he couldn't. Not yet. She was too angry to hear how deep he dug his hole.

Kara wiped her eyes in quick motions, practically slapping at her face as she sniffled. "When you're ready to tell me what's going on, come find me. Otherwise, leave me alone." She thrust an arm through her purse strap and stormed off without another word.

"Be careful," he whispered.

Edward watched her disappear beyond the campground gate. He ran his hand through his hair and sighed. As his gaze retreated along the path she walked, he realized he wasn't the only one watching her go. A landscaper dressed in a blue and khaki campground uniform was looking in Kara's direction from up the path. Edward was too distraught to care that they made a scene, or that someone heard Kara shout his list of crimes.

But then Edward noticed something odd. He thought it could be the shadows or a trick of his tear-stricken eyes, but the man appeared to glow. It was a faint blue, similar to what he saw on the French-Canadian with the canoe. Though at the time, he convinced himself it was only an illusion of campfire smoke.

He rubbed his eyes and blinked, yet the effect didn't fade. Edward stared, mesmerized by what he saw, as the man set down his rake, brushed his hands on his pants, and walked off toward town.

Kara descended the hill from the campground toward the Arno River, where tourists choked the streets, flowing toward the Pitti Palace in segregated flocks. Sunburned Americans, Europeans, and Chinese marched past, oblivious of anyone not in their group. Twice, her feet were stepped upon. Not once did she receive an apology.

She skirted the crowd to Ponte Vecchio, the city's famed medieval bridge where centuries-old jewelry shops lined its sides in a jumble of two-story squares and taller rectangles bulging outward over the river. The tawny geometry reminded her of Picasso's disjointed *Girl with Mandolin*, an unwelcome comparison she pushed from her mind.

The bulwark of stores gave way to a plaza in the center of the bridge. Kara threaded the crowd and paused to take in the upstream view.

The Arno's banks were lined with ochre-colored apartment buildings, shining like gold in the sun as the water twinkled below. It was a view unlike any she'd seen in her travels, yet her camera remained tucked away. Kara leaned against the ancient stone rail, resting her chin atop her hands, unsure what to do, where to go.

Her wrists smelled of the perfume she bought in Paris, reminding her of the night she had planned for her and Edward, and the dress she bought to celebrate reaching the City of Light—a dress she now wore, alone. She sighed, knowing there'd be no sunset atop the Eiffel Tower or gourmet meals on Place Dauphine. Gazing downward, her chest heaving for what should have been, she rubbed the dress's crimson floral pattern between her fingers, as if doing so could dull its cheerfulness.

Amongst the crowd surging around her, Kara felt someone looking at her, as if waiting to approach. It was probably Edward, she thought, knowing how incapable he was of giving her space when she wanted it most. She turned to tell him to leave her alone, only to see a couple pushing a pair of fully loaded touring bicycles toward her.

"*Mi scusi,*" the woman said, holding out her phone. "Photo, *per favore?*" Her voice cracked with the hesitation of one who knows only a dozen words of the local language. Kara knew the feeling well.

"Sure," she said, nodding. Kara made room for them to pose, then raised the smartphone. On the screen stood a fifty-something couple with their arms around one another, their smiles as broad as Ponte Vecchio's overhead arches. Their bikes leaned against them, the panniers decorated with stickers of international flags.

Kara stared at the screen, struggling to tap the button, her fingers refusing to give what should have been hers. It was the photo of her dreams, the type she'd imagined hanging over their bed, or using as Christmas cards, or getting printed on a coffee mug. She and Edward had been traveling for more than three months, but never posed like this. Not once did they ask someone to take their picture.

She tapped the button. Hard. The blurry image necessitated a do-over, forcing her to linger, to focus.

The screen blinked, searing the image of the couple in her mind. *Will we even be together in twenty years? Ten?* Kara squeezed her eyes shut and thrust the phone at the woman. She took off across the bridge, pushing and shoving her way through the throng, trying to outrun her envy.

Kara fled into the historic quarter of Florence, not slowing until the crowd was behind her. Side streets named after a who's who of saints and apostles beckoned with quaint storefronts and immaculate herringbone brickwork. But her mood favored the shattered pavement of the main road, her feet at home on the warts of its lumpy asphalt patches. She proceeded, flanked by graffitied shutters, windows encased in rusted burglar bars, and the orange netting of so much unfinished construction. And she wore the ugliness like a shawl.

Blocks later, in no mood to sightsee and craving a snack, Kara stepped inside a *gelateria*. *"Bonjour,"* she said upon entering.

"Ciao," the clerk said pointedly, as if tired of dealing with tourists who didn't speak Italian.

Kara blushed, remembering she was no longer in France. "Sorry. *Ciao*, of course."

"Ah, English," he said. "What would you like?"

Two dozen varieties of gelato provided a palette of colors piled high in oblong stainless steel bins, their flavors labeled in Italian. Normally, she'd be happy to be somewhere without bilingual menus, evidence it wasn't just a place for tourists. But now? She wanted familiar. And rows of unpronounceable flavors and a balding, forty-something man in a pinstriped vest and bow tie was anything but typical for an ice cream shop.

Where's the Chunky Monkey when you need it?

"Uhh …" she said, hesitating, pointing from one bin to the next, guessing at the translation of *stracciatella, amarena,* and *croccantino* as the colors and foreign words blurred in a kaleidoscope of thoughts and emotions. Kara felt herself quailing under the pressure. Not just of choosing a flavor, but of the suddenness of swapping countries, languages, and customs—and navigating it alone.

Behind the counter, the clerk held his ice cream scoop in a manner that betrayed his impatience. Kara wanted only to avoid seeming ignorant. "I'll have the pistachio," she said, an impulsive selection.

"Mi scusi, but that's not a wise choice." The voice, masculine and confident, came from behind her. Kara startled, not realizing someone had entered the store.

She turned, facing a man with wavy black hair, an aquiline nose, and sharp jaw. His clean-shaven face had the complexion of someone who spent a good deal of time outdoors. His broad chest and muscular arms reinforced the notion. Yet despite this—and the grass stains on his khaki pants—she sensed an air of refinement.

"Why is that?" she asked, deciding to humor him.

"Look at the color. It is false. The color of good pistachio," he said, halving its syllables as he spoke, pronouncing the word *pi-stash,* "should be a marriage, as much the tan of the shell as the green of the nut."

Kara asked the clerk if this was true.

He shrugged, turning up his hands and bobbing his head, like a man not wanting to lie, but unwilling to defend his employer's product. Kara turned back to the pistachio expert. "So, which flavor should I get?"

"The pistachio is the barometer. If it's no good, you leave. All of Italy knows this." He moved to the door, and pushed it open with one hand. "Come with me."

Kara took a step back and raised her hands, laughing in a you-got-to-be-kidding-me kind of way.

She turned to the clerk. "Two scoops of chocolate," she said, pointing at the bin marked *cioccolato.* "On a waffle cone." Watching him scoop the gelato, Kara noticed Mr. Pistachio's blue shirt reflecting back at her from the glass case. She took a half step away, checking the reflection for a glimpse of his face, to gauge what interested him, but the angle was all wrong.

Kara withdrew her wallet from her purse. As she did, a tanned arm reached past and placed three euros on the counter. *"Per la signora,"* the man said.

"Oh, no, that's not necessary," she said, thrusting a five at the clerk.

He was beside her now. "It is the least I can do for insulting the pistachio." He plucked two napkins from the dispenser and handed them to her, gazing at her with a roguish smile. "A risky choice for a lady in white."

Kara looked at the chocolate gelato, a drip already forming, and smiled sheepishly. *Well, if someone hadn't distracted me ...* "Thank you," she said, taking the napkins. She returned the wallet to her purse as the men conversed in Italian. Kara felt them sneaking glances at her as they spoke, the clerk clearly referring to her as *il turista*. Typical men, she thought, turning to leave.

Kara wasn't the least bit surprised when Mr. Pistachio followed her out the door without ordering. When she pointed this out to him, he dismissed it with a wave.

"So, what brings you to Florence?"

Kara was in no mood to chat, or be hit on for that matter, but the sweetness of the gelato and the warm, buttery smells of the waffle softened her resistance. Still, his question cut close to the bone. *My asshole husband,* she thought with a sigh. "I'm not really sure, to be honest."

"Most come to see the museums. And the Duomo, of course."

Kara crinkled her face and looked away. An immature reaction, she knew, but didn't care.

"Someone who didn't come for the art? I don't believe it."

"I *wanted* to see the art in Madrid."

"Madrid?" The man sounded baffled.

"Yes, Madrid," she said sarcastically. "Dali? Picasso?" Kara licked her gelato. The cream seemed to coat her tongue in a layer of fudge.

The man nodded, but his brow furrowed ever so slightly as he did. To Kara, he looked confused, as if he'd never heard of two of the most famous painters of the last century. *Maybe he didn't know they were Spaniards,* she thought, giving him the benefit of the doubt.

Together, they meandered their way through the historic quarter, Kara taking the lead, turning at random. Though part of her wanted to lose him, she didn't have the energy to be rid of him—that, and she liked his accent.

"So, why not go to Madrid?"

"My husband brought us here instead," she said. Kara watched him out the corner of her eye, wondering how he'd react to her being married.

He stayed silent for several steps then said, "Not an easy mistake to make."

"Well … it wasn't a mistake." Though she didn't turn to look at him, she sensed his smile.

They continued walking as Kara ate her gelato, eventually arriving back at Ponte Vecchio.

"Do you see the corridor atop the bridge? It goes straight to the Uffizi Museum. It has been many years since I've been, but perhaps I can give you a tour. I once knew the museum quite well."

Kara scrunched her face. "No thanks, I'm not really into portraits of dead Catholics."

A storm flashed in the man's eyes ever so briefly, but he quickly calmed it by clutching his chest and feigning mortal pain.

"No offense," she said, making a note to bite her tongue in the future. "I'm Kara, by the way."

"Kara," he said, softening it as he repeated it. "*Mia cara, Kara.*"

The dulcet tones of his Italian rose and fell, as if reciting poetry. She watched him, waiting for the next line, then, covering her lapse, blurted out, "Hey, that's the logo of the campground we're staying at." She pointed at the embroidered image of a tent and sun on his chest.

"Ah, you're staying at the *campeggio*. I work there. *Mi chiamo Alessio.*"

"Nice meeting you," she said, hoping he'd continue speaking in Italian.

"The pleasure is mine." He took her hand in his, raised it slowly to his lips and kissed it, not taking his eyes from her.

Kara felt herself gasp, then made a half-hearted attempt to remove her hand from his lingering lips. "I'm not used to that," she said, as the heat of the moment rose in her. She felt herself leaning toward him, melting, offering her wrist, her arm …

"You should be," he said, with a glint in his eye. He straightened and released her hand.

She recovered quickly and looked all around, the guilt of her prior infidelity rushing in, as it always did when she was alone with another man. But nothing happened. She told herself that him kissing her hand was nothing more than long lost chivalry. *Are you sure?* She wasn't. As much as she'd love to believe it, she couldn't deny what had transpired. In that moment, in his eyes, his touch, she felt a connection on a deeper plane. Familiar and true.

Kara balled the napkins in her hand, trying to look anywhere but into his eyes, dismissing the attraction as a result of feeling lonely and sorry for herself. *Just like last time.*

She wanted to believe that's all it was, but he kept staring at her, smiling, reveling in the effect he had on her.

"I must return to work. Would you care to accompany me?"

"Oh, I …" she stammered, taking a step back.

"Ah, you've not yet tired of seeing the sights. Perhaps you can join me for dinner at the *campeggio trattoria*."

Absolutely. "I'm sorry, but I shouldn't," she said, spinning her wedding ring nervously on her finger.

Alessio laughed. "It's not like that. Bring your husband. My colleague Hiromasa will join us."

Kara bit her lip, thinking.

"Eight o'clock?"

"I'll see," she said, deciding right then that she'd be there.

"I do hope you come, *cara*," he said, again softening her name into a term of endearment. He made like he was going to kiss her hand, but paused, smirking, as if he knew the effect he had on her and wanted to tease it out.

He tilted his head in a slight bow and winked. "*Ciao*."

A neon board announced the campground's nightly special in fluorescent block lettering. As Edward read the sign, wondering what *Spaghetti alla Carbonara* was, the door swung open, releasing a din reminiscent of a college cafeteria. *Here? This is where Kara wants to eat our first meal in Italy?*

A young couple exited the restaurant, immediately lighting cigarettes once outside. The man stopped to stare at Kara behind the lighter's flickering flame, squinting as he inhaled, eying her up and down. Edward followed his gaze, taking in the cut of Kara's new dress, the way her hips moved as she walked, and he wondered how many other heads she turned that day.

"They're probably inside," Kara said, not paying her admirer any attention.

Edward trailed behind, feeling like an afterthought, stuck in the backseat with no power to steer the evening ahead. He had spent the day washing bicycles, doing laundry, and rehearsing his apology, hoping to earn a chance to explain himself over dinner. But it would have to wait. For when Kara finally returned, she already had plans. He could come, she said, if he wanted.

What choice did he have?

Inside, teenagers crowded around tables draped in candy-striped vinyl, sipping beers, and sharing pizza. Elsewhere, moms and dads slouched, absently twirling pasta, unable to mask their exhaustion beneath the fluorescent lighting, as their kids slalomed between the tables at full speed.

Without hesitation, or a glance back at Edward, Kara took off across the checkered tile floor, weaving between the tables, craning her neck.

At a corner table, a man stood and waved. Edward hurried after Kara as suspicion balled in his gut. It was him, the groundskeeper Edward caught watching them argue earlier that day. The man had changed into a pair of black jeans and a gray V-neck shirt, but there was no mistaking him.

"Buonasera, cara."

"Good evening, right?" Kara asked, smiling as she leaned into his air-kisses.

Edward looked to Kara, hoping to share a silent laugh over how the guy pronounced her name, the absurdity of his honeyed Italian accent. But Kara didn't look his way.

"This is my friend, Hiromasa," the Italian said, introducing a man who, until that moment, Edward hadn't noticed. Hiromasa stood and shook hands with Kara, who appeared to blush upon seeing him. Hiromasa wore a clean campground shirt with jeans and had short, black hair and a soft, fleshy face. His features and bright smile gave him the look of someone who could be trusted—at least compared to the wolf standing beside him.

Edward cleared his throat as the greetings gave way to small talk, hailing Kara's attention, however briefly. "Oh," she said, "This is Alessio." Edward shot Kara a frustrated look. "I'm Edward. Kara's husband," he said, extending his hand to Alessio, annoyed that Kara didn't introduce him.

"Ciao." Alessio shook his hand, his gaze never straying from Kara.

Edward stared at Alessio, clenching his jaw, restraining himself from saying something that would upset Kara.

"Please sit," Hiromasa said. Kara took the seat opposite Alessio, while Edward sat beside her, facing Hiromasa.

"Our first meal in Italy. I can't wait," Kara said.

Edward held his tongue, opting not to mention that he invited her to dinner hours ago.

Alessio whistled the attention of a server, then shouted across the brightly lit room in Italian, gesturing at the table as he spoke. A waiter arrived with two bottles of mineral water and four glasses as Alessio described the night's pasta special. He poured as he talked, emptying the first bottle into glasses for himself, Hiromasa, and Kara.

"You forgot one," Hiromasa said.

Alessio passed the unopened bottle to Edward, who took it, glaring at the man. Edward poured himself some water and made a point of setting the bottle down at his end of the table. If Kara wanted more, he'd be the one pouring.

When Edward turned back from Kara, he noticed Hiromasa staring at him curiously. Edward smiled politely, which must have been interpreted as a willingness to talk.

"You are American?" Hiromasa asked, his speech slow.

"Uh-huh. Born and raised."

"And what year were you born?"

"Eighty-five," Edward said, not wanting to be rude, but hoping to avoid being stuck on a conversation island with Mr. Twenty Questions while Kara sailed off with Alessio.

"And this is your first time to Italy?"

What's with this guy? "Yep."

"But only because you brought Kara to the wrong city," Alessio interrupted, grinning as he spoke, making no effort to hide the mockery in his tone.

Edward fought to conceal his shock. He turned to Kara, wondering what else she told him, how long they talked. She sipped her water and returned his glance with a shrug, challenging him to deny it.

"It's complicated," Edward said through clenched teeth, trying to maintain calm.

"I don't know," Alessio said. "A beautiful woman wants to visit Spain and you take her to Italy? That sounds very simple to me." Alessio raised his eyebrows and stared at him.

Edward's skin tightened around him, armoring him as his pulse quickened, keeping pace with the barrage of threats and insults he wanted to hurl. His toes curled in anger as his chest ballooned. "It's between my wife and me," he said, hoping she wouldn't leave him alone in this. A nudge of her foot, a hand on his knee, perhaps.

Nothing.

"What do you do for work, Edward?"

He ignored Hiromasa's question, unwilling to have his fuse cut before it could be sparked. He glared at Alessio while cracking his knuckles under the table, silently daring him to make another comment, begging for a reason to knock the smirk off his face.

"He was in venture capital," Kara said, drawing Edward's attention. Her voice carried the urgency of someone hoping to change the conversation. "Investing," she added.

Hiromasa nodded then tilted his head, eying Edward with suspicion. "Was?"

"He lost his job in February," she said, looking away.

Edward stiffened as she repeated the story but was distracted by the response from Alessio and Hiromasa, who quickly turned to one another, their eyes bulging with private recognition. Hiromasa leaned to whisper something to Alessio who, in turn, nodded his understanding while glancing out the corner of his eyes at Edward.

Edward looked to Kara, the one person who knew how much he hated people whispering in front of him, but she merely shrugged and looked up as the waiter arrived with four plates of pasta.

"Wow, that was fast," she said.

"They prepare large quantities early in the evening," Hiromasa said. "Much goes to waste on many nights." He shook his head with disapproval as Alessio spoke to the waiter in Italian, twirling his finger overhead.

The table fell quiet as everyone turned their attention to the food. The silence was a relief and the peppery scent of the Parmesan a balm for Edward's nerves. He was on his third bite of the egg-coated spaghetti when the sterile overhead lighting was dimmed. Alessio's request, no doubt.

"Can I have the water?" Kara asked.

"Of course," Edward said, chewing as he spoke. But as he paused to wipe his mouth with a napkin, an arm reached across his plate, grabbing the bottle. Alessio's blatant disrespect was startling—Edward nearly laughed at the absurdity—and his reflexes wouldn't tolerate it.

Edward grabbed hold of the bottle too and tugged. "I got it." Only then did he see the blue fringe surrounding Alessio's arm, the solar flares of light on his fingertips dancing and arcing toward Edward's hand. He hadn't noticed it with the fluorescents on, but now it was as clear as the hair on his arms.

A memory of Jean-Benac appeared in Edward's mind, only to vanish as Alessio pulled on the bottle, catching Edward in an impromptu tug-of-war. His eyes locked on the bottle, on Alessio's hand, and the light growing in intensity.

"Peace, gentlemen," Hiromasa said, seizing the neck of the bottle and lifting.

The glow dimmed as Edward and Alessio let go, but Hiromasa's hand continued to emit the same faint bluish glow and, thanks to the shift in lighting, Edward could see that both men had a slight glow around their entire beings. He rubbed his eyes, watching Hiromasa pour the water, his aura-like glow visible all around him.

The light was reaching for me.

Edward turned to Kara and whispered. "Did you see that?"

"I saw you acting ridiculous," she said, shaking her head.

Was he seeing things? Across the table, Hiromasa resumed eating, but Edward could tell he was watching him, studying.

"So, Alessio, what do you do at the campground?" asked Kara, snapping Edward's attention back.

Alessio finished chewing then explained his daily maintenance and landscaping duties with disdain. For the first time since they arrived, Alessio wasn't charming or disrespectful of their marriage, too absorbed in complaining to keep up the game. Kara listened politely, but Edward could tell she was sorry she asked.

"What about you, Kara? Do you have a profession?" Hiromasa asked.

"I'm in graphic design."

"She's also an incredible painter," Edward said, putting his arm around Kara as he did. "Her paintings are amazing."

Alessio's face brightened as he leaned forward on his elbows. "I used to own a gallery in Malta."

The hell you did.

"Really?" Kara shifted in her seat, her voice rising with interest as she slid out from under Edward's outstretched arm, causing it to clunk onto the chairback.

Edward dragged his hand across Kara's back in an effort to retract it gracefully. His jealousy spiked as he felt the absence of a bra strap, knowing how seldom she went without. "So, how does an art dealer end up cleaning toilets?" Edward asked, hoping to mask his hostility in the tone of the curious.

"It is, as you said, *complicated.*" Alessio barely shifted his gaze from Kara, who failed to stifle her giggle.

Edward bit down on his lip as he fought against the tug of his sinking heart. He couldn't breathe, as if his body refused to exhale the last lingering scent of Kara's perfume—perfume and makeup she refreshed before dinner. Her laugh echoed in his ears as memories of the past months spiraled in his mind. All the lies, the shouting, the tears spilled. He wanted only to give her everything she could want—and now he feared she only wanted another.

Dizzy with guilt and disappointment, Edward sat clutching his knees, staring at the salt and pepper shakers as he wondered how he could make it up to her, hoping she'd give him the chance.

"How long will you be in Florence?" Hiromasa asked, staring at Edward.

They answered simultaneously. "Maybe a week," Kara said.

"Till tomorrow," Edward said.

"What about your knee?" Kara asked, her voice laced with phony concern. "I thought you needed time off the bike."

He mouthed his apology. *I'm sorry.* It was a start, he hoped, of a conversation they could continue later. Kara looked away.

"Ah, you're injured. That is too bad."

"I'm not—"

"You should rest. But don't worry. Maybe I will show Kara around Florence," Alessio said.

Kara coughed in her water, then uttered something noncommittal.

Through a red haze boiling within him, engulfing him, Edward noticed Hiromasa shaking his head ever so slightly, sending a signal. Hiromasa's clamped lips, sucked inward with nervousness, rang like an alarm bell.

Edward tilted his head and narrowed his gaze at Hiromasa, wondering if he was imagining things.

Hiromasa dipped his head in acknowledgment.

"It will be fun. We can climb the steps of the Duomo," Alessio said, ignoring the other men, his lecherous eyes locked on Kara.

The cathedral's dome was visible from outside the campground, and all Edward could picture was Kara climbing its stairs in her new dress, with this creep lagging behind, eye level with her ass, ogling her thighs, licking his lips, planning his move.

"Don't you have a lawn to mow?" It came out every bit the insult Edward had meant, only he didn't intend to say it quite so loud.

"Edward!" Kara's hand went to his knee, pressing it, calming him, a silent rebuke and reprimand, and an order to lighten up. Still, it was the first contact he'd felt from her since leaving Paris.

Her touch was a life raft in rough seas. It wasn't salvation, but it was hope.

Chapter 23

SATURDAY, JUNE 20 — FLORENCE, ITALY

Edward picked anxiously at the label on the jar of instant coffee as he waited for the water to boil, for Kara to return. He had wanted to get it over with last night, to come clean after dinner—about the contest, Florence, everything—but Kara was tired. "It can wait till morning," she said.

What little relief he felt was gone by sunrise.

Steam sent the pot lid rattling as Kara approached in flip-flops, carrying her towel and toiletries, her damp hair combed back, and the purple highlights long gone. She wore capri pants and a wine-colored sleeveless blouse she saved for days spent sightseeing.

"Would you like some coffee?"

"Yes, please," she said, her back to him.

He watched as she draped the towel on the clothesline, then returned his attention to the coffee. Spooning the crystals into their mugs, he felt her hand upon his shoulder. He froze, welcoming his good fortune, relishing her touch, as if she was a butterfly that alighted on an outstretched palm. That she was merely using him for balance as she changed her shoes didn't matter. She could have leaned upon a lamppost or sat in her chair. Instead, she chose him.

He swallowed hard and extended her mug. "Can we talk?"

"Thanks," she said, taking it. She adjusted the angle of her chair so it wasn't directly facing him, then sat. He watched her blow on the coffee, delaying, searching for her response in the twisting clouds of steam.

"I want to explain—"

"Now's not a good time," she interrupted. Then, looking embarrassed, as if aware she was denying him the chance to provide what she demanded. "I'm heading into town."

He opened his mouth to speak, but could only manage the sound of stunned silence. *What happened to making up?*

"You didn't give me a say in coming to Florence, but since we're here," she cocked her head to the side as her voice took on a determined edge, "I'm gonna make the most of it."

"I'm confused. I thought you said—"

"I know what I said. Later, okay?"

Edward swallowed. "Are you going to the Duomo?" He left off the part he was really concerned with, about Alessio.

Kara checked her watch and, as if not really paying attention, said, "I don't know. Maybe. The gardens open around eight. I want to be there while the light's good." Kara looked around, searching for a place to set her mug. She'd only taken a few sips.

He searched her eyes for a hint of the spark he'd always seen. "Will you be back for dinner?"

"Yeah. We'll talk then," she said, after a pause that seemed to last all morning.

Edward waited until Kara was well on her way before retrieving the Blackberry. The morning hadn't gone as he'd hoped, but now that he knew she'd be having dinner with him—and only him—he was determined to find someplace romantic. He plopped himself in the chair, cradling Kara's still warm coffee mug in one hand and the phone in the other.

The phone felt awkward. The tool he used to hammer a wedge between them would now be relied upon to span a chasm. He looked up as a golf cart drove past, a shovel and rake flanked a pair of trash cans mounted on the rear. Alessio glanced his way before accelerating down the dirt path, the tires kicking up dust as he went.

Edward craned his neck as Alessio honked the cart's cartoonish horn. "Who's he beeping at?" Edward wondered aloud, lying to himself. He knew damn well who.

He stood in time to see Kara disappear over the crest of the hill outside the campground gate as Alessio parked the cart near the office. Edward relaxed, glad to see Alessio was working, only to see him toss his gloves on the seat and leave the campground, walking briskly after her.

What the …?

Initially, Edward thought she had lied to him, that she had arranged to meet Alessio behind his back. The thought tortured his empty stomach, but it was instantly replaced by the memory of Hiromasa shaking his head, as if to warn him about Alessio.

Edward dashed into the tent, gathered his wallet and passport, and thrust them along with the phone into his pockets. He tossed the chairs and stove into the vestibule and took off running.

Keeping Alessio in view, Edward stuck to the opposite side of the street as he followed him down the hill into town. A motley lineup of compact cars crowded the curving road, providing ample cover for Edward, who walked in a crouch, feeling his way after Alessio, moving between the pollen-dusted vehicles.

Edward's chest tightened as they passed signs pointing to *Giardino delle Rose* and another for *Giardino Bardini*. Kara had mentioned visiting a garden, and he knew there were probably dozens in a city like Florence, but the farther they walked, the more he feared she had lied.

The road meandered past a fort and several villas en route to the river, where, even at this early hour, the street was alive with tourists. Edward expected a turn to the right, to cross the river into old town, but Alessio cut left, forcing Edward to dodge behind a van to avoid being seen. Through the window he saw Kara in the distance, standing on a corner studying a map.

Edward knelt, spinning his wedding ring around his finger, wondering if Alessio had marked a spot for them to meet. Then they were off again. She rounded the corner toward a massive stone palace the color of sand and the length of a city block. Pitti Palace was fronted by a sweeping plaza with little to hide behind. Lucky for Edward, Alessio's royal blue shirt was easy to spot in the sea of earth tone travel wear, allowing him to keep his distance.

Ahead, Kara approached a ticket office. Edward couldn't see her face or how many tickets she bought, but he was relieved when she didn't look back, didn't wait. She disappeared beyond the entrance alone. The sign above listed a number of museums and attractions, including the Boboli Gardens.

She hadn't lied.

Then he saw Alessio hurry to join the line for tickets. Any comfort Edward felt believing Kara hadn't arranged to meet Alessio was replaced by a darker realization: Alessio was stalking his wife.

Edward peered out from behind an ornate lamppost, clenching his fists as the magnitude of Alessio's arrogance hit home. He acted as if he could pursue Kara with impunity, not once looking over his shoulder to see if Edward was following.

He didn't know how he'd confront Alessio, but Edward knew he wouldn't allow him near her.

The queue for admission was growing by the minute. Edward waited until Alessio reached the ticket counter then joined the line ten people behind him, thankful he brought his wallet.

Once inside, Edward hurried after Alessio. The main garden path spanned the width of a street, was arrow-straight and flanked by columns of towering cypress trees, a detail gleaned from the garden map Edward wielded to shield his face from detection. Statues guarded numerous paths leading deeper into the gardens. Alessio paused at each, as if studying their detail, but Edward could tell he was merely waiting for Kara, biding his time.

Gravel crunched underfoot with every step, igniting Edward's nerves, bringing him closer to ... he had no idea. As Kara slowed, so did Alessio, and thus Edward in a chain reaction of cat and mouse—and dog, Edward thought, flattering himself in the apex role.

Kara strolled along, zigzagging across the path, photographing the statues and trees, her delight visible from forty yards. Though largely convinced she had no idea she was being followed, Edward was unsure how she would react upon seeing Alessio. Would she welcome his sudden appearance—he'd no doubt pretend it was a happy coincidence—or would she see through his ruse?

Again, Edward thought of the warning from Hiromasa.

He imagined Alessio wanting to trap Kara in an isolated corner of the garden, between the hedges, screened from view. He envisioned him grabbing her by the arm, pawing at her, pulling her behind a statue ...

"I'll kill him if he touches her," he said through gritted teeth, feeling the heat rise in his face as he suspected Alessio was playing with her, just as he toyed with Edward at dinner. His breathing turned deeper, noisier, as he recalled Alessio all but asking Kara on a date right in front of him.

He had to do something. *Wanted* to do something. But what? Edward typically avoided confrontation and couldn't recall laying hands on someone since elementary school. Still, he knew he had the size advantage, not to mention youth and strength were on his side if he had to guess. At the very least, he'd threaten him. He hoped it wouldn't come to that.

Kara continued around a reflecting pond, past a statue of a giant cracked face, to a thicket of gnarled trees that arched overhead, their limbs entwined, blocking the sunlight. Edward watched her disappear into the darkened, tunnel-like pathway with Alessio not far behind, lurking beyond a hedgerow that ran perpendicular.

Ahead, three women posed for selfies near the far end of the path, their backs to Kara. No one else was near. He had to act fast.

Edward rushed forward and grabbed Alessio by the wrist, pulling him onto a side path, out of view.

Alessio spun in surprise, his eyes flashing wide with anger, before settling into a veneer of manufactured friendliness.

"What the hell are you doing?" Edward demanded, steeling himself.

Alessio yanked his wrist free of Edward's grip. "Enjoying the gardens—"

"Bullshit. You're following my wife."

Alessio shrugged.

"You followed her yesterday too. I know what you're up to with this artsy Italian bullshit. Stay away from her," Edward said, jabbing his finger at Alessio. As he did, the blue glow of Alessio's face seemed to flow down his brow, over his nose, and toward Edward's finger, as if being drawn magnetically. Edward struggled not to appear distracted, but couldn't help watching in awe.

"Or what?" Alessio asked, leaning forward.

Or what?

It was a good question. Edward stared at Alessio, trying to ignore the flickering blue light, and clenched his fists, racking his brain for a response.

"What will you do?" Alessio said, pushing Edward in the chest.

Edward swatted the hand away and shifted his stance.

Menace flooded Alessio's eyes as he sneered, "You *turista*. You *stranieri*. You come to my city and follow me? You grab my arm—"

"You're stalking my wife!"

Alessio laughed. "And you think you can keep my Sylvia from me? You believe you can protect her?"

Alessio was talking madness. Edward shot him a puzzled look as his leg quivered.

"Don't play games," Alessio said.

"I don't know who the hell you're talking about, but you better stay away from Kara," he said, shoving Alessio with both hands.

Alessio stumbled backwards, shouting at him in Italian, waving his hands in the air.

The outburst drew the attention of a small crowd, and Edward became acutely aware of the circle forming around them, murmuring in languages he couldn't understand. He felt outnumbered, a soldier in enemy territory. "Leave her alone." His voice sounded thin and feeble.

Alessio smoothed his shirt and approached, his teeth bared. A vein in his forehead pulsed and the whites of his eyes spread wild like those of the Medusa statue they passed earlier. *This is what crazy looks like,* Edward thought.

He paused alongside Edward and whispered, "I'll release her. Kara. Sylvia. Isabelle. Her name is of no consequence. We will be returned."

Edward stood, holding his breath until Alessio retreated toward the exit. Then he collapsed forward, his panic hissing out of him in a lengthy sigh, as Alessio's words thundered his nerves. Sweat coated his skin and stung his eyes as he slumped with his hands on his knees, wondering what lunacy his deception had exposed them to.

It wasn't long before the miles spent pounding the paving stones yesterday caught up to her, as did her lack of breakfast. After two hours at the gardens, Kara had seen enough. She exited onto Via Romana, a narrow one-lane road crowded with parked scooters and dumpsters and couples walking hand-in-hand. Three-story buildings loomed above, plunging the street into a trench-like shadow.

A sign up ahead advertised a *trattoria,* a word she'd heard before. It was what Alessio called the campground restaurant. The thought of last night's dinner made her uneasy, and not just because of the food, though she was sure she'd tasted better pasta in Eau Claire. She merely wanted a diversion, another person to ease the tension between her and Edward. She'd never seen anyone get under Edward's skin like that before.

It would have been easier if Alessio couldn't speak English, she thought, recalling their meal with Jean-Benac, hoping he was okay. Kara sighed, wondering when they'd run into some female travelers, someone who might be able to relate to her plight.

"Table for one?" a goateed server asked, offering Kara a menu. Behind him, a dozen tables sat empty. A bad sign.

Kara bit her lower lip and shook her head in a sorry, but no thank you gesture.

"On the terrace, if you prefer," the server said, motioning skyward, where the heads of several diners were visible. It was too early for lunch, but she was starving. He escorted her to a rooftop garden, where a cozy collection of tables sat occupied, all save for one. Hers.

She requested a half carafe of the house white and settled into the chair, her legs crossed beneath the table. The sun's warmth radiated off the whitewashed walls of the adjacent, taller buildings, as the shadow line slowly dropped away. A small fan gave the air just enough circulation to feel refreshing without messing her hair.

When the waiter returned with her wine, she ordered the *insalata caprese* (a safe choice, but perfect for an early summer lunch, she thought) and the *carpaccio con rucola e parmigiano,* unsure what *rucola* was.

Conversation surrounded her, mostly in Italian and English, but other languages as well. At the adjacent table, a woman told the waiter she and her friend were visiting from Buenos Aires. Yes, first time to

Europe. Florence is *beautiful*, she said, stretching each syllable to its breaking point. The women resumed their conversation in Spanish after the server left.

Trying to distract herself, Kara reached for her book, only to realize she'd left it in the tent. Instead, she paged through her passport, but every *-isima, -ito* and *-eria* floated across to her table, the Spanish words sticking in her throat like a swallowed fly.

Since arriving in Florence, she had sought to make the best of it, to distance herself from Edward, and not to dwell on his lies. But there was no getting over it. She stared at the Argentinian women, watching their plump, cabernet lips share indecipherable gossip, and realized any reference to Spain would forever remind Kara of her husband's betrayal.

Forever?

She wondered as much as she gulped her wine, hoping it wasn't so.

The waiter soon arrived with her salad and *carpaccio*. Kara twirled the beef on her fork, watching a drip of honey course its way through the tines, down along the handle, onto her finger. She licked it off, detecting a hint of pepper amongst the sweetness.

But as conversation progressed at the nearby table, Kara found it impossible to enjoy her meal. She couldn't wait any longer. She needed to hear his explanation, to test the ground upon which their marriage stood. She hurried through her meal and set off for the campground.

Kara had nearly crested the hill when she spotted him. Edward paced along the sidewalk, chopping at the air, talking to himself. His hair was tousled and face pale. He had the nervous air of someone who felt he was being watched—or worse.

She took a deep breath, slid her purse behind her hip, and crossed the street to him.

"Kara. Thank God. I was hoping I'd catch you."

"You were waiting for me? What's wrong?" Kara nearly commented on his appearance, then recalled how he looked in Paris, right before he told her they were leaving that night.

"We need to talk."

"Yeah, that's why I came back."

Edward nodded as his eyes darted back and forth anxiously. "Not at the campground. Come this way," he said, leading her by the hand across the street to *Piazzale Michelangelo*.

Kara followed him through the parking lot, dodging tour buses as they went. He ushered her to the quiet upstream end of the plaza, away from the gaggles of tourists, ice cream kiosks, and merchants hawking postcards and faux leather notebooks embossed with the Florentine lily, red on a white field. To Kara, the lily reminded her of the *fleur-de-lis*, and France, where they should have been.

Still, the view was impeccable, even for midday.

Kara made a note to return at sunset, anticipating the sight of the Arno flowing into the descending sun, a swirl of Bellini pinks and oranges reflecting off its mirror-like waters. Even with the sun directly overhead, the view of the Duomo and the sea of sun burnt rooftops lapping against its marble walls was hard to ignore.

Edward took a seat without mentioning the view.

Kara sat beside him, her back to the overlook, and fixed her gaze on a crack in the pavement, listening with all her senses.

He sighed as he ran his hands through his already messy hair. "I'm sorry."

She dipped her head in acknowledgment, unsure what she hoped to hear, knowing she only wanted a return to normalcy, to how they were when they first married, before he became obsessed with his work, began lying to her. *Lying to one another.*

"I can explain everything. It's hard though. I've never kept secrets from you."

Kara raised her eyebrows. *And …*

"Or lied before. I was an ass, and I screwed everything up."

Kara nodded again, vigorously this time, but willed herself to remain silent. She could feel him squirming next to her.

"You're not going to make this easy on me, are you?"

"Should I?" she asked, turning to face him.

"No. I suppose not," he said, his voice cracking as he picked at a cuticle. "But I can explain. Really. I'll tell you all the stupid reasons why I lied and why I've been hurrying us along ever since ..." His voice trailed off.

I knew it, she thought. She'd suspected him of being up to something long before the train ride to Florence. He had a lot to explain. The flight to London, the long days in Canada, the Netherlands. Kara turned on the bench, her knees pointing toward his, and urged him to continue.

"God, I hope you understand," he said, as if talking to himself. His knees bounced as he continued. "I'm so sorry and I can explain why we ended up here. I'll tell you everything. But it has to wait."

"Uh, no it can't," she said, shooting him a threatening look.

"We need to leave Florence."

"What!" Kara shouted, leaping to her feet. "Again?"

"Maybe just ride to Siena. We can get there by dark if we break camp fast."

Kara shook her head in disbelief, her hands on her hips, not knowing whether to laugh or cry, or do both.

"Okay, fine, not Siena. We'll take the train to Madrid, for real this time, I swear, but we've got to go—"

"Why?"

Kara watched as a curtain spun from the threads of shame and nervousness descended upon Edward's face. It was a look she'd never seen on him before. "It's that guy. Alessio."

She guffawed, a spontaneous laugh that she regretted the moment it happened.

"It's not funny."

"You're jealous?"

Edward looked away for a moment then gazed up at her, his eyes puffy. "I'm worried, Kara. The guy's dangerous."

"Dangerous? You're ridiculous, you know that? First you lie about ... about everything, probably, and then—"

"He followed you today," he said, interrupting her.

She flinched. "How do you know that?"

"Because I tracked him. I caught up to him in the gardens."

"You went to the gardens?"

"I didn't intend to follow you, I swear. But when I saw him take off after you ..." He stood facing her. "Listen, Kara, he was stalking you. I confronted him by the hedges, when you were alone in that tunnel of trees, and I'm telling you, the guy's up to no good."

Kara remembered that particular path clearly, how dark it was, how isolated. The thought of being stalked made her skin crawl. *But Alessio?* She wondered if he had followed her yesterday, but recalled how much of a gentleman he was.

"He's harmless," she said, wondering if this was just another one of Edward's lies, a story he concocted to rush her from yet another city.

"You didn't see what I saw. You didn't hear what he said. He told me I couldn't keep you safe," Edward pleaded, grabbing her by the shoulders.

"He's taunting you. He's Italian. It's all bravado and bluster." Kara placed her hands atop his, lifting them from her shoulders, trying not to laugh. "Don't tell me you let him scare you?"

"He said—"

Edward was interrupted by a sudden symphonic chime. The ring of a telephone filled the air as the lump in Edward's pocket vibrated. Kara stumbled back in surprise.

"Shit, shit, shit," Edward repeated, fumbling at the pocket, squeezing it, slapping it as Kara watched, and feeling herself scowl. He pulled a ringing Blackberry from his pocket, one of the older ones with a tiny keyboard and a ball in the center.

Kara's entire body went itchy. "Whose is that?"

Edward hit the red button, silencing the device, but not before Kara could read the screen: Unknown Caller. She watched him shove it back in his pocket, wondering why he didn't answer.

"Tom gave it to me."

The name didn't register, not at first. But it wasn't long before a picture came into focus, a collage depicting their every decision dating back to Minnesota.

"Why didn't you tell me you had a phone?"

Edward stammered in his search for an answer.

Kara's face puckered, so sour were the thoughts coming to mind. "Does this have to do with us not going to Cape Cod? Or Spain?"

He slumped in shame, then nodded. "You would have never understood—"

"You bastard," she said, balling her fists as her rage drowned out his cascade of pleas and promises to explain everything. The phone already had.

Edward chased after Kara with an awkward gait, all hips and ankles, not wanting to run, but calling for her to slow down. He'd explain. Just give him a chance.

She didn't slow. Kara never once looked back.

The phone rubbed against his leg as he pursued her. He wanted to tear it from his pocket and smash it to pieces, but he didn't. He could barely remember why it was on him in the first place, the morning felt so long ago. Something about a restaurant, he thought, and then ...

Alessio!

Alarm punched him in the gut, forcing him to quicken, knowing Kara was headed back to the campground, toward Alessio. Forgetting his reluctance to make a scene, he sprinted after her, shouting her name as he raced to their campsite.

Ahead, Kara halted steps from their tent, her hands flying to her face as she gasped. "The bikes," she yelled, her voice shattering with horror and dismay.

Edward followed her gaze and saw their bicycles, slumping against the locks that bound them to a lamppost, like two prisoners who died shackled to the walls of a dungeon.

He ran to the bikes and lifted the one nearest him. His? Hers? He propped it against the post, gently, as his heart sank. The wheels were demolished, the spokes broken, the rims bent into tacos. The tires suffered lengthy gashes in the sidewalls.

He rubbed his hand along the downtube, to where the derailleur cables had been cut, their frayed ends pointing this way and that like an electrified cowlick. A wire punctured his skin and Edward squeezed a pinprick of blood from his finger, feeling as if he was squeezing his entire heart through the eye of a needle.

There was other damage as well. Brake cables, the leather seat, the front racks. Looking away, unable to take the sight of it, he saw the other bike—his bike—had been equally tortured.

As the torrent of blood rushed to his face, amidst the roar of his inner rage, he heard Kara behind him. Sobbing, trying to make sense of it. "Why? Why?" she begged. "Who would do this?"

Edward knew. He grabbed a fragment of the shattered shifter and hurled it into the overhead netting. He was apoplectic in his fury.

"You know who did this."

Kara's eyes widened as she took a small step back, confused.

She still doesn't see it, he thought.

"Alessio! I told you he was dangerous. Now do you believe me?"

Kara shook her head as if she couldn't process what she was hearing. "You really think he did this?"

"Of course he did it. He told me I couldn't keep you safe. He said he'd release you. Whatever the hell that meant."

"He wouldn't do this," she said, shaking her head, but Edward saw fear in her eyes.

"How would you know?"

"Because he wouldn't. He works here, for one thing," she said, controlling her sobs.

"That's right, he does." Edward's thirst for revenge sharpened as he envisioned grabbing hold of Alessio and stomping him in the gut just as he must have done to their bicycle wheels. "Where's he staying?"

"How should I know?" Kara stiffened, glaring at him.

"Don't act like you don't know."

"I don't. Why would I?"

"Fine. I'll find him myself."

"Edward, no. What are you going to do? Beat him up? Get yourself arrested? You don't even have proof!" Kara stepped in front of him and held her arm out, begging for him to stop.

He hesitated as her words sank home. *Arrested? Then I couldn't protect her. Holy shit, was that his plan?*

"Maybe there's a security camera," she said. "Or maybe another camper saw something."

Edward took a deep breath and pumped his fists five times in quick succession, but the moment his eyes landed on the bikes, his simmering temper boiled up once again.

Memories flooded his mind: the nights spent assembling the bikes, the nervous excitement of setting out from Alki Beach in Seattle, the freedom he felt rocketing down the Continental Divide. The bikes were practically the only things they owned.

"Can you fix them?"

He looked at the wheels and sighed. They were custom. "I can probably order most of the parts, but the wheels are toast." He closed his eyes and wished the past five months away, wishing more than anything for a proper vacation. Maybe a cruise.

"So, a couple of days then?"

"At least," he said. He looked at his watch. It was Saturday afternoon. "The shops might be closed until Monday."

He saw her staring at the pocket containing the phone.

She stiffened as she collected herself, wiping at the last of her tears, purposefully stroking her eyes with a single finger in a slow, thoughtful manner. Edward could sense her remembering why she'd raced ahead, alone, ignoring him.

"Might as well call around for parts. Or is that phone only good for calling Tom?"

Chapter 24

SATURDAY, JUNE 20 — FLORENCE, ITALY

Alessio set the faucet to full blast and slapped at the soap dispenser. Pink liquid oozed past the metal plunger into his grease-stained hand. As he scrubbed at the black smears, adrenaline drained from him like air escaping a tire pierced by a thorn. Not like the rubber he stabbed with a tent stake, where the air burst free in an explosive *whoomp*, but in a gentle hiss that left the frame of his excitement upright, ridable.

The cold water stung as it penetrated the grated skin of his knuckles, the nicks and cuts from where the bicycles bit back in defense. He picked at a sliver of wire that jutted from his palm, eyes fixed in concentration on the silver splinter as his mind focused on the day ahead.

The plan was in motion.

Behind him, coins plunked into a metal box, a dial was wound, and a shower run. A man's voice, groggy despite the midday hour, cursed the cold water.

Alessio's gaze drifted toward the sound, to a shower door with a towel draped over the top. A thrill rippled through him, coalescing in his groin as he recalled lingering inside the doorway to the lady's bath house early that morning. Kara had been the first camper awake. He spotted her during his rounds and waited out of sight till he heard the water running. The stall door descended to her calf, limiting his view, but he stared as the soap bubbled down her legs, pooling atop her painted toenails. Under the guise of emptying the trash, he gawked at what was revealed and used his imagination—and memories of Sylvia—to paint in the rest.

The memory thrilled him, but he couldn't afford to waste any time. He had much to do before nightfall.

Alessio hurried to the shed, hoping to gather the rope he'd need before Hiromasa returned from lunch. But the door was open when he arrived, and the landscaper's cart he'd been driving that morning parked nearby.

Inside, Hiromasa busied himself, his back to the door, bent over, loading a bucket of equipment. Scattered around him lay a variety of gardening tools. Alessio noticed the unsheathed soil knife and frowned at the sight of its serrated edge resting beneath a trowel and weeder.

"Thought you'd still be eating," Alessio said, smirking when Hiromasa jumped at the sound of his voice.

Hiromasa aimed to collect himself, but failed to hide his embarrassment at being so easily startled. "Ah, Alessio. I was looking for you earlier." He tossed the tools into the bucket and stood.

Alessio stared at him, unsure whether to share his plan, the expedited timeline. He grabbed a shovel that hung from a hook and turned the tool over in his hands as he thought. The shovel felt powerful in his grip, deadly. The sensation emboldened him. "I followed Kara into town."

Hiromasa's eyes widened, betraying his surprise. "And do you still believe she is related to Sylvia, that she can help you somehow?"

"She left before I could speak with her."

"I see."

Alessio clenched the wooden handle, holding it in his right hand like a hatchet, recalling the husband's interruption. "But tonight will be different." His voice was raspy, and his lip curled as he spoke. In the damp silence of the shed, Hiromasa exhaled long and slow. Outside, a breeze blew. The painted barn-style door creaked on its hinges, and the daylight shrank to a mere rectangle. "Can you pass me that?" Hiromasa asked, pointing to a spray can on the shelf, seeming to change the subject.

Alessio returned the shovel to the hook and placed the can into the bucket. While bent, he picked up the soil knife, pinching the blade tip between two fingers, lifting it slowly, swinging it like a pendulum. "Have you decided to return with us?"

Hiromasa followed the swaying handle with his eyes, but said nothing. Between them, dust floated in the dank air, sparkling in the scant sunlight.

"Well? You asked to sleep on it." He had explained his thinking to Hiromasa last night, after dinner, as they lay in their cots. Sensing that Kara had felt a connection to him was all the convincing he needed. Their bodies were merely shells, false vessels imprisoning the souls meant to unite. If his theory was right, releasing their souls would send them back to their rightful era—and this time he'd be sure to keep Sylvia by his side.

"She won't go along with it."

Alessio sneered. "She has no choice."

"But Kara is no more Sylvia than she is Isabelle. Maybe your ideas would work if performed on Sylvia, but she's an innocent woman—"

"I'm willing to take that chance," Alessio interrupted. It had been five weeks since he and Hiromasa volleyed explanations across the table, before Hiromasa served up his soul mates suggestion. Ever since, Alessio had dreamed of finding Sylvia, of setting them free, returning home with their love renewed. "And if proven correct, I won't make the same mistakes as I did," he said, a reminder to himself.

Hiromasa spun the bucket in his hand by the handle, oscillating it slowly back and forth as the objects knocked about. "When are you planning to do it? She and her husband may not stay very long."

"They're not going anywhere," he laughed. "I saw to that."

Hiromasa's eyes shifted, as if searching for something, an escape perhaps. Alessio realized he was silhouetted against the doorway, and that Hiromasa had grown intimidated, uncomfortable in his presence. He tucked the soil knife in his belt, hooking it by its hilt.

"You seem nervous, Hiromasa."

"Your plan frightens me."

"Don't you want to return to your rightful time? To at least test my theory?"

Hiromasa sighed. "I don't know. Life was hard back then—"

"It's harder now," Alessio interrupted, raising his voice, recalling the decades he spent alone after Sylvia abandoned him.

"But people didn't live as long back then. You and I were lucky to see fifty."

"We were brought to this time to set the order right, to correct the wrongs."

"But why would God want you to harm yourself, or another person, as a way of penance? It makes no sense."

"The bodies are irrelevant. And our souls feel no pain. We've been through this."

"I don't know," Hiromasa said quietly, shaking his head. "Pardon me," he said, crossing the shed. The plywood floor bowed under their collective weight as Alessio refused to move.

Alessio stared at him nose to nose, their gazes colliding. "Your Isabelle's soul is here too. In Kara."

Hiromasa grunted, a sound Alessio accepted as a reluctant admission of someone caught facing an undeniable truism.

"Join us. We can return to our rightful times and leave this godforsaken place."

Hiromasa opened his mouth to speak, but made no sound, looking as if the decision bore him physical pain.

"Don't you yearn for your Isabelle?" Alessio asked. He picked up a pair of snips on the workbench and thumbed the safety lever back and forth, unlocking and relocking the blades. "You know you've wished for a way to stop her from leaving you."

"I have. But ..." Hiromasa's voice faded as his face twitched in the shadows.

Alessio's lips pressed into a tight smile as he stood taller, enjoying the smell of fear wafting off Hiromasa. He set the snips down and stepped aside, allowing Hiromasa to pass. "It will work."

Hiromasa hurried past him, scurrying toward daylight, the bucket bouncing plaintively against his leg. Before he left, he stopped, and without turning around, issued Alessio a warning.

"For your sake, it better. There are worse places than purgatory."

Chapter 25

SATURDAY, JUNE 20 — FLORENCE, ITALY

With her Hemingway paperback tucked under an arm, Kara slid a plastic tray along the cafeteria rails and helped herself to the day's two remaining *cornetti,* not caring whether the croissant-like pastries were still fresh. She ordered a cappuccino and flicked the necessary coins onto the counter without eye contact. She'd already eaten lunch, but even greater than her cyclist's appetite was the desire to dunk the agony of the last hour in something sweet.

She carried her snacks to a postage stamp garden hemmed in by rhododendron and sat at a limestone pedestal table barely larger than a birdbath. Her metal chair, more decorative than comfortable, sank unevenly in the grass under her weight.

Elbow on the table and head in her hand, she submerged the first of her pastries into the froth, coating it in the cinnamon and sugar sprinkled atop the foam. She flipped open her dog-eared copy of *The Sun Also Rises,* tasting nothing, and stared at the page. Jake was in San Sebastian and had returned to his hotel for supper, where a group of bicycle racers were holding court. *Figures.* As Hemingway's narrator described the cyclists' thirst for wine and women, Kara's mind drifted to her damaged bike across the campground.

She shoved the book aside and took a sip of the cappuccino, picturing a couple of would-be thieves who, upon failing to cut the bike locks, opted to vandalize what they couldn't steal. And it wouldn't have happened if Edward hadn't followed her.

Kara wondered if they should bother calling the police, a springboard from which her mind leaped to the ringing phone in Edward's pocket. "Tom gave it to me," Kara said with a snort, imitating Edward's voice. But why? For safety? *Maybe.* But wouldn't Brenda have said something? After all, Tom didn't strike Kara as the kind of guy to worry. Something was definitely going on between them. She was sure of it.

"What a dumpster fire this trip turned out to be," she said in the snark-laced vernacular of her coworkers.

Knowing she'd be stuck in Florence for at least a few days while Edward repaired the bikes, she opted to take out the tourist pamphlet and find something to do. Hiromasa entered the garden carrying a lunch tray shortly after she spread the map across the table. His demeanor shifted upon spotting Kara, and he hurried over, an anxious look on his face.

"May I join you?"

Kara didn't want to be rude. "Sure."

She folded the pamphlet before even looking it over and set it atop her book to make room for his tray. She considered it odd that he wanted to sit with her, given that he barely spoke to her at dinner. In fact, he seemed downright bashful around her.

He set his plate and bottle of soda on the table and leaned the tray against his chair leg. "Forgive my intrusion, but I must speak with you."

His formality struck her as odd. Especially given the campground atmosphere. But, to humor him, she affected her best business posture and folded her hands over the table's edge. "What can I help you with?"

Hiromasa scanned the small garden, as if checking for eavesdroppers, then leaned forward. His voice was hushed, whispering like a summer breeze through tall grass. His cheeks were slightly flushed. "Have you seen Alessio today?"

"Not at all."

"Very good." His face relaxed. "Please don't tell him I said so, but you must avoid him."

"You too?" she asked. "Did Edward put you up to this?" Kara's voice rose with frustration as she suspected yet another attempt to trick her.

Hiromasa flinched from her question, as if confused, but he recovered and reached for her hands. Kara pulled them away, not wanting him to touch her. It was an urge that saddened her for a reason she couldn't explain.

"Please, believe me. You must stay away from him."

She paused, wanting to leave, but curious why Alessio's own friend would warn her to avoid him. Even if Edward was involved. "Why?"

Hiromasa glanced over his shoulder. "He's dangerous. He has … ideas."

"All men have ideas" she said, brushing the comment aside.

"He thinks you are someone else. A woman who once harmed him. You should leave Florence." His voice was firm, but compassionate, like that of an older brother warning about the dangers of going to parties with boys. But Kara was no teenager. She stiffened in her chair. "Let me guess, I should hurry off to Siena?" She rolled her eyes.

Hiromasa sighed and leaned back. He studied Kara for several awkward seconds, then lifted his panini to his mouth. He set it back on the paper plate without taking a bite. His mouth hung open, as if waiting for the right moment to speak.

"Go on. Might as well say it."

"It's my English," he said, sheepishly. "I am unsure how to put it delicately."

Kara took a long sip of her cappuccino, wanting to finish and leave. Her eyes drifted to the tourist pamphlet, where an advertisement announced discount admission to the Uffizi Museum.

"Were you going to leave Edward?"

"What? No. And that's none of your business."

Hiromasa stared, observing her, his hands tented, fingertips tapping against one another. He raised his eyebrows slightly as he nodded his head in a knowing manner, a gesture she took to mean he was willing to wait for her answer—and already knew the response.

"I mean, sure, I'm mad that he tricked me into coming to Florence, but I'm not going to divorce him over it." Then, under her breath, she added, "It's complicated," parroting Edward's line from the prior night.

"Not now. When he lost his job. In February."

Kara squirmed in her seat and felt the color drain from her face as her head swam. How could he know? She told no one, not even her girlfriends at work. A sense of dread inched its way up her spine. It had to have been Edward. He must have sensed it.

"I apologize. I don't wish to frighten you."

Kara wilted under Hiromasa's gaze, feeling judged. Though she knew she had every right to walk that path if she chose, she couldn't stand to have it exposed by this stranger. She felt violated. "Why are you asking me this?"

"So, it is true?"

Kara looked away. Her nose itched, allergic to the scrutiny.

"And Edward stopped it?" He asked, his voice hopeful.

"Obviously," she said, flipping her wrist in the air. She sought relief from his questions, but a part of her also felt relieved to share the burden of her secret. "If you must know, I was going to leave him if he didn't cut back his hours at the office. Not that he would have noticed."

Hiromasa nodded his head slowly with what appeared to be a look of barely concealed delight. His stare unnerved her, but his eyes did not condemn.

Kara crumpled the paper her *cornetti* had sat upon and stood.

"I'm leaving. Tell Edward, when you see him, which I'm sure will be right away, that I'm going to the Uffizi. And the next time he wants to talk to me, tell him to do it himself."

Kara ascended the grand staircase, carried on a wave of tourists to the Uffizi's top floor. After waiting nearly an hour to buy a ticket, she had almost given up. And she would have if she could've thought of somewhere else to go—or so she'd tell Edward if he asked. But she waited, knowing deep down that she'd regret leaving town without paying a visit to one of the world's great art museums. And personal tastes aside, Florence was still very much *Florence*.

All around her, couples pooled and eddied in the corridor and gallery halls, some studying their museum brochures, others leaning in, conjoined by the tinny speaker of their overpriced audio guide. Men walked with practiced posture, their hands clasped behind their backs and chins jutted in contemplation, as women nodded thoughtfully by their side.

Kara advanced through the centuries, from the Byzantine to the Gothic to the Early Renaissance, each gallery a reminder of the Jesus story. Crucifixions hung from every wall, forlorn portraits in crackling plaster and oils dulled by time, their wooden frames perfuming the museum with musty aromatics reminiscent of a Midwestern church basement.

Ahead, she caught a partial glimpse of *The Birth of Venus*, a mere fragment of Botticelli's seashell, a pasty white leg, and a wisp of Venus' flowing locks, before receiving an elbow to the midsection.

"Excuse you!" Kara snapped at the man who paid her no attention, shoved as he was by the crowd flocking to their shepherd, the guide's red pennant held aloft on a stick.

Leonardo da Vinci's name drew her into the next hall, but a cursory lap was all she could muster. Impersonating the gravelly monotone of the priests she endured in her youth, Kara took to entertaining herself. "Crucifixion, annunciation, crucifixion, adoration, repetition, repetition."

Two women dressed in flowy skirts and loose-fitting, striped blouses, turned and laughed. "*Tu es très drôle,*" one said, her hand covering her laugh. They looked Kara's age.

"*Merci beaucoup,*" Kara replied. It wasn't often someone thought her funny. "*Ciao.*"

Kara strolled along the corridor, past endless marble busts, slowing to peek in at the Renaissance works, disregarding them as more of the same. Ahead, a windowed wall offered sweeping views of the Arno River. She looked to the hill on the far bank, toward the campground where her bike doubtlessly slumped, damaged and limp. And toward Edward, the other half of her crumbling marriage.

She leaned on the windowsill, her head pressed against the warm glass, recalling her turbulent winter, the pressure building for months, until February, when Edward rescued them from divorce with a vacation of her dreams. She'd been fighting a headwind ever since.

A museum attendant approached, heels clacking on the tile floor, finger wagging in time with her shaking head, warning not to lean on the windows. Kara noticed a sweat smear on the glass before hurrying away, embarrassed.

She meandered along the corridor, drifting aimlessly downstream on the current of museumgoers, unable to focus on the art, blurred as it was by the gauzy recollections of her arguments with Edward, the peculiarity of Hiromasa's warning.

A cranberry-colored room caught her attention. The area was dominated by a Roman sculpture, a lady in recline, a breast exposed. She was drawn further into the room, enchanted by the stark brilliance of the colors in a circular painting on the far wall.

She looked at the nameplate: Michelangelo's *Doni Tondo*. It was the only painting of his remaining in Florence. "How could that be?" she wondered aloud as she soaked in the colors, a palette of the most brilliant blues and pinks and yellows she'd seen. The near-fluorescent pigments cut through the dreariness of her mood, shattering her malaise.

Kara stepped back to better absorb the warmth of the colors, the comfort of the flowing garbs adorning the Holy Family.

Feeling someone trying to get her attention, she noticed the two French women she had seen earlier off to her side, staring. One gestured for her to look beyond her, a flick of the eyes and subtle lift of the chin. "*Vous avez un admirateur,*" she whispered.

Kara feigned nervous surprise as she placed her hand on her heart and mouthed her gratitude. The woman's glance suggested he was coming this way, and judging by her arched eyebrows and devilish wink, she thought he was hot.

Edward. He'd always been attractive in a classical sense, but the months on the road had sharpened his features, given him a masculine edge she found suited him, irresistible.

When he's not being a jackass. She punctuated the thought with a snort and stepped to the side, leaving room for him to approach. Whether to report on the bikes or tour the museum with her, she didn't care. That he knew where to find her only confirmed her suspicions that he put Hiromasa up to confronting her about Alessio.

"Michelangelo only used the rarest, most expensive pigments available in Italy," the voice behind her said. "*Spettacolare.*"

Surprise swirled a tinge of fright as Alessio stepped beside her. "Oh. It's you," she stammered, caught off-guard. *Dammit, Edward.*

Alessio's two-day scruff complemented the olive-bronze tan of his skin. Instead of the campground polo shirt, he wore a slim-fitting collared shirt, the top three buttons undone. His black jeans, Kara noticed, flushing, were clean. Tight.

He sure cleans up well, she caught herself thinking.

"His only painting on wood that remains."

She turned back to the *Doni Tondo,* impressed by his knowledge, distracted by the comforting familiarity she felt bubbling inside her. "It's beautiful," she said, immediately embarrassed for having allowed such banality to escape her lips.

"But I saw you were not so impressed with the others."

Kara's breath caught in her throat as Edward's warning rang in her ears. *He's stalking you. He's dangerous.* She glanced at Alessio, who stood studying the painting with his chin in his hand, and recalled how harmlessly he accompanied her yesterday. Still, she knew she had to be careful. She shifted a small step away and noticed the other women were nowhere to be seen.

"Religion doesn't interest me," Kara said, before turning to exit the hall, unsurprised when he followed.

"But the Renaissance has so much to teach us," he said, falling in step beside her in the western corridor.

"Sure. In terms of technique—"

"And emotion," he interjected.

"Yes, emotion too, I suppose," she added. "But it was so stodgy. So staid. The Renaissance only stands out in history because of the misery that preceded it." It was a retort she'd first heard from a classmate in her Survey of Western Art class and had been repeating the line ever since.

"You speak of the black death?"

"Well, of course," she said, noticing his tone had grown defensive.

Kara believed the true value of art lay in its role as a wellspring for contention. As Alessio leaned on the piety of the era's patrons to justify the subject matter—and Kara indelicately compared them to pagans— she couldn't help thinking of the philosophical debates she had tried to engage Edward in over the years. But his was a world of numbers, hard truths, and ledger sheets without room for interpretation, a monochrome environment unable to process the Technicolor of her thoughts.

As they spoke, Alessio held back to allow a tour group past, gently placing his hand on the small of Kara's back; he escorted her, shielding her from being bumped. His touch rippled up her spine, ringing her vertebrae like a xylophone. His hand lingered several steps longer than necessary as his finger stroked the material of her shirt. The gesture leaped past chivalry into the zone of familiarity. Desire. Kara indulged in the attention a moment longer than necessary, then stepped to maintain some separation.

"Okay, maybe not like pagans. But seriously, Michelangelo, Titian, and Raphael were all great painters, but their work was prosaic. What the Renaissance needed was a woman's touch."

"Ah, you believe there were no female painters."

Kara shrugged, then noticed they had returned to the windows overlooking the river and hilltop campground in the distance. And Edward. She turned her back to the view and leaned against the sill. She lowered her voice, as if afraid her husband would hear her. "We ladies just like to see one another succeed."

Alessio looked around. "One moment, please." He approached a museum guard stationed in the corner.

Kara couldn't hear the conversation, but judging by the man's body language, whatever Alessio was asking was out of the question. Kara watched with curiosity as Alessio pulled a blue bill—twenty euros— from his pocket and handed it over. The man looked around, frowning as Kara locked eyes with him, then pocketed the money. Alessio waved Kara over.

The guard spoke rapidly, annoyed, as if berating them in advance for the trouble they would undoubtedly cause. Kara couldn't understand a word the man spoke, but his tone suggested a list of dos and don'ts. They were led to a pair of handsome wooden doors, at least twelve feet tall, with red handles. The guard waited for a family to pass, then backed through the doors. Kara braced for an alarm that never rang and followed.

"Where are we going?" she whispered to Alessio, who merely smiled, his eyes sparkling with the joy of a surprise yet to be sprung.

The guard, clad in navy polyester pants and plain burgundy jacket, led them down a flight of stairs to an arched hallway lined with portraits. Alessio handed him an additional ten euros, saying *"Due minuti, per favore."* Then, to Kara, "Come. It shouldn't be much further." He cupped her elbow, guiding her down the hall.

Kara gave a hesitant glance to the security guard, then continued, warming with each step, anxious to see what the bribery had bought them.

"This is the Vasari Corridor, where the Medici traveled privately above Ponte Vecchio, between their palace and offices." Alessio scanned the portrait-lined walls, ushering her onward, swiveling his head back and forth before stopping beneath a darkened painting. In it, a woman in black robes with an alabaster shirt stared at them, her blond hair pulled tight against her scalp. She held a piece of paper and a quill.

"Allow me to introduce Sofonisba Anguissola," Alessio said with esteem.

Kara never heard of her. "Your mistress?" she joked, immediately regretting the innuendo.

Alessio smiled a wolfish grin. "She was before my time."

Kara detected a hint of longing in the way he said it and approached the painting, craning her neck to inspect the brush strokes.

"It is a self-portrait. Sofonisba was among the most famous women of the Renaissance."

Kara nodded, genuinely impressed, as much by the information as she was Alessio's knowledge.

"Michelangelo himself helped to nurture her talent. Sofonisba went to Spain, to serve as the lady-in-waiting for King Philip II's third wife."

"At least someone got to go to Madrid," Kara said, looking away, ashamed how whiny the comment sounded.

"Yes. I'm sorry. I forgot."

Doubtful.

Behind them, the security guard said something in Italian, his voice echoing through the hall. Alessio held a solitary finger and resumed his lesson.

As he explained the painting's history, Kara became distracted by the thoughts going through her mind. Comparisons of this moment and those times at the SAM with Edward—and his cell phone. Few exhibits were more interesting to him than his email. And here was this man, a stranger willing to bribe his way into a special area. For her.

Kara whispered empty praise as her face sagged with regret, wondering if she had given up her dream too soon.

Which one?

"Even the Pope is said to have commissioned a painting from her," Alessio continued.

Kara turned to him, surprised. She couldn't look away. A part of her suspected he was seducing her vulnerability, using her story about Spain, her anger at Edward, to crack her defenses. *Everything he said could be made up,* she reminded herself. *But how many landscapers know where a rare painting is located in a secure part of a museum?*

The guard cleared his throat and began tapping his watch. "We should get going," she said, no longer trusting herself, knowing Edward was right to want her to stay clear of Alessio.

Together, they walked back through the museum, passing a dizzying array of exhibits they barely glanced at. They talked at length about Kara's art, why she gave up traditional media for the dazzling world of designing business cards and do-it-yourself book cover templates. Though Alessio seemed to have little understanding of what she said, he never let the conversation falter, and never brought it to himself. It was the kind of conversation Kara wished could have gone on all day, the kind where one topic led naturally to the other, and witty observations were volleyed back and forth with the ball always coming to rest on her side of the court, her interests. Her plans, her dreams.

Kara slowed her pace, allowing each foot to hang in the air, dangling, before finding the floor, as if she was trying to hold back time. She was swept up in the moment, trying to convince herself of its innocence, knowing it would end soon. And then what? The past hour had felt more and more like a date with each passing artwork.

From within the hall nearest the stairs, a towering depiction of the Virgin Mary appraised Kara with side-eyed scrutiny. Kara felt the heat of the Madonna's glare, judging her, reading her thoughts. She hurried down the stairs, wanting Alessio to stay behind, but thrilling at the sound of his shoes on the steps behind her.

Outside, Kara crossed the street, wondering where to go, suspecting Alessio would follow. She stopped beneath the loggia, shaded by the stone columns.

"Well, thank you for showing me the Sofonisba." She wasn't sure what to say. Only knew she had to leave.

"It was my pleasure." Alessio stood an arm's length away, his eyes locked on hers.

"So, I guess I'll see you around the campground."

"You most certainly will."

Alessio took a step toward Kara who, in turn, backed up incrementally, feeling for the stone column behind her. She leaned against the fluted marble as he placed a hand against it, beside her shoulder. He leaned in, smiling.

Kara's heart beat faster as the air warmed around her. The murmur of the tourists waiting to get into the museum disappeared, taking with it the noise of the hawkers and ubiquitous *polizia* sirens.

He brushed his hand across her face as he moved in to kiss her, and at once his hand was around her shoulders, pulling her to his lips. She gave in, instantly, with her whole body, and yielded to his advance.

And for two of the longest seconds she could remember, her heart thundered as her knees went weak, and she kissed with the verve of passion and sin—and the cresting realization that this thing that could never happen again, had in fact happened.

Kara pushed Alessio away, her eyes wide. "No. I can't."

His hand ran the length of her arm, to her wrist. Which he grasped loosely. "Kara."

Her eyes followed the stitching of his clothes, from his sleeve to his collar, dropping to the hairs of his chest protruding from the open buttons.

"*Cara*," he said, repeating her name softer, taking her hand in his calloused fingers.

"I'm flattered," she said, shaking her head, pulling her hand free. "But I'm married." Her voice cracked as she turned and ran in the direction of the campground, cursing herself for not taking Edward's advice.

Chapter 26

SATURDAY, JUNE 20 — FLORENCE, ITALY

"We need to talk."

Edward looked up from the flattened cardboard on which he'd spread the salvageable parts, wondering what prompted her urgent tone. Kara appeared flustered, winded, as if she'd pedaled a mountain pass. *Where had she been?* He wanted to ask, but the sight of her crossed arms and tapping foot told him not to bother.

He tore open a foil packet and withdrew a makeup removal wipe to clean his hands. The smears of bicycle grease soon vanished, leaving only dueling inky crescents under his fingernails and cuticles. "Should have swiped more of these from that hotel in Amsterdam," he said, holding the empty packet up for show.

"Why did Tom give you a phone?"

Edward took a deep breath and stood, grimacing as the sudden change in position fanned the fire in his thighs. He'd been squatting for the better part of an hour. He balled the wrapper with the blackened wipe and tossed the trash onto the cardboard, where it rolled to a stop against a bicycle chain that lay coiled like a snake.

"To check in. We made a bet," he said, delaying, searching for the explanation he'd rehearsed that morning. Before the trip to the gardens, the damage to the bikes.

"What kind of bet?"

Edward ran a nervous hand though his hair, "It was more of a contest. It turns out that Tom knows Ron Madsen and he recognized me from our profile picture ... Do you remember that magazine I was in?" Edward paused for acknowledgment, but Kara merely twirled her hand, ushering him to the point.

"He wanted me to come work for him—"

"In Minnesota?" she interrupted, her voice rising with incredulity.

"No. In Seattle."

Kara stared at him, her face pursed in concentration. She seemed to be analyzing every word he said, anticipating and slotting each syllable into a grid, as if every argument and lie he'd told her were a Sudoku to be solved by his coming explanation.

He knew he had to get this right.

"Tom offered me my own office, my own staff," he continued, growing wistful for what could have been. "Private wealth management. Great money and strictly nine to five once I got set up."

"Fantastic. So, why hide it from me?"

His gaze fell to her feet, where her toes clawed the soles of her sandals, as if bracing for the blast of his secret. "He wanted me to start in six months." As the truth hung in the air, Edward thought back to all the times he'd heard people say how relieved they felt after confessing a secret guilt. Unburdened. *Bullshit.* The words of his revelation clamped down upon his shoulders like a yoke, hitching him to the immovable heft of his deceit. He willed himself to look her in the eyes.

It was the hardest thing he'd ever done.

"And you *agreed* to this?" Kara's mouth fell open, her disbelief spilling out in an exasperated sigh.

"No. Not at first. I was flattered, sure, but when I told him how long the trip would take ..." His voice softened. "He said he wouldn't wait."

"And?"

"I knew I'd never get an offer like that again. Hell, I'd be lucky to get another job in VC anywhere. And three years out of work would be too long, I'd be forgotten." In his words, Edward heard the same rationale Tom used against him that night on the dock, and he shivered despite the Tuscan summer, feeling again the dread of an uncertain future.

"I don't believe you said yes." Kara rubbed her head as she spoke.

"I needed to be back in Seattle by October."

Kara took a step backward, and though she looked toward her bicycle lying upside-down in the dirt, Edward could sense her recalling the flight to London, the train to Florence. He could almost hear the puzzle pieces clicking together in her mind.

"I thought it was possible. A compromise. Six months to travel the world," he said, doling out excuses in a staccato that matched his rising pulse. "A dream house to come home to. Your own art studio. You wouldn't have to work anymore—"

"You still don't get it," she said, cutting in, her voice wavering.

Edward turned his hands over, gesturing for her to fill him in as he struggled to ignore the nausea boiling in his stomach.

"Remember when I asked if you knew why I wanted to take this trip?"

He waited for her to continue, then realized he should say something. He took a guess. "You were bored with your job, wanted to shake things up—"

"I was sick of coming second."

"But you were the best—"

"Oh, for chrissake. Not at my job. *To yours!*"

He didn't understand, but tried to soothe her. "Kara, you were never second to anything—"

"You put everything before me! Your company. Your clients. They always came first. This trip was my dream. And what did you do? You ruined it the first chance you got."

"The only reason I worked those hours was for you, for our future. Even the contest …" He tried explaining but stopped, hating how inadequate the words sounded.

Kara closed her eyes and took a deep breath. "Know where I was today?"

A bird swooped down from a tree and landed briefly on the tent, drawing his attention, rescuing him from having to risk another guess. When he looked to Kara, he saw tears welling in her eyes.

"While you were fixing the bikes, trying to hurry us off to Siena or Rome, or, I don't know, probably Tokyo if you got your way, I was at the museum." She swallowed slowly, the movement drawing his attention to a single tear that had coursed its way over her cheek and down her neck. "With Alessio."

Edward's stomach clenched, absorbing the gut shot as he forced himself to stay quiet, to hear her out.

"I wasn't in the mood for company—I was so upset about the phone and the bikes—but we started talking about art. And religion. Then, before I knew it, he was bribing a security guard to let us into an old Medici corridor."

"Did he hurt you?" Edward asked, feeling his hair stand on end.

"What? No. He was a perfect gentleman. He wanted to show me a portrait of a Renaissance artist I hadn't heard of. A woman," she said sniffling.

The thought of Kara alone with the man he warned her about; the one he was certain had vandalized their bicycles; the one who threatened him, was almost too much to bear. "So, why are you crying?"

"Because I kissed him."

Edward stumbled backward as his thoughts spun like a vortex, sucking up the ground beneath him, unbalancing his world. He grabbed a fistful of his shirt, trying to hold himself upright while processing what he heard.

"He initiated it. It was quick. I stopped him—"

"After I told you he was dangerous?"

Kara looked away. When she turned back, her face was stony, her breathing forceful. The sudden shift took Edward by surprise. Her lack of apparent remorse chilled him.

He rubbed his face, but there was no blocking the visions that formed in his mind, nor the scent of her perfume wafting toward him on a breeze laced with lawn clippings and fertilizer. Real or imagined, he couldn't tell. Didn't care. Every breath filled him with the thought of his wife kissing that groundskeeper. Yet it was the way she looked at him that concerned him most. She wouldn't have hurried back to admit only to a simple kiss.

"What else?" he asked, his voice hard, suspecting whatever occurred was likely his fault. Even if he couldn't forgive her for it.

Kara looked as if he slapped her. "I told you we only kissed. What are you—"

"No, not about him. What else do you have to say? You've been holding something back for months. I kept telling myself it was nothing, but ..." he said, hoping he was wrong.

Kara took a deep breath and squeezed herself, rubbing her bare arms as she did. She had goose bumps despite the warmth of the late afternoon sun. Their shadows had seemed to double in length since she'd gotten back.

"I guess there's no point in denying it, since you already had Hiromasa ask me," she said.

Edward had no idea what she was talking about and told her as much. He hadn't spoken to Hiromasa since last night's dinner, and only then out of politeness.

"He asked me if I was going to divorce you in February. Why else would he have thought that if you didn't put him up to it?"

Edward gasped. "What?"

"Please don't make this harder than it is. You must have told him something."

"No, I didn't. And why would I think that? Sure, we went through a rough patch, but I never thought you were going to leave me." His voice rose in pitch as he spoke, his vocal chords drawn tight.

"Then how did he know—"

"Hold on. Were you really going to divorce me?" Edward's eyes widened with shock.

Kara looked everywhere but at her husband, and he could tell, in her silence, what her answer would be. "I was considering it," she said.

Her words pierced his heart, sapping his strength and his breath. He felt himself collapsing inward, wondering what went wrong. He'd committed himself fully to their marriage, for six years he had chased every opportunity that crossed his periphery, taking on the most difficult clients, angling for every promotion, seizing every risk. He'd sacrificed time with friends, his hobbies, even his health on occasion, all so she'd never have to want for anything.

And it wasn't good enough, he thought, unwilling to admit to a conclusion that was growing inescapable, that he may have been loving her wrong. He felt his face twist in confusion as he stared at her, clenching the pit in his stomach, silently demanding an explanation.

"What did you expect? How long did you think I'd sit around waiting for you? Alone. Forever? The constant late nights, the weekends with clients. Did you think I enjoyed fending for myself, having to ask friends to join me for dinner, or to go to parties with, or ..."

As Kara's words ran together, a cacophony of accusations, Edward moved across the campsite, in search of a chair, needing to sit down. As he walked, he bumped the cardboard with his foot. A solitary dirt-caked pedal lolled to the side as the crankset rolled a quarter turn. Behind him, Kara continued, counting off the litany of charges brought, the times he canceled their plans on account of work. Right then, something she said rang clear, penetrating the fog.

"What did you just say?" he asked, looking at her askance.

She mumbled something incomprehensible as she took a step back, stunned.

"Something about a camping trip."

"No, I—"

"I heard it. You mentioned going camping without me." He took a step closer. "That happened once. Why bring it up now?"

Kara stuttered, backpedaling in her complaints, trying to shove off from the sandbar where she herself had run the conversation aground.

"It was last fall, when those investors came up from California on short notice. There was a mountain bike festival that weekend, right?"

Kara nodded slowly as the truth surfaced in her face.

"And you went alone."

Her chest heaved with nervous breaths. He stared at her, not wanting to see her cry, hoping her venom would return, knowing he could shoulder enough guilt for the team, and learn from his mistakes, but unsure if he could forgive what he feared she had done.

Tears streamed down her face, yet she remained silent.

"That's about the time you started mentioning this bike trip. Isn't it?"

Kara didn't move, didn't look at him.

"Answer me!" he yelled.

She nodded.

Edward pumped his fists, squeezing them till his fingertips ached. He looked away, to the treetops, the tent, their bicycles, searching for an escape from his fate, but he couldn't ignore the question scorching his heart.

He tried to ask what she had done, but his voice caught on the lump in his throat.

Kara shook her head, sobbing. "I was so lonely. And I was terrified of being unfaithful to you. It's why I wanted to do the trip, why I thought of a divorce. I needed you to quit your job. I never wanted it to happen again."

"Who was he?" The words hissed through his clenched teeth.

"I don't know. Some guy. I've hated myself ever since."

Edward felt his heart ripping in two, as if his insides had spilled across the ground, the years of their togetherness disassembled for all to see.

"I'm so sorry," she said, reaching for him, her bloodshot eyes as red as his panniers. "I love you so much. I'm so, so sorry," she said, pleading.

He raised his hands to stop her, as if he could ward off her betrayal, then squeezed his eyes shut and bit down on his lip, screaming in his mind, wanting to kick and punch and destroy something, anything, so that he alone didn't have to suffer the torture he was enduring. A thousand memories flooded his mind, dreams and recollections of their lives together, each of them feeling counterfeit, as if he were merely a stand-in for some faceless, nameless guy she'd fuck the minute he wasn't around.

The taste of iron hit his tongue, salty droplets of blood pumped by his surging adrenaline, leaking from his shattered soul. Kara's demands for forgiveness sounded distant, but too close. He needed to get away. Away from her. He raised his hands again, obscuring his view, blotting out the short-term memory of her face. "I need to be alone," he said, backing away. "I can't be around you."

Chapter 27

SUNDAY, JUNE 21 — FLORENCE, ITALY

Edward walked the streets of Florence for hours, losing himself in the pubs of the San Niccolò neighborhood. At each stop, he ordered a Negroni, embracing the perfect bitter companion to his jealousy, swallowing his grief drop by drop as he sucked the Campari from ice cubes that were slow to cool his seething anger.

The sting of Kara's betrayal stuck with him through the night, a barb that worked itself deeper with every thought, splintering all notion of the life they had together.

He put off returning as long as he could, hoping to outlast her inevitable desire to wait up for him. It was past two in the morning when he finally dragged himself up the hill to the campground, spurred by the onset of rain and a desperate need to lie down. The campground disco had ceased its nightly racket, and even the cicadas had concluded it was too late to sing.

Isolated by the silence, he paused outside the campground gate, as the rainwater dripped from his hair, and wondered if they both wouldn't be better off if he stayed away for good. He granted himself a moment of self-pity, then shrugged away the thought and made for bed.

But even in the haze of his drunk, he could hear the tent's vestibule door flapping in the breeze, a snapping accompaniment to the patter of raindrops on nylon.

Edward stiffened, realizing Kara had probably gone to the bathroom—it was the only reason they ever left the door unzipped without rolling it. He'd have to talk to her, after all. But before he could corral his emotions into words, the faint light of a distant campground street lamp revealed their campsite in a state of disarray.

Their camp chairs lay upside down and their bikes were once again knocked on their sides. The clothesline had fallen on one end, their towels now lying limp and wet in an expanding puddle of mud, the map case drowning nearby.

Edward's head ached as he grasped for possible explanations. Maybe a storm had blown through. Or perhaps they were robbed by whoever had damaged their bikes. Or maybe, he thought, Kara threw a fit on account of his walking off.

Then he noticed the footprints. They were too numerous, their size too large to be Kara's alone. The prints went this way and that, revealing a trail of chaos in the damp dirt. Slicing through them were two narrow streaks, as if someone petite had been dragged by the heels.

Edward called his wife's name and stood stock-still, listening, hoping she was nearby, and straining to hear over the sound of his breathing and the rain.

Nothing.

Near one of the chairs he found a piece of crinkled paper that appeared to be from Kara's journal, the dirty tread of a boot print stamped across the message.

He bent to lift it and swayed as a rush of blood flooded his throbbing head. The letter was addressed to him, written in Kara's unique blend of block printed vowels and looping consonants. He broke out in a cold sweat.

Edward backed toward the tent as he struggled to read the soggy paper in his hands, and fell onto the floor of the vestibule, having tripped over a tent stake. The tent's inner door, the last barrier to their home, was also unzipped. Kara's sleeping bag lay untouched, her pajamas folded atop the pillow, just as she left them every morning.

He pulled his headlamp from the pocket near his pillow, flicked on the light, and read.

Dear Edward,

I know nothing I can write will ever undo the pain I caused you. But you must understand that I've been hurting for some time. You've strayed too. Maybe not in the traditional sense, but I've been backseat to your career since the day you got hired on at Madsen. All I ever wanted was to spend time with you, my best friend. It was the reason I chose to get married so young. But your time was the one thing you could never give.

I thought this trip would bring us closer. That it would make up for all the time we missed. I was wrong. I don't know where we go from here, but

The letter ended unfinished, the pen having been dragged askew. Interrupted. Edward's heart raced as the stray line and the muddy boot print on the letter coalesced in a terrifying scene.

Kara needed him.

Edward sprinted straight to the campground office, the light of his headlamp bobbing back and forth across the path, reflecting from tents, cars, and travel trailers. *She must have yelled for help. Why didn't anyone call the police?*

The office lights were out and the doors locked, but a campground map taped to the door showed an unnumbered collection of cabins circled with the words "For Emergency" written in multiple languages.

The circled area was just past the restaurant. Four canvas cabins squared off in pairs, their lights out, the doors to three of them sealed tight. The landscaper's cart was parked in front of the fourth, one whose screen door stood ajar, creaking in the wind. *Were Alessio and Hiromasa involved?* Edward poked his head into their cabin and called Kara's name. The space was empty except for some clothing piled neatly on a shelf, winter sweaters by the looks of it, along with several blue uniform shirts.

"Kara!" he yelled into the night. "Kara!" he shouted, praying she'd answer, receiving only a chorus of drowsy Italian grousing in response, the other campers no doubt telling him to shut up.

Edward considered banging on the other cabin doors, but was gripped by the thought of Kara returning to the campsite, only to find him not there. He knew it was unlikely, but he had to hope. He raced back to the tent, his belief in her being there rising with each step.

Alone.

He decided to call the police, and even got as far as dialing 112, the European emergency number, but quickly hung up when the operator answered in incomprehensible Italian. He froze on the spot, too nervous to ask if she spoke English. Besides, he thought, excusing himself after the fact, they wouldn't do anything for twenty-four hours anyway. Especially once he admitted that they'd been arguing. That he had walked off fuming.

Could she have left me?

No. The letter, the footprints and mess …

"At least then I'd know she was safe."

He sighed, hating his helplessness, his guilt in all of this. He took to pacing the path past the adjacent campsites, ignoring the snoring emanating from the other tents. On each pass, he'd reach the lamppost, check his watch, then return the other way, only to look over his shoulder, convinced Kara would be there.

But he was alone.

"I couldn't protect her."

Edward pressed his knuckles against his head as he walked, trying to imagine where she could be, inventing reasons why this was all perfectly ordinary and he was overreacting. He brought his hands down, slamming his fists against his legs for lack of anything more solid to hit.

His right fist struck hard against something in his pocket. But not just a thing, *the* thing. The root of his problem. The phone. If only the phone hadn't rung in the plaza, he would have had time to explain himself, to get them out of Florence. "Damn it," he said, cursing his luck.

But that wasn't true and he knew it. The problem was him. The contest. It was his decision to sabotage Kara's dream, his willingness to prioritize Tom's ridiculous schedule over his own wife's desires.

Tom, Edward thought. *That's right.* "He's the one who got me into this, maybe he knows someone who can help me out."

He shook the doubts from his mind, turned on the phone, and called Tom. "Pick up, pick it up," Edward urged, after three rings went unanswered.

"Yeah?"

"Tom, it's Edward—"

"I know who it is. You're aware it's not Thursday, right?"

"Yeah. Tom, listen, I need your help."

"I'm busy right now, Ed."

"It's Kara. She's missing. I think she's in trouble," Edward said, struggling to keep his breath.

"And what do you expect me to do about it?"

"I'm not sure. I'm in Florence. Italy. And—"

"I know where Florence is," Tom interrupted, sounding like he might hang up.

"Right. Of course. I was hoping you might know someone who—."

"If you think she's in trouble, call the police. But if you're worried she might be shacking up with some Italian playboy, then get used to it."

Edward recoiled from the verbal sucker punch. "Get used to it?" His head swirled with nausea as the images he tried to keep from forming in his mind took shape. Kara, an anonymous other, his hands on her body, kissing, feeling …

Edward paced as he tore at the cuticle of his thumb, the fresh sting distracting him from the tryst in his mind.

"Half the guys in the office are divorced, and the rest should be," Tom said, with the casualness of a waiter announcing the daily special.

"You're not helping."

"I'm just telling you how it is. Jobs like ours make it easy to attract the prettiest birds, but they sure do fly away quick if you leave them alone long enough." Tom laughed as Edward raged quietly. "Now, how about an update on your office search? I expected some info from you by now. What the hell's taking so long?"

Edward held the phone away from him and silently screamed at the night sky.

"Edward, you better not be trying to stall—"

As he squeezed the Blackberry in his hand, feeling the plastic case buckle in his grip, Edward wished it was Tom's neck. "Stall? I called you worried about my wife! You think I give a shit about office space? Go to hell!" Edward shouted.

He stuffed the phone in his pocket, hating Tom more than ever, despising him for revealing what Edward should have seen long ago.

Edward stirred beneath the hand on his shoulder. It had landed with the heft of a fog settling before the dawn. He opened his eyes to the darkness, waking to the rain-blurred letter dissolving in his hands, to the puddled divots carved by the heels of his shoes.

He couldn't have been asleep for more than a few minutes. *But still?*

A thought came to him as he sat slumped in the chair, in the moments before he rose to shed his blanket of suffering, relieved to feel what was surely Kara's hand. He imagined himself as she saw him then: pathetic.

There was no question of forgiveness. It was he who needed to apologize. If she cheated, it was because he had strayed first. If she wanted a divorce, it was his actions that drew up the papers. Tom's comments helped him see this now.

He turned in the chair slowly, like a second hand swinging to the bottom of the hour, buying time to find the words that would set them straight.

But the hand that roused him glowed blue. Hiromasa.

"You?" Edward knocked the chair over as he rose and grabbed him by the shirt. "What are you doing here? Where's Kara?" He shook him. "Where is she?"

"With Alessio," Hiromasa said, cringing. His left eye was swollen shut and puffy. Blood leaked from a gash in his brow and streaked down his rain-soaked face, glistening in the faint light.

Edward surged with rage as he jostled the smaller man. "Where are they?"

"He brought her to an apartment across the river. He couldn't get in. He's crazy. I tried stopping him."

Edward relaxed his grip, but didn't let go. It was the one thing he felt he had under his control. "Stop him from what?" His mind ran with possibilities he hadn't before imagined, not truly believing Alessio posed a threat other than to Kara's fidelity. But seeing Hiromasa in his bludgeoned state changed everything.

"He plans to kill her, so they can be together."

Edward's face froze in paralyzed confusion as his body strained to act. The words were slow to penetrate, like an axe bouncing from an elm log before finally biting, splitting the grains of Edward's understanding.

His lips trembled as he recalled the worst of everything he'd ever said and done in their relationship. Of it all, nothing compared to tricking Kara into coming to Florence. He bunched his fists in Hiromasa's shirt as his breathing intensified, stoking his determination. He couldn't live with himself if anything happened to her. He'd risk everything to keep her safe.

Through the din of the myriad questions shouting in his mind, he noticed Hiromasa struggling to speak, and released him. Once freed, Hiromasa massaged his throat, catching his breath as Edward interrogated him, demanding an explanation, a location.

"Alessio was wronged a long time ago by a woman named Sylvia—"

"What does this have to do with Kara?" Edward interrupted.

"He believes they're the same person. That Sylvia's soul is alive in Kara."

Edward gnashed his teeth, growing impatient, but let him continue.

"Sylvia broke his heart. She tricked him. And now, Alessio thinks by killing himself and Kara, he and Sylvia can return to the past. Together."

A chill rippled through Edward as he recalled Alessio's comment in the gardens. He said he'd release her. "What do you mean *the past?*"

"Alessio and I …" Hiromasa shook his head, then abandoned the effort. "You won't believe me."

Edward wasn't about to press for details. Whatever madness the two had shared wasn't his concern. "You said he couldn't break into an apartment. Where else would he take her?

"I'm not sure. When we couldn't get into the apartment building, he grew hostile, then mentioned a place in Oltrarno." Hiromasa hesitated as he spoke. Whether truly uncertain or playing coy, Edward couldn't tell. "He wanted me to join them. But when I tried to untie her, he attacked me."

"She's tied up?" His eyes bulged at the realization.

"Her wrists," he said, dropping his gaze.

"Why didn't you call the police?"

"No *polizia*. It's too complicated," he said, shaking his head. Hiromasa looked at his watch. "But we have time. Alessio plans to wait until 3:23." He rubbed a hand across his face. "That's when we returned to Florence."

Edward let the comment sail by, another in a series of remarks that made little sense. It was almost three. "Think! You've got to know where he's taking her."

Hiromasa scrunched his face in thought, causing the cut on his forehead to pulse a fresh trickle of blood. "Maybe to Santo Spirito. It's where I woke. Not far from here."

"Good. Let's go," Edward said. Then, surprising himself, he thought back to the bar in Montana, when the ranchers asked him if he was packing a gun. He couldn't have imagined needing a weapon back then, but now he understood.

"There are things I must know about you and Kara."

"Later."

"It cannot wait. I must know what happened in February."

Edward stiffened, not caring for the reference to his losing his job. "What did Kara tell you?"

"Nothing I couldn't guess. I swear," he added, perhaps sensing Edward's rising temper. "But I have a theory we must discuss."

"Then we'll talk on the way. First, show me where you keep your tools."

Chapter 28

SUNDAY, JUNE 21 — FLORENCE, ITALY

Edward's nerves vibrated like piano strings as he led the way down the hill into the slumbering city. Charcoal clouds hung overhead, soaking up the city's ambient amber light, wringing themselves empty.

Hiromasa talked incessantly, inquiring about Edward's marriage, the bicycle tour, and the events of that February day. He appeared to slot the information into an equation only he could see. That was, until Edward told him about the baseball, getting fired, and his cowardly offer to take the bike trip.

"That's it," Hiromasa announced. "That must have been the trigger!"

"What are you talking about?"

He grinned with the satisfaction of a man who'd solved the impossible. "It's what brought us back. Your offer to take the trip broke the cycle. You avoided the rejection that Alessio and I could not."

"What rejection?"

"My friend," he said with somber compassion, "that was the day Kara intended to divorce you."

The revelation plunged into Edward's gut like a shovel, lifting and doubling the void he felt without her. *Could it be?* Hiromasa continued talking as Edward's attention returned to that fateful afternoon in their Seattle apartment, when he thrust the map and champagne at Kara the moment she got home. But her hands were full with a gym bag in one, a manila envelope in the other. He thought it was junk mail.

"I've been so blind." But it didn't matter now. He licked the rain from his lips and turned to Hiromasa. "How much further?"

"Just past the bridge," he said, crossing the street. "We need to move fast, though, it's almost time."

"About that—"

"Alessio and I woke at 3:23." He gave Edward a sidelong glance, as if to check he was paying attention. "I had no way of knowing the time, but Alessio saw a clock and remembers it vividly. He thinks it holds significance."

"And what do you believe?"

Hiromasa rubbed his chin. "I think Kara is in grave danger. We should hurry."

Edward quickened his pace, following behind Hiromasa as he jogged. It was already past three, and the bustling streets of Florence had been soothed to sleep by the early summer rain. That they were in a well-lit part of town was both blessing and curse. The street lamps would make Alessio easier to spot, but he didn't want any witnesses if it came to blows. Or worse, he thought, feeling the weapon shift in his rear pocket.

Movement flashed up ahead, on Ponte Vecchio. He pointed.

"Come. Quickly," Hiromasa hissed, ducking into the shadows on the darkened downstream side of the bridge.

"I see you," the voice called out. "You disappoint me, Hiromasa."

Edward stepped from behind the corner of a jewelry shop. Any lingering hope that this was all a misunderstanding, or that Kara was somewhere safe, vanished in a blink. Alessio stood alongside a stone column near the center of the bridge, holding a knife to Kara's throat.

"Edward," Kara yelled, her voice shattering the night, as she tried to twist out from Alessio's grasp.

"Let her go. Now!"

Alessio laughed and pulled her closer. "Why? You're going to lose her either way."

Edward shook his head, knowing he'd never let it happen. Not again. He'd stake his life on it. "Dying won't bring you back," Edward said, surprising himself by giving into Hiromasa's story.

"He's right, Alessio, it won't work," Hiromasa shouted.

"You know nothing. Neither of you! You've no concept of the suffering I endured for years because of her. Because of you," Alessio snarled at Kara, shaking her by the neck.

Edward advanced, but Alessio froze him with a threatening look. "You don't get to win. Sylvia was mine. I lost her, but God himself has granted me this chance!"

"What's he talking about? Why is he calling me Sylvia?"

Edward saw the confusion in Kara's eyes, and the terror she fought to suppress. He stood fifteen yards away, close enough to read the panic on her face and to see her knees trembling, but too far to comfort her, to whisper that he loved her—that he was sorry for everything.

"We're connected," Hiromasa said. "All of us. And maybe many others. You and Edward are soul mates, Kara. As were we once."

Edward snapped his head in Hiromasa's direction.

"I knew you as Isabelle. In my time, four hundred years ago. And to Alessio, you were a Florentine woman named Sylvia. For others, you were ..." he shrugged.

"Claudette," Kara said, her voice barely audible.

Edward recalled the gravestone they'd found in the woods, the French-Canadian who flirted openly with Kara as if he knew her. He thought of all the encounters he'd had on this trip, replaying the journey back to the body of the Blackfoot.

Was he the first? Or did the bond stretch even further back in time?

"Alessio," Hiromasa called out, "You must face the truth. Sylvia married another because you abandoned her. You chose Malta and your gallery over her."

Alessio looked away in denial, and Edward took two quick steps closer.

"And Isabelle bid me farewell because my heart belonged to God." Hiromasa turned to Edward and lifted his chin, encouraging him.

Edward inched forward, his eyes locked on his wife. "And Kara, you wanted to divorce me because I wasn't there for you." He swallowed, trying to moisten his dry mouth. "But then I lost my job."

Kara struggled against Alessio's grip. "What does this matter now?"

Edward motioned for her to remain calm, afraid what Alessio would do if he got nervous. "Hiromasa thinks that by taking the trip, we broke some sort of continuum—"

"This makes no sense."

"I know, babe, I know. But we should believe him. He says our souls have fallen in love countless times throughout history. We're meant to be together, but each time ..." Edward choked on the words, unearthing the truth buried in the absurdity. "I didn't know how lonely you were."

Kara looked to Edward, her eyes moist with understanding, as she mouthed the words *I still love you.* And he knew right then that he was going to undo this. He'd get his second chance.

And he was almost within range.

"Enough!" Alessio checked his watch, then whispered in Kara's ear. Her eyes went wild as she struggled again to break free, but Alessio tightened his grip, dimpling the hollow of her neck with the knife's tip.

"It's not going to work, Alessio." Hiromasa cried out. "Death is death. There's no returning to 1845. You'll only be murdering an innocent woman. And yourself."

Alessio laughed his response.

Edward spotted a security camera above Alessio, beyond an awning dripping with rain, but couldn't tell if Alessio was in view. If the police had seen him, they were on their way.

"Two minutes," Hiromasa whispered.

Edward strafed right, attempting to flank Alessio, to bait him into the camera's view. But Alessio shifted away, sidling around the corner of the shop, keeping the wall behind him and Kara.

Alessio shifted from foot to foot, fidgeting with the knife, seemingly fighting his own inner doubt. Though Hiromasa pleaded for Alessio to abandon his plan, Edward's focus was on Kara, the knife, and what he must do.

Holding her gaze, he mouthed the word *butterflies*.

Kara looked confused, so he silently spoke the word again and bulged his eyes for emphasis, willing her to close her eyes. At last, Kara understood.

Edward pulled the cold metal cylinder from behind his back and spun it in his hand. He sprang forward, raising the weapon, as his finger squeezed the flimsy trigger—but nothing happened. The plastic resisted, blocked by the safety tab.

Alessio opened his stance and readied himself to slash at Edward. But the tab gave way in time, and a stream of hornet spray shot from Edward's hand, jetting straight at Alessio's face. He shrieked and clawed at the foaming poison now drenching his face, blinding him, filling his mouth as he screamed. In his fit, he seemed to lose track of Kara, but Edward couldn't take any chances.

He lunged, tackling Alessio away from Kara and knocking the knife from his grasp. Edward maintained his assault, squeezing the trigger with all his might, as his adrenaline armored him against the stinging backsplash and filtered the fumes from his awareness.

Alessio choked and writhed, but Edward wouldn't stop.

He plowed forward, driving Alessio back as he emptied every ounce of hornet killer into the face of the man who threatened to murder his wife. Alessio struck the bridge railing off-balance, hitting the waist-high stone wall clumsily. Before Edward could react, before it could be prevented, Alessio's momentum carried him backward over the railing.

And then he was gone.

A moment of silence, then a splash.

Alessio was dead before he even hit the water.

Chapter 29

SUNDAY, JUNE 21 — FLORENCE, ITALY

Gasping for air, Edward leaned against the bridge's stone railing, dizzy from the poison he'd ingested. His swollen tongue tasted of dental fillings and citronella, and his stomach bubbled with nausea. A searing heat engulfed his face, as if the toxic backsplash had ignited, scorching his nose and eyes.

Yet, as he stared at the inky waters flowing beneath him, trying to catch his breath, he could only think of the light. For in that fleeting moment before Alessio hit the water, a tremendous flash blinded him. A singular blue strobe so intense it knocked the wind from Edward as it washed over him—into him.

Edward dropped the empty canister over the edge and stood in silence. Beyond the dripping of the rain and a motorcycle's distant whine, Florence was quiet. No cry of sirens or shouting, no slapping of a policeman's shoes on wet paving stones.

He'd remember this forever. The moment he killed Alessio. The night he saved Kara's life.

Kara!

Edward hurried to her side. Ignoring the fear of what she'd now think of him, having seen what he's capable of, he pulled her into his arms.

"You're safe," he said, summoning a calm tone, as much for his benefit as hers.

Kara choked on her words as she interlaced her fingers in his. Never before had Edward felt as relieved as when she buried her head in the nook of his shoulder. Her love was like a string-tied balloon that nearly floated away, and he gripped her tighter than ever as he reeled it in.

Their nervous breathing calmed and fell into sync as they sat intertwined on the cold, damp stones of Ponte-Vecchio, slumped against a centuries-old storefront, with Edward whispering assurances of safety, devotion.

Hiromasa approached. "We must leave." he said, and motioned to cut the rope from Kara's wrists. Edward nodded. Once done, Hiromasa threw the rope and knife into the river and helped the couple to their feet. "We shouldn't loiter here. You can rest in my cabin."

Kara took a steadying breath and dusted her pants off. "He's right. We better go."

Edward stared at Hiromasa, unsurprised to see him glowing brighter than before, as if the dimming of Alessio's light increased the wattage of Hiromasa's soul. He sought to say something, but couldn't find the words—and the questions were too numerous.

Edward lay awake when Hiromasa entered the cabin, carrying a tray of pastries and coffee. Kara remained asleep, curled beside him, the two nestled together in Hiromasa's twin bed. Judging by the angle of daylight shining through the screen door, it had to be at least eight in the morning.

"Thank you," Edward whispered, watching Hiromasa set the tray down atop a small table. "Anybody ask about …" his voice trailed off as he gestured at Alessio's empty bed.

"I explained he had to travel on short notice." Hiromasa said.

Edward pondered the comment, rooting around in the surface of the lie for the truth sown below. But if it was true, if he and Alessio had traveled through time and were somehow related to him—to his soul—then he had to accept the rest of their story as well: that even soul mates can break one another's hearts. He recalled the sight of Kara on the bridge, the horror of seeing a knife to her throat, the paralyzing knowledge that Alessio would have killed her if Hiromasa hadn't found him. He fixed his gaze on Hiromasa and admitted, "I don't know what to say."

"You can agree to cover his shift. It's best to start with the toilets."

Edward recoiled, but Hiromasa's sudden laughter spared him from having to reply. Cracking jokes about a dead man made Edward squirm, but he couldn't resist giving in to the moment. A snicker quickly built to a belly laugh that blew the lid off the pressure cooker of the prior night.

Kara stirred beside him, awakened by the noise.

Perhaps sensing Edward's unease or wanting Kara to hear his words, Hiromasa said, "You mustn't feel guilty about what happened. Alessio was a danger. But it was only thanks to you that he got to experience a life beyond death. Beyond his time. We both have."

The gratitude in Hiromasa's voice rang as deep as the bells of the Duomo. Whether Edward believed in the fantastic didn't matter, Hiromasa certainly did. And thanks to that, Edward found relief. Few even knew who Alessio was; nobody would miss him.

"What will you do?" Kara asked, yawning as she rose to sit. Edward pulled a blanket across her shoulders and mouthed his good morning as he swung his feet to the floor. They both wore their clothes from the previous night.

"I'm planning to return to Japan in the fall. I read on the Internet that Emperor Meiji ended the Christian persecution many years ago." He clapped his hands together. "These are amazing times to be alive."

Edward and Kara exchanged confused looks, neither knowing much about Hiromasa's past or Japanese history.

"I never thought it would be safe for me to return home," Hiromasa said, his tone wistful. After a beat, he continued. "But what about you? Where are you cycling to next?"

"Well …" Kara began. Edward chewed his lower lip and listened as she handled the onion of an answer without slicing too many layers, keeping the core at arm's length to avoid tears.

"I can tell you have much to discuss. I will leave you to it."

Edward and Kara rose in unison to say their goodbyes. Edward extended his hand to Hiromasa, then thought better of it. He wrapped the smaller man in a bear hug and thanked him for helping to rescue Kara, for showing how to save their marriage.

Edward stepped aside as Kara approached.

"Thank you so much," she said, gently placing her hand on his bruised face. "For everything."

Kara hugged Hiromasa goodbye as he bent to whisper in her ear. A pang of jealousy stabbed at Edward as he watched Kara blush upon receiving a secret farewell from a man who claimed to have once been her soul's mate in another life.

Edward could only hope that one day in the future, if he's lucky, she'd tell him what he said. But he knew better than to ask—and suspected she'd never forget.

The couple ate in silence after Hiromasa left the cabin. Whether it would be the last meal they'd eat together or the first of thousands to follow was uncertain. But Edward knew they had to open up, and not just about the trip or their secrets, but about the way they live and love together. When they finally spoke, they did so in unison.

"We need to talk," Kara said.

"Let's take a walk," Edward suggested simultaneously. She nodded.

Edward led the way out of the campground, taking care to avoid the campsite where their damaged bikes and the trauma of the prior night lay. They took turns making innocent remarks about the weather, how tired they were, and the Italian architecture as they wandered the streets of Oltrarno, unwilling to glance toward the river or Ponte Vecchio, reluctant to embrace the conversation they so needed to have. Finally, Edward guided them up the hill to the overlook at Piazza Michelangelo, where only two long nights earlier he sufficiently turned a mess into a disaster.

This time the words came easily.

"I'll never lie to you again. I promise," he began, cutting to the chase.

"Me too," she said under her breath.

"I've been a fool. A horrible husband." Kara shook her head, but Edward continued. "I only wanted to provide. Like my father."

"I never cared how much money we had."

"I know that now. I read your letter." He said it fast, spitting out the words quickly to avoid the toxic aftertaste. "But losing my job made me feel like such a failure. I was paranoid of telling you. Of what you'd think."

"It's okay to fail. Especially in your career. Better that than your personal life." She balled his hands in hers and met his gaze. "Or your marriage."

"God, Kara, the thought of you wanting a divorce. I don't know what I'd do without you. I'm so sorry."

"I'm sorry too—"

"I know you are," he said, holding a finger to her lips. "You don't need to say it. Maybe one day in the future, but not now. Right now, I only need to know if you'll continue this trip with me."

"Are you sure that's what you want?"

"I've never wanted anything more in my life. We'll get the bikes working and go wherever you want. And whatever you want to do, we'll do. I promise."

"That's what you said in February." Kara sighed.

"I know. And I screwed it all up. But you've gotta believe me that I only agreed to Tom's stupid contest for you. Everything I've done, I did for you."

Kara took a deep breath and straightened, sending chills up Edward's spine. "I love you, Edward. I really do. But I cannot allow myself to stay married to you if things don't change. If *you* don't change."

"Okay, I'll do whatever—"

"Let me finish. This is hard enough without you interrupting me." She blinked several times, then continued. "I know you worked really hard to get your degree and want to have a big house and drive a fancy car, and that's fine. But I don't. I want a friend. I *need* companionship."

Edward felt his breathing quicken as he braced for the worst.

"I want to believe what Hiromasa said was true. That you and I are meant to be together. But you have to promise that I'm never going to come second to your career again. Even if it means we have to move someplace else, a different lifestyle, I need you to be there for me."

Edward nodded slowly, packing her plea tighter into his memory with each dip of his head.

"I will." He moved to kiss her, but was shocked solid when the phone in his pocket rang out. Kara pulled back, her smile drooping into a crease of incredulity.

Edward yanked the phone from his pocket and showed her the screen. "It's Tom."

"And?"

Edward cracked a sly grin. "I quit," he said, then whirled and flung the phone as far as he could. The ringing Blackberry went silent upon crashing through trees and shrubs far down the hillside.

Kara smiled briefly, then exhaled into a slump.

"What is it?"

"This has been so much harder than I expected. I feel like we've been pedaling into a headwind ever since leaving Seattle."

Edward bit his lower lip. He'd felt it too, but knew it wouldn't last. It couldn't. He put his arm around her and smiled in the mischievous manner she thought so annoyingly cute. "There's a summer breeze on the way. And I hear it's all tailwinds past Florence."

Chapter 30

FOURTEEN MONTHS LATER …

Kara's head lolled as the hammock swayed. The sudden movement may have startled her weeks ago, but she'd since made a habit of napping while her *batik* paintings dried—and waking to the evening wind had become a favorite pastime.

She opened her eyes to the wide brim of a straw hat pulled low over her brow and listened as the rice plants rustled in the breeze. Lifting the hat, she peered beyond the swimming pool, across the rice field to the west, to where the sun had all but disappeared behind the papaya trees.

Oh, crap!

"Edward?" She called for him as she swung her feet to the ground, wondering how late it was. As if in answer to her question, the sandalwood scent of the neighbor's evening offering wafted through the bamboo as she listened for a response.

She removed her hat and the denim apron she wore as a smock, and hung them on a hook in the covered patio that served as her studio. They'd been living in Bali for two months, and she'd taken to painting in the afternoons, after it got too hot to work digitally at the open-air co-op in town.

"You home?" She opened the door leading inside and yelled as she checked the clock. Again, no reply.

She'd grown used to the pliable concept of time in Bali, a place where punctuality meant arriving within hours of when one said they would, but restaurants were different. They had a reservation for the Sunday buffet at a nearby vegetarian café—as they did every week—and he was late.

Kara smoothed the wrinkles in her sundress as she paced the outdoor kitchen, her agitation growing by the minute. And not even the cooling touch of the tile floor on her feet could chill her temper.

"Did he forget?"

Barefoot and braless, Kara snatched her phone from the kitchen table and strode around the side of the house. There she stared along the crumbling concrete walk that snaked between an irrigation channel and the steep embankment leading down to the lower rice fields.

The throaty, sickly roar of Edward's rented scooter echoed in the distance, straining as he climbed the ramp from the main street. Kara waited, tapping an invisible wristwatch, blocking his path.

Edward soon rounded the corner wearing a white helmet with a peeling green decal and a smile as wide as the visor. Bundles of passion fruit hung from the handlebars, swaying with every bounce of the scooter. He rode with his legs extended, kicking off the ground for balance in his flip-flops, practically propelling the scooter forward by foot.

"Sorry I'm late."

"Our reservation's for six. Where have you been?"

"I'll hurry. It was Wayan again." He pulled off his helmet and gave Kara a peck on the cheek. "The guy shows up every day with another dozen questions."

"About the delivery service?"

"No, the other one. Wayan with the taxi."

"You should've told him you had someplace to be."

"I tried. But you know how it is. Besides, he wanted to pay me."

Kara stumbled backward in melodramatic shock. Edward had been consulting with local micro-businesses for a few weeks now, and though the locals, half of whom were named Wayan or Made, were quick to recommend him to their friends and brothers, he'd yet to see a dime for his effort. And while Bali was certainly cheaper than Seattle, her freelance work was barely enough to get by. "How much?"

Edward lowered the kickstand and hoisted the two bundles of passion fruit. "You're looking at it!"

Kara covered her mouth in attempt to stifle a giggle, but couldn't. "Figures," she said, taking the fruit and leading the way back to the house. Behind her, the seat of the scooter slammed shut on the small storage compartment.

"I also stopped for these," Edward said. And before she could turn to face him, he wrapped an arm around her waist from behind while raising a bouquet of exotic, sweet-smelling flowers to her nose. "I tried asking for daffodils, but it got lost in translation."

Kara inhaled deeply, luxuriating in the intoxicating fragrance of the cempaka. And as she did, she looked across the horizon of lemon-yellow petals to her husband and suggested a change of plans. "Let's eat in tonight."

STAY IN TOUCH

Reviews are critical to an author's success and improvement. Please consider leaving an honest review on Goodreads or at the storefront where you purchased this book. Thank you.

Sign up at dougwalsh.com for alerts concerning upcoming releases and special offers. All mailing list subscribers receive a free book download.

ACKNOWLEDGMENTS

Authoring this book took longer than the trip that inspired it, a two-year journey from Seattle to Singapore by bicycle and ship. It was at a dinner party in London, that I sat, deflated, listening as the other guests all-but ridiculed my then-secret desire to write the next great travel memoir. A book about cycling the globe was passé, one said. The last thing the world needed, another commented.

Deep inside, I suspected they were right.

My wife and I pedaled for the coast the following morning and sailed to Denmark. Six borders later, atop a mountain pass in Spain, I furiously scribbled the premise for this novel. Like the adventure that inspired it, it wasn't possible without the help of many, many people I'm fortunate to have in my life.

To David Anderson, Taylor Arthur, Chenelle Bremont, Sari Gallegos, Shandara Larson, and Jeff Weaver: This book owes what it is to you allowing me into your lives.

To Natalie French: Your addition to our group couldn't have come at a better time.

To Sandra Rosner: I fear the day you collect on the debt I owe you.

To Edward Bittner, Joseph Epstein, Jennifer Lesher, and Staci Roberts: Your time and effort in helping me improve this story is forever appreciated.

To Jessica Walsh-Jadach: Your long-distance enthusiasm is like a *doppio* to the veins.

To my editor, Timothy Fitzpatrick: I only wish I wrote faster, so we can work together more often.

To the Pacific Northwest Writer's Association: I wouldn't know half the people mentioned in these pages if not for this organization.

To everyone who cheered us on and opened their homes and refrigerators to two exhausted cyclists: Thank you! The publication of this book is the final chapter in the Two Far Gone journey, but another has already begun.

And, lastly, to Kristin: You're the only one I need betting on me.

CPSIA information can be obtained
at www.ICGtesting.com
Printed in the USA
FFHW02n0626231018
48945502-53190FF